"I'm Just a Comic Book Boy"

"I'm Just a Comic Book Boy"

Essays on the Intersection of Comics and Punk

Edited by Christopher B. Field,
Keegan Lannon,
Michael David MacBride
and Christopher C. Douglas

McFarland & Company, Inc., Publishers
Jefferson, North Carolina

COME ON NOW
By JEFFREY HYMAN, JOHN CUMMINGS and DOUGLAS COLVIN
(c) WB MUSIC CORP. (ASCAP) & TACO TUNES, INC. (ASCAP)
All Rights on Behalf of TACO TUNES, INC. (ASCAP).
Administered by WB MUSIC CORP. (ASCAP)
All Rights Reserved

LIBRARY OF CONGRESS CATALOGUING-IN-PUBLICATION DATA

Names: Field, Christopher B., 1980– editor. | Lannon, Keegan, 1980–
   editor. | MacBride, Michael, editor. | Douglas, Christopher C., 1982–
   editor.
Title: I'm just a comic book boy : essays on the intersection of comics
   and punk / edited by Christopher B. Field, Keegan Lannon,
   Michael David MacBride and Christopher C. Douglas.
Other titles: I am just a comic book boy
Description: Jefferson, North Carolina : McFarland & Company, Inc.,
   Publishers, 2019 | Includes bibliographical references and index.
Identifiers: LCCN 2018059828 | ISBN 9780786496419
   (softcover : acid free paper) ∞
Subjects: LCSH: Comic books, strips, etc.—History and criticism. |
   Punk rock music—History and criticism. | Music and literature. |
   Music, Influence of. | Punk culture and art. | Music in literature.
Classification: LCC PN6714 .I37 2019 | DDC 741.5/9—dc23
LC record available at https://lccn.loc.gov/2018059828

BRITISH LIBRARY CATALOGUING DATA ARE AVAILABLE

ISBN (print) 978-0-7864-9641-9
ISBN (ebook) 978-1-4766-3498-2

© 2019 Christopher B. Field, Keegan Lannon,
Michael David MacBride and Christopher C. Douglas.
All rights reserved

*No part of this book may be reproduced or transmitted in any form
or by any means, electronic or mechanical, including photocopying
or recording, or by any information storage and retrieval system,
without permission in writing from the publisher.*

Front cover illustration © 2019 Shutterstock

Printed in the United States of America

McFarland & Company, Inc., Publishers
   Box 611, Jefferson, North Carolina 28640
      www.mcfarlandpub.com

Acknowledgments

We'd like to thank Marvel, Raymond Pettibon, Bob Adelman, Justin Green, Diego A. Manrique, Juan Rodriguez Ortega, Bülent Üstün, Memo Tembelçizer, Square Enix, Glenat and Viz Media for permitting us to publish their illustrations in this collection.

Christopher B. Field dedicates this book to everyone who will never read it. You have no idea what you're missing. He also thanks his coeditors for all of the work they have put in to this project, and he wants to give a special acknowledgment to Michael MacBride for coming up with the original idea for the class that eventually led to this book. He also wishes to thank Tennessee State University's Office of Research and Sponsored Programs for funding that helped in part to finish this project.

Keegan Lannon dedicates this book to Q101 and WONC for soundtracking my formative years. And to Catherine for tolerating the stupidly loud music. He also wishes to thank Kelsey Morehead and Ceylan Kosker for their translation skills, which helped to acquire the French and Turkish permissions, respectively.

Michael David MacBride would like to thank his former students (for being engaged with the course material that this project grew from), the Comic Arts Conference at the San Diego Comic Con (for accepting the panel that grew from that class), and his fellow coeditors and copanelists for making this project possible. But, above all, thanks go out to Christopher B. Field for introducing Michael to Justin Green's work (which was the spark for all of this).

Christopher C. Douglas dedicates this book to anyone still listening to ska bands: You're not alone. Unless it's just me. It might be just me.

Table of Contents

Acknowledgments — v

Introduction — 1

Part I: Punk Superhero Comics

One Man Artistic Corps: Jack Kirby's *OMAC*
as Punk Precursor
    CHRISTOPHER B. FIELD — 19

Captain America: All-American Punk
    JILL DAHLMAN — 29

Part II: Vertigo Punk Comics

No Future: John Constantine, *Hellblazer* and the '70s Punk
Rocker in the 21st Century
    SPENCER CHALIFOUR — 49

"I Hate It Here": Spider Jerusalem as Punk Anti-Hero
    JODIE CHILDERS — 61

24-Hour Murder People: The Punk Iconography
in Grant Morrison's *The Invisibles*
    KEEGAN LANNON — 75

Anarchy at the Alamo: The Creation of a 21st Century
American Punk-Western in Garth Ennis
and Steve Dillon's *Preacher*
    RUSSELL WEBER — 88

Part III: Underground Punk Comics

Aspiring Revolutionaries and "Petty" Conflicts: The Penis in the Punk Movement and *Binky Brown*
  MICHAEL DAVID MACBRIDE 113

Reinventing a Carnivalesque Public Sphere: (Re)imagining and (Re)drawing Madrid in the Long 1970s
  LOUIE DEAN VALENCIA-GARCÍA 134

Drawing Istanbul's Asshole: Turkish Punk Comics
  CAN YALÇINKAYA 153

Part IV: Punk Manga

Bōsōzoku Motorcycle Gangs, the Bubble Economy and Psychic Children: Reaffirming *Giri* Through Ōtomo Katsuhiro's *Akira* (1988)
  CHRISTOPHER C. DOUGLAS 171

Schoolgirls and *Sukeban*: Representations of Punk Women in Contemporary Japanese Manga
  ALICE VERNON 188

Punk Bodies and the "Do It Yourself" Philosophy
  FRANCESCO-ALESSIO URSINI 205

About the Contributors 223

Index 225

Introduction

If one truism were to come from this book it would be that punk, at its best, is difficult to talk about and, at its worst, aggressively resists the kind of academic inquiry undertaken here. Punk seems to adamantly refuse to *be* anything (or share anything, or borrow anything).

It is a movement of opposition, defined more by what it is against (authority, hegemony, "the man") than what it is for (most often, simply, anarchy).

It is a movement of contradictions and paradoxes: it claims to be illiterate while making references to avant-garde literature, cinema and art; it seeks to gather and unite people with a shared sense of alienation; it rejects authority but refuses to be ideologically positioned or to suggest what should replace that authority. In short, punk just doesn't give a fuck.

It is this attitude that pairs punk so well with comics, an art form that eternally resists codification. Just when it seems like comics are a certain way, say after the forced sterilization in American comics stemming from Fredric Wertham's *Seduction of the Innocent*, then it will morph into something wholly unthought-of, like the San Francisco underground comics of the 1960s.

As with punk, moral outrage, political censorship and concerned citizen brigades tried to corner comics, and every single time comics eluded these societal forces to grow into something new and equally as confrontational.

One would be well within his or her rights to throw hands in the air and refuse, like punk and comics, to the terms set forth by books like these. This reaction, though, misses the point. Punk and comics endure, they adapt and change according to the demands put upon them by outside organizations, and they shrug off attempts to pigeon-hole; we, too, should strive to resist the resistance, contain the uncontainable, and understand the openly, aggressively obstinate.

So here goes…

Tracing the Roots of Punk

We take punk music as our starting point for the punk movement in this compilation. While we could easily tie in myriad other mediums of popular culture which adopted a punk ethos—such as fashion or art—as an influence in the coalescence of the punk movement, we limit our discussion here to the music that was instrumental in founding the movement both for the sake of brevity and because we attribute the greatest influence in the foundation of the movement to punk music. So, what is "punk"?

Perhaps the simplest definition is the opposite of convention. Thus, to name it and to define it is to defeat the purpose. It isn't so much a concrete set of words and terms, as an amorphous idea. What punk means has changed over the centuries, and, as Seth Kahn-Egan rightly points out, in "Pedagogy of the Pissed: Punk Pedagogy in the First-Year Writing Classroom" (1998), "There is no Platonic ideal of 'punkness' from which we can extract a definition" (99). But, of course people have attempted to define it. A quick look at the *Oxford English Dictionary* reveals the fluid nature of the word: the earliest use is denoting a prostitute (1575). Then, in 1698, punk means, "a young boy or young man kept by an older man as a (typically passive) sexual partner." In 1893, it means, a "despicable or contemptible person ... petty criminal; a hoodlum." By 1920, it's "an amateur"; in 1935 a "homosexual"; and, in 1939, "a coward." This sexual element of these early definitions is dropped from the modern usage, but certainly is an essential element in "punk music" or "punk culture." The modern definition of "punk" stems from 1970, and there's a debate about who coined it first. Again, the *OED* offers the following: a concert flyer for the band Suicide (November 20, 1970), and Ed Sanders (founder of the band the Fugs) in a *Chicago Tribune* article dated March 22, 1970. In this article, Sanders coins the term to describe the music on his new album, which he describes as, "punk rock—redneck sentimentality—my own past updated to present day reality."[1] Sanders' album *Sanders' Truckstop* definitely leans more toward "redneck sentimentality" than anything modern listeners would call "punk rock," and Suicide is an early electronic music duo sharing more in common with the keyboard-driven Doors music than, say, the Sex Pistols. But, what's really important here is that these two very divergent musicians were looking for an alternative classification to their music and both happened upon the term "punk rock" in 1970.

By 1970, JFK, MLK, and RFK were dead. So were Janis Joplin and Jimi Hendrix (Jim Morrison would join them in 1971). Woodstock was over, and the "Woodstock West" (aka: Altamont Free Concert) had effectively killed the "summer of love" with its violence and Hells Angels "security" guards. Lenny Bruce had been arrested for obscenity, and George Carlin was working on the material for "Seven Words You Can Never Say on Television." Public opinion over Vietnam had officially changed tide—Eddie Adams' photograph of Nguyen Ngoc Loan killing a handcuffed Nguyen Van Lem didn't help. The Kent State and Jackson State shootings had happened, shaking the resolve of the peaceful nonviolent protesters. The Beatles broke up. The U.S. began its invasion of Cambodia. The Stonewall Riots signaled the "official" start of the gay rights movement, and the Civil Rights movement was well under way. Military coups were occurring all over Africa, Latin America, and the Middle East. China was undergoing its Cultural Revolution, and the "troubles" in Ireland were reaching a fever pitch. Black Sabbath released its first and second album in 1970, and in the process ushered out the happy sounds of the hippies and introduced the world to the brooding of heavy metal. This is the world in which Ed Sanders and Suicide found themselves coining a new descriptor. "Rock" was no longer sufficient to describe the diversity of music emerging in the post–Summer of Love reality, let alone the shaken public consciousness of that world.

By the following year, "punk" was being more clearly defined and spreading around the world. The *OED* offers the current usage as, "rock music played in a fast, aggressive, or unpolished manner," and cites the following for reference points: *Rag* magazine (Apr. 12, 1971), *Rolling Stone* (Apr. 15, 1971), *Creem* (Nov. 1972), *The New Yorker* (May 20, 1974), *New Musical Express* (July 10, 1976), *Melody Maker* (Sept. 11, 1976), *New Statesman* (Dec. 17, 1976), and *Time* (July 30, 1979). This definition is typical and does seem to form the foundation for understanding what "punk" is. Mark Perry, in *Sniffin' Glue* (2009), recalls seeing the Ramones for the first time: "I had never heard anything so exciting ... they played at breakneck speed." Similarly, Adrian Boot and Chris Salewicz, in *Punk: The Illustrated History of a Music Revolution* (1996), point to the, "frenetic urgency of [their] songs," when speaking of the Sex Pistols and New York Dolls (13). Though the sound of Suicide and *Sanders' Truckstop* might not fit this definition, these bands certainly helped to coin a term for other artists to aspire to. Punk was the label that music writers needed to classify the sounds they heard from the MC5, The Stooges, and the New York Dolls. It gave a sense of cohesion to an otherwise diverse and unpredictable sound.

However, there was something to "punk" that went beyond the simple sound or speed at which the music was played—that "something" was the attitude that came with the performance. George Gimarc, in his *Punk Diary* (1994), suggests that the first punk band is The Stooges and begins his catalog of punk performances with their show on August 1970. For Gimarc, The Stooges offered an alternative to the "too polished, too packed, too produced" sounds of the '60s, and instead put forth the ethos of bringing the music back to, "the street level," allowing "a new generation of disenfranchised kids" to find their voice (vii). This group of disenfranchised kids were "the punks.

Troublemakers. Attitude incarnate," and "they had nothing but disrespect for those before them ... they were homely, unkempt and generally couldn't play worth a damn" (vii). This was punk; the *OED* was missing the word "attitude" from its definition. Rather than a lack of musicianship being an obstacle to overcome, punk offered an opportunity to the "unskilled." In fact, Throbbing Gristle's Genesis P-Orridge went so far in 1969 as to suggest that, "the future of music lies in non-musicians" (qtd. in Reynolds 226). P-Orridge, and the punk purists, believed that music had stagnated and it was only through a nontraditional shot in the arm that it might evolve beyond where it had come by 1970.

Later punk, the "new wave" in particular, offered a much more polished sound, but for the "protopunk" bands, the "unpolished" sound was a hallmark. It conveyed urgency of message and indicated to the listeners that this was "real" and "pure," not studio magic. As Lester Bangs writes, in "Protopunk: The Garage Bands" (1980), "Given the greatest garage bands could barely play we may assume not only that virtuosity has nothing to do with the form, but also that the utopian dream of everyman an artist can come true right here" (261). Punk offered the antithesis of the progressive rock movement and of the pop tunes heard on the radio; listeners were encouraged that they too could do this. Griel Marcus, in "Anarchy in the U.K." (1980), suggests that, "People cut singles not so much on the off-chance that they would hit but to join in, to be heard, to establish a new identity" (457). Singles were a sort of currency that could be "cut" to join in the conversation. Geoffrey Sirc, in "Never Mind the Tagmemics, Where's the Sex Pistols?" (1997), echoes Marcus, saying, "Listening to Punk was only a 'preliminary stage'; it was music you listened to in order to take further action, records to play en route to the ultimate rejection of records, in favor of making one's own music" (22). It wasn't about making "good" music; it was just about making music, and being heard. Overproducing and overthinking it killed the art and the expression.

Lack of polish went beyond the simple quality of the recordings, and it included the language that was used and way the music was performed live. For Simon Reynolds, in *Rip It Up and Start Again* (2006), the thing that initially grabbed him about punk music was the "profanity," but beyond "the naughty words themselves ... it was the vehemence and virulence of Rotten's delivery" (xiii). It was this combination of uncensored language and unrestrained performance that attracted youth to the punk movement. Of course, this wasn't new. Musicians frequently pushed the boundaries of decency and reaped the benefits of the interest it generated. Guitarists like Jimi Hendrix and Pete Townshend smashed guitars. Keith Moon smashed his drums. Ira Louvin used to smash mandolins that were out of tune in the late '50s and early '60s. Jerry Lee Lewis, and Paul Revere and the Raiders destroyed pianos in the '50s and early '60s. And, of course, Jim Morrison was famously charged with indecency. Simply put, destruction, sex, and swearing, sell. Punk frequently combined all of these elements, but, rather than simply being a marketing device, punk bands fully embraced these elements as being an essential ethos of "punk." While the Doors, the Who, and others were under investigation by the FBI for their behaviors, punk bands escaped the notice (or interest) of the government. It's difficult to know why exactly—perhaps because their music was direct and unambiguous, or maybe simply because punk music didn't "chart" the way the other acts did.

Ironically, the song that was investigated most during the "protopunk" era was the Kingsmen's classic "Louie Louie." This song was investigated for its lyrics and potential lewdness. The problem was, though the FBI heard complaints from the public, they could not officially determine what was being said in the song. An FBI report, dated February 17, 1964, declares, "the words are hard to recognize" and asks that the, "Laboratory is requested to determine if enclosed record, 'Louie Louie,' can be considered obscene for purposes of prosecution." No such luck. As Dave Marsh reports, in *Louie Louie* (2004), "the record ... was played at various speeds but none of the speeds assisted in determining the words of the song on the record" (116). Marsh argues, as others have as well, that "Louie Louie" is the first punk song, but he goes a step further suggesting it's not the song itself, but the way the Kingsmen performed it that made it "punk." By comparing the versions by the Kingsmen and Paul Revere and the Raiders, Marsh's argument is clear.[2] The Paul Revere version is clean-sounding, the lyrics are clear, and the attitude is toned-down. Whereas the Kingsmen's version sounds hastily made, fuzzy, and the lyrics are slurred—as if made by amateurs, which it was. Paul Revere and the Raiders were gifted musicians, they were the old guard, and the Kingsmen were the youthful upstarts. And punk is definitely a youthful endeavor.

Youth, attitude, boundary pushing, aggressive performance, and the idea that music is an inclusive activity, rather than an exclusive club of talented musicians, are all essential elements in defining "punk." Though Kahn-Egan states there's no "Platonic ideal of punkness," he offers a pretty thoughtful definition; according to Kahn-Egan, punk requires:

> (1) The Do-It-Yourself (DIY) ethic, which demands that we do our own work ... (2) a sense of anger and passion that finally drives a writer to say what's really on his or her mind; (3) a sense of destructiveness that calls for attacking institutions when those institutions are oppressive, or even dislikeable; (4) a willingness to endure or even pursue pain to make oneself heard or noticed; (5) a pursuit of the 'pleasure principle,' a reveling in some kind of Nietzchean chasm [100].

Thus, our definition of punk, which we have derived from the musicians that founded the punk movement, is one that places a premium on an aggressive confrontation with social mores, a DIY ethos, and a regard for substance over style, although the style itself later takes on a stylized affect once stylistic aesthetics within the movement start to coalesce.

Intersections Between Punk and Comics

The Ramones' 1981 album *Pleasant Dreams* represented a sea change for the band and their fanbase. The trend away from "punk" and more towards a pop-oriented sound began with *End of the Century* (1980), took root with *Pleasant Dreams*, and spilled over into *Subterranean Jungle* (1983). While the former and the latter have redeemed themselves in the minds of most Ramones fans, *Pleasant Dreams* is much more difficult to place. Of the ten Ramones albums reviewed in the *Rolling Stone* reader poll, it placed dead last. A piece in *New York Magazine* entitled "Johnny Ramone Grades the Ramones," which was published on March 18, 2012, years after his death, contains the "grades" that Johnny Ramone would have given each Ramones album, and even Johnny Ramone gave the album a B-, a grade shared with *Animal Boy* (1986), *Halfway to Sanity* (1987), and *Acid Eaters* (1993)—all albums that barely rank on top lists by fans—and the only albums to score worse were *Brain Drain* (1989) and *Mondo Bizarro* (1992)—a C for each album from the guitarist. In his comments about the album, Johnny wrote, "Nobody in the band was speaking, and I didn't write any songs with Dee Dee, so it has no real punk songs on it. It's too light." Despite fan dissatisfaction and Johnny's own disparaging comments, *Pleasant Dreams* was the third highest charting album the Ramones put out: *End of the Century* (1980) hit 44, *Rocket to Russia* (1977) hit 49, and *Pleasant Dreams* (1981) came in at 58 on the Billboard 200. *Subterranean Jungle* aside, no other Ramones albums broke the top 100—and it barely made it at 83.

This is the first album where the band members vied for individual songwriting credits, and it's also the first time that Dee Dee Ramone is not responsible for most of the writing—Joey gets credit for seven of the tracks, and Dee Dee gets credit for the remaining five (including "Come On Now").[3] By most accounts, Dee Dee was *the* punk in the band, and perhaps him taking a backseat to Joey accounts for part of the lack of "punk" sound on the album. In many ways, though Joey and Johnny get much of the credit for the sound of the Ramones, Dee Dee is the heart and soul of the band. It was Dee Dee that named the band, came up with the 1-2-3-4 introductions to each song, and who was the principal songwriter. However, the bigger issue than Dee Dee taking a backseat is that the band was being pressured by the record company to find the elusive "big" radio hit. After years on the road, and seeing their peers succeed, the Ramones wanted that recognition, too.

Instead, the album threatened to tear the band apart and to lose them fans. The songs ranged from the first single from the album and opening track, "We Want the Airwaves"—which could have been a Judas Priest song—to "Come On Now" that would have been in good company with "any track by The Dave Clark Five" (True 167)—to the third single from the album "The KKK Took My Baby Away" (a song frequently cited as being the sole redeeming track on the album). Even the album art left the band members unsatisfied. Johnny recalled, "We had a better cover that looked kinda like a horror movie poster, which I thought was great. The record company saw it and said it was the worst cover they've ever seen" (Melnick 210–11). The horror movie poster look would have been right at home with the rest of the "low culture" that is referenced throughout the album, and because of the band's love of film in general. The lyrics refer to: TV (Uncle Floyd and talk shows), film (Allan Arkush, Roger Corman, Clint Eastwood, and Jack Nicholson), radio (Phil Spector, 10cc, and Vin Scelsa), fiction (Stephen King), 7-11s and junk food, the subway and New York bus system, freak shows, roller coasters, listening to records (and rock 'n' roll in general), video games (*Space Invaders*), sniffing glue, and comic books.

Though the style of the music may have veered from their original punk roots, the Ramones were at least consistent in their focus on the things they held near and dear. When asked about their influences, Tommy Ramone immediately responded, "we were influenced by comic books, movies, the Andy Warhol scene, and avant garde films. I was a big *Mad Magazine* fan myself" (Colegrave 67). Their longtime roadie, Monte Melnick, also recalled the band, "had a song called 'Pinhead' [which was] inspired by the movie *Freaks* and Zippy the Pinhead" (96). There was even a Pinhead character included in the film *Rock 'n' Roll High School* (1979) and it soon became, "tradition for the drum roadie to put on the Pinhead mask and run out during the song to dance onstage with the 'Gabba Gabba Hey' sign" (96). So, it shouldn't have been a surprise when the Ramones appeared on *The Simpsons* and they looked right at home.[4] With their adopted names and uniform (haircut, t-shirt, leather jacket, and blue jeans), it was almost as if the Ramones had always been a cartoon and it was more about illustrators finally catching on.

On *Pleasant Dreams*, Dee Dee's song "Come On Now" makes the most direct reference to comics with the simple admission: "I'm just a comic book boy." Though autobiographically accurate, Dee Dee was a "comic book boy" and indeed the Ramones were "comic book" boys, the line also speaks directly to the heavy burden the Ramones felt on their shoulders. The burden to live up to expectations of the fans, to be "true" to their roots, to sell albums, to keep the record company alive, to finally, and deservedly, receive some acknowledgment for all they had accomplished, and to maybe make enough money to take a break from the road (they performed over 2,200 concerts in 22 years, and many of those years they spent over 300 days on the road).

8   Introduction

We have taken that song lyric—"I'm just a comic book boy"—for the title of our collection for several reasons, but chief among those reasons is that the lyric represents an inherent contradiction. Whereas at its onset punk acts like the Ramones typically opted for a heavier and faster style of playing, this song utilizes a more pop-influenced sound that slows down the tempo of the song. This style is juxtaposed with lyrics that can only be described as classically punk, which emphasize the influences of consumer culture such as junk food, roller coasters, and, in the lyric that we use for our title, comic books. Comic books, the classic emblem of disposable consumer culture, which are meant to be devoured and discarded, are listed as a major influence for shaping identity in this lyric. This demonstrates a clear influence from comics on punk music.

However, there's still that contradiction. The lyrics indicate punk, but the music indicates a more polished pop sound. What should we make of that? We interpret this as a valuable entry point into our discussion of punk comics. Comics produced in the U.S. market during the height of the punk movement—and even today—typically followed/follow one of two trajectories: (1) they are either produced commercially for mass market consumption by a corporate publisher; or, (2) they are "underground" comics (or comix) produced on a smaller scale, often by one individual or a limited group of people, in a system that resembles the DIY production ethos of the punk movement. The mass market comics were typically superhero comics with watered down content so they could adhere to the comics industry's self-censorship Comics Code which limited violent and sexually suggestive imagery. In contrast, the DIY production and distribution method of underground comics typically gave them the freedom to explore more lurid content. For us, then, "Come On Now" represents a critical parallel between punk and comics. The lyrics indicate a self-aware nature that would align the punk genre with underground comics; however, the polished pop sheen of the music indicates a genre that is influenced by corporate capitalist aims to make the music as marketable as possible. Thus, this is the perfect song to introduce a collection where the contributors examine comics that range from the most mainstream productions to the most obscure underground comics in order to examine the punk aesthetics incorporated therein.

Manga and Punk

One of the areas that we were adamant about including in this collection is the influence of punk on one of the fastest growing segments of contemporary comics, Japanese comics, hereafter referred to as manga.[5] The context of manga's development is obviously different from Western comics, and

Introduction   9

some of these differences should be made clear. Of increasing popularity outside of Japan in the twenty-first century, the origins of modern Japanese manga are found in the postwar reconstruction of Japan, with the publication of works such as Hasegawa Machiko's (1920–92) *Sazae-san* (サザエさん) which ran in the *Asahi Shimbun* newspaper from 1946 to 1974. *Sazae-san* forms an exemplar of very early Japanese manga. The comic was short, confined to only four panels, and dealt with humorous, slice-of-life issues. Although almost unknown outside of Japan, this manga is the basis for the longest-running animated television series in the world as noted by *Guinness World Records*, airing on Fuji TV from 1969 to the present ("Longest Running Animated TV Series"). Other manga appeared in magazine anthologies of comics, mostly meant for a younger audience. The most influential manga writer and artist of this early era is Tezuka Osamu (1928–89). Tezuka is the creator of *Astro Boy* (鉄腕アトム; 1952–68), *Phoenix* (火の鳥; 1967–88), and *Black Jack* (ブラック・ジャック; 1973–83), among a large number of other works. His works differed greatly from Machiko's as his storylines lasted for at least several pages, and the focus was not placed simply on humor, but on science fiction action and adventure in works such as *Astro Boy*, a lengthy exploration of the ideas of life, death and reincarnation in *Phoenix*, and most relevant to scholars interested in punk comics, on a renegade doctor who uses his skills to punish the unjust from the margins of society in *Black Jack*.[6]

To trace out the entire creative growth of manga across the last sixty years is beyond the scope of this introduction. However, it would be remiss to not mention the publication of two more authors' works, as they are highly influential in establishing a punk or cyberpunk aesthetic in Japanese manga. The first manga creator is Nagai Gō (1945–present), who helped to pioneer a number of manga genres in the 1960s and '70s, including the giant robot genre with his work *Marzinger Z* (マジンガーZ; 1972–74). Most notable for this collection is his work *Devilman* (デビルマン; 1972–73) and *Shin Devilman* (新デビルマン; 1979–81). *Shin Devilman* was published in English as *Devilman* by Glenn Danzig, founding member of The Misfits, as a part of his Verotik comic book publishing line. The original *Devilman* is remarkable, not only for its violence and focus on youth-led rebellion and social anarchy, but also for its treatment of the quintessential social outcast, an intersex Satan, who in the series has shown to have rebelled against the ultimate authority, God, in an attempt to prevent the world from being destroyed, realizing only too late that the actions taken by demons against humanity have mirrored what God had intended for the demons themselves (5: 204–11). Sadly, this original work has never been completely and officially translated into English. The second manga creator who helped establish a punk aesthetic is Ōtomo Katsuhiro (1954–present), who is best known for his cyberpunk series *Akira* (1982–90), which appeared in *Weekly Young Magazine* (週刊ヤングマガジン), a publication meant for young adult men. This work is widely considered to be highly influential in generating interest in Japanese animation and manga to a Western audience (Napier 41). Every essay in this collection which deals with manga discusses Ōtomo's work in some capacity. In addition to the above, in his essay, Christopher C. Douglas discusses some of the backgrounds for the young rebellious man in Japanese culture, which also provides more context for understanding punk conceits in a Japanese context.

From the time that Tezuka was publishing his first works, to Ōtomo's publication of *Akira*, the audience for Japanese manga had grown from mostly children to include an audience of young adults and adults. In today's Japan, manga is read by a wide variety of people, across age groups. For many manga, the head writer is likewise the head artist, although collaborations between artists and writers also exist. Unlike their American counterparts, Japanese manga is not typically published as standalone projects, at least during the initial publication phase. Japanese manga goes through two radically different publication schemes. In the initial stage, a weekly, bi-weekly, or monthly magazine collection of many different manga by many different creators is published, with each manga having approximately twenty pages published at a time, although this can differ widely; four-panel comics, such as were popularized by *Sazae-san*, are still commonly published in addition to longer works. These manga anthologies are mostly published in black and white, with colored plates reserved only for the most popular series, and even then used very sparingly. These magazines typically have a target audience ranging from young boys or young girls (*shōnen/shōjo*) to older males or females (*seinen/josei*), to pornographic works meant either for an adult male or female audience. After this stage of publication, most manga are collected into anthologies dedicated to a single work, called *tankōbon* (単行本). The average *tankōbon* will include around two-hundred pages worth of an individual manga, and retail for less than ¥600 (approximately $5.50), although exceptions to this rule do exist, making them affordable even to young children. Thanks to this publication system, while it is very easy to have access to an entire manga series, access to the original form of publication, the magazine anthologies, is very uncommon: the large size and their multi-story nature discourage collection. A popular anthology may have twenty or more manga being published in each issue, with some titles being published for ten or more years.[7] Because of this, when referring to a manga title, the *tankōbon* anthology is referenced, instead of the original format of publication.

Contents

Before we proceed any further, we, the editors, must acknowledge our failure. Punk has had a lasting influence on both mainstream and underground comics that persists to this day. There are a number of comics creators—such as Gary Panter and Los Bros Hernandez (Mario, Gilbert, and Jaime)—who have produced canonical punk comics with punk aesthetics. There are also a number of punk themes and submovements within the larger classification of punk that have been explored in comics. There have been so many comics that could be classified as punk that we knew when we embarked on this project that there would be no way we could include essays that examined all of the comics with punk themes and/or aesthetics. Rather, we wanted to use this collection as a way of opening up a larger conversation concerning punk comics. We found that the conversation concerning punk comics is limited to the production of two main publishing cultures—the U.S. and the UK—in much the same way that conversations concerning punk music focus on those same two cultures. Our goal was to open up the discussion to the output of punk comics from other countries so that we could have a more inclusive examination of punk comics that no other large-scale study had attempted. So, we acknowledge our deficiencies at the outset of our discussion, and we invite future scholars to add to the discussion with anything they believe we have omitted here. What has been assembled here, though, is a comprehensive look at intersections between the punk movement and comics. Spanning from U.S. superhero comics to underground comics published internationally, we have gathered an eclectic mix of articles that we hope provides a thorough examination of punk comics.

Superhero comics might not seem the most likely place to find punk aesthetics, considering both Marvel and DC (the two biggest U.S. publishers of superhero comics) are massive corporations who are, in a very real sense, the controlling authority in the world of comics. Regardless, some subversive comics managed to come from these two industry giants. Christopher B. Field's essay, "One Man Artistic Corps: Jack Kirby's *OMAC* as a Punk Precursor," examines the strange, futuristic comic and the mohawked OMAC in particular. Field stops short of claiming Kirby was directly influenced by punk, but instead suggests that the anti-authoritarian undertones and use of punk aesthetics (particularly OMAC's mohawk) stem from Kirby's sense of alienation and disenfranchisement, much like the punk movement. *OMAC*, then, is a precursor to the later punk comics, such as *The Invisibles*, *Preacher*, and *Constantine* discussed in other essays.

In a similar vein, Jill Dahlman's essay, "Captain America: All-American Punk," makes the paradoxical argument that Marvel's Captain America, particularly in the Silver Age, embodied the punk ideology. Coining the phrase

"Patriotic Punk," Dahlman argues that Captain America's revolutionary tendencies place him squarely in the punk camp. While it is true that Captain America's central goal was to represent all that was great about America, Dahlman argues that his definition of "great" was not always prescribed by the establishment. Captain America would resist the government and authorities when either interfered with his agenda, be it by punching Hitler or fighting the Superhero Registration Act. For Dahlman, Captain America represents a unique facet of the punk movement in which the heroes applied the punk ideology to nationalist pride.

Likely, the most obvious punk to come from the mainstream U.S. publishers would be DC's dark antihero, John Constantine. Part of Constantine's backstory includes a stint in a punk band. This aspect of Constantine is the central focus for Spencer Chalifour's essay "No Future: John Constantine, *Hellblazer* and the '70s Punk Rocker in the 21st Century." Chalifour examines Jason Aaron and Peter Milligan's run on *Hellblazer*, specifically two issues in which Constantine's punk background are at the center of the narrative. For Chalifour, Constantine represents an uneasy balance in contemporary conceptions of punk music, a musical art form which is both subversive and commodified, authentic and mythical.

Another essay examining Vertigo comics, Jodie Childers' "'I Hate It Here': Spider Jerusalem as Punk Anti-Hero," looks at Warren Ellis and Darick Robertson's cyberpunk comic, *Transmetropolitan*. Childers is particularly interested in the central character, Spider Jerusalem, a gonzo-reporter who frustrates those in power. For Childers, Spider Jerusalem represents the same dichotomic ideological tensions as does the punk movement. She argues that Spider Jerusalem, like punk music, wants to both destroy society and, paradoxically, make a better one. Both are driven by an impulse to create a Utopia, and both are willing to take whatever means are necessary to do so.

Keegan Lannon's essay, "24-Hour Murder People: The Punk Iconography in Grant Morrison's *The Invisibles*," examines one of Vertigo's first series, and Grant Morrison's first creator-owned work. Considering Morrison's interest in punk and the critical consensus that *The Invisibles* is, at the least, partially autobiography, Lannon argues that punk has greatly influenced the nature of the series. He focuses his discussion on the first issue, "Dead Beatles," and delineates to key areas in which punk has clearly informed the content and style of the comics. He asserts that these early indications can be extrapolated across the series as a new approach to Morrison's seminal work.

Like Dahlman's examination of Captain America, Russell Weber's essay "Anarchy at the Alamo: The Creation of a 21st Century American Punk-Western in Garth Ennis and Steve Dillon's *Preacher*," is interested in how punk aesthetics and ideologies can be blended into a seemingly disparate genre. Weber examines *Preacher*, yet another Vertigo comic, claiming that the series creates the punk–Western, which embodies both the mythology of the American Western and the subversive tendencies of the punk movement. Weber contends that the book's central anti-hero, Jesse Custer, is equally informed by a hallucination of John Wayne, the epitome of the Western hero, and Custer's friend Proinsias Cassidy, an anti-authoritarian Irish vampire. It is in Custer that Weber sees the perfect amalgamation of punk and Western ideologies which creates the punk–Western hero aptly suited for a showdown with God.

Michael David MacBride discusses *Binky Brown Meets the Holy Virgin*, a key text in American underground comix, in "Aspiring Revolutionaries and 'Petty' Conflicts: The Penis in the Punk Movement and *Binky Brown*." MacBride is interested in how Justin Green's comic and the latent punk movement (particularly the album and poster art of Raymond Pettibon) both fixate, almost compulsively, on penises. MacBride argues that this use of phallic symbols and euphemisms, or actual representations of the artist's penis in Green's comic, is meant to shock the audience and open conversations about uncomfortable or taboo subject matter, such as Green's own anxieties about his art. Ultimately, MacBride maintains that any discussion of *Binky Brown* which does not at least recognize the recurring images does not fully engage with the work.

Moving to Spain, Louie Dean Valencia-García's essay, "Reinventing a Carnivalesque Public Sphere: (Re)Imagining and (Re)Drawing Madrid in the Long 1970s" explores the comics published following the death of dictator Francisco Franco in 1975. Valencia-García explores how young Spaniards created an underground movement which blended Spanish youth culture with the punk scenes in both the U.S. and UK. The comics which were associated with this movement resisted the conservative policies of the dictator's ruling party by resurrecting the "carnivalesque" atmosphere made popular by the *Movida Madrileña*, or Madrid Movement. Valencia-García argues that these comics helped to drive a wedge between the exiting conservative regime, and the new, consumer-driven youth culture.

In Turkey, a similar youth uprising was taking place in the early 1980s, as discussed in Can Yalçınkaya's essay, "Drawing Istanbul's Asshole: Turkish Punk Comics." It might seem strange to find a punk movement in Turkey, an Islamic country with a secular government. Yalcinkaya's essay investigates the two punk magazines, *L-Manyak* and *Lombak*, and the comics therein. He argues that the cartoonists featured in these magazines fostered an attitude of resistance, filtering the subculture through a lens of seemingly harmless humor magazines. For Yalçınkaya, the cartoonists and their comics were a harbinger for the global punk scenes, which instilled a culture of resistance in the young readership until it was coopted by the mainstream culture.

A key thread which ties together each of the works in the final section of this collection is Ōtomo Katsuhiro's highly influential *Akira* manga and the film version, which was also written and directed by Ōtomo; Ōtomo popularized a movement in anti-establishment youth culture in Japanese comics and animation during and after his series' publication. Christopher C. Douglas, in "*Bōsōzoku* Motorcycle Gangs, the Bubble Economy and Psychic Children: Reaffirming *Giri* through Ōtomo Katsuhiro's *Akira* (1988)" specifically explores the cinematic version of Ōtomo's work, placing it in its historical and cultural context. Closely examining the idea of *giri*, or social obligation, in Japanese culture, the development of the isolated young man who cannot fit into society, and the era of the Japanese Bubble Economy, Douglas shows how a cultural concern over the future of Japan worked its way into this particular version of Ōtomo's work, which was created before his manga was completed, and which also diverges greatly from the storyline of the manga. Douglas argues that the ultimate message of *Akira* is a conservative one, seeking to reaffirm a traditional understanding of social relations. Set into its social and historical context, the movie's radical prevision of the manga's yet-unpublished end shows how it is only a concern for the well-being of others that would permit Japan a way to move forward, a message which is not present at the conclusion of the manga's serialization, after the Bubble Economy had burst.

Likewise, Alice Vernon also explores the cultural context of several punk texts and gender relations in "Schoolgirls and *Sukeban*: Representations of Punk Women in Contemporary Japanese Manga." Vernon closely analyzes the representations of women in a number of highly popular manga, including Ōtomo's *Akira*, Ōkubo Atsushi's *Soul Eater*, and Narita Ryōgo's *Durarara!!* Vernon shows how, in a series of texts that borrow heavily from the punk movement, what should have been a liberating space for female characters, instead managed to constrain those women who do appear in their pages. In marking out the female who fails to conform to strict expectations of gender standards as either the object of sexualization or as a literal monster, these punk texts serve to reaffirm Japanese society's boundaries. Contrary to what might be the expectations of a punk-influenced text, the traditional ideal of the *ryōsai kenbo*, or virtuous mother, is upheld in these manga as the cultural ideal of femininity. Vernon's explication of Hayashida Q's *Dorohedoro*, however, proves to be an example of a punk manga which breaks gender expectations instead of reaffirming them, discussing how the punk aesthetic can not only be borrowed superficially, but also developed to reimagine gender roles in a particularly Japanese context.

Francesco-Alessio Ursini in "Punk Bodies and the 'Do It Yourself' Philosophy" looks at a wide range of texts, Japanese, American, and European, to explore the concept of how punk comics utilize characters who seek to reshape the world around them through the ideals of independence, authenticity, and creativity. The trajectory of the main characters of these comics is laid out, tracing the growth of punk from traumatized individuals into rebels seeking to alter their own lives, and finally into characters who seek to alter the lives of the world around them for the better. Ursini carefully shows how and where punk ideals came to influence the actions of characters in pre-punk movement texts such as Ishinomori Shōtarō's *Cyborg 009*, which he argues lack a true do-it-yourself principle; in contrast, Ursini argues that less-frequently discussed punk texts such as Ōtomo's *Akira*, Stefano Tamburini and Tanino Liberatore's *RanXerox*, and Grant Morrison's *Doom Patrol*, show how these texts develop a true punk aesthetic closely tied to the desire to change the individual, and later the world.

Notes

1. See Sanders (404) for a short discussion of his memory regarding this article.
2. See Marsh (81–101).
3. During his time with the band, Dee Dee was the most prolific songwriter, and even after he quit he continued to write songs (at least three for each album).
4. Season 5, episode 4 "Rosebud," originally airing October 21, 1993.
5. All Japanese words and names in this collection follow the Modified Hepburn method of romanization, with a few key deviations where a standard English spelling has come into common use, most notably for the word "Tokyo." This is the romanization style preferred by the Library of Congress and the American Association of Libraries. The names of Japanese persons retain the Japanese naming order, wherein the family name precedes any given name. Words in common use, such as "manga" ("comic") and "anime" ("animation"), and proper nouns, such as "Tokyo" or "Ōtomo Katsuhiro," are not italicized, but uncommon words not in regular use in English, such as *giri* ("social obligation") and *sukeban* ("delinquent girl") are italicized.
6. Also, considering *Black Jack* and the do-it-yourself approach, not only does Black Jack successfully perform surgery on himself in the middle of the Australian bushland, he does so while under attack by a pack of wild dingoes (3: 63- 72). He also makes a daughter for himself out of the extraneous organs present in a teratoma cyst, excised from a woman's body (1: 50–68).
7. For example, *Weekly Shōnen Jump* (週刊少年ジャンプ) has published Akimoto Osamu's *Kochira Katsushika-ku Kameari Kōen Mae Hashutsujo* (こちら葛飾区亀有公園前派出所) on a regular basis since 1976 (T. Ohara). Collecting nearly forty years of bulky paperback anthologies for this single text would be simply prohibitive for most fans.

Works Cited

Adelman, Bob. *Tijuana Bibles: Art and Wit in America's Forbidden Funnies, 1930s–1950s.* Simon & Schuster, 1997.
Armstrong, John. *Guilty of Everything.* New Star Books, 2001.
Bangs, Lester. "Protopunk: The Garage Bands." *The Rolling Stone: Illustrated History of Rock & Roll*, edited by Jim Miller, Random House, 1980, pp. 261–4.
Boot, Adrian, and Chris Salewicz. *Punk: The Illustrated History of a Music Revolution.* Broadwall House, 1996.
Chute, Hillary. "Temporality and Seriality in Spiegelman's In the Shadow of No Towers." *American Periodicals: A Journal of History, Criticism, and Biography*, vol. 17, no. 2, 2007, pp. 228–44. Project Muse. Accessed 7 May 2013.
Colegrave, Stephen, and Chris Sullivan. *Punk: the Definitive Record of a Revolution.* Da Capo Press, 2005.

Duncan, Randy, and Matthew J. Smith. *The Power of Comics: History, Form & Culture*. Continuum, 2009.
el Refaie, Elisabeth. "Life Writing from the Colorful Margins." *Autobiographical Comics*. Mississippi UP, 2012, pp. 11–48.
Gabilliet, Jean-Paul. *Of Comics and Men*. Translated by Bart Beaty and Nick Nguyen. Mississippi UP, 2010.
Gardner, Jared. "Autography's Biography, 1972–2007." *Biography*, vol. 31, no. 1, 2008, pp. 1–26. *Project Muse*. Accessed 7 May 2013.
Gimarc, George. *Punk Diary: The Ultimate Trainspotter's Guide to Underground Rock 1970–1982*. Backbeat Books, 2005.
Green, Grass. "The Strange World of Snappy Sammy Smoot: An Interview with Skip Williamson." *The Comics Journal*, no. 104, 1986, pp. 50–75.
Hasegawa, Michiko. *The Wonderful World of Sazae-san* (サザエさん). Kodansha International, 2006, 12 vols.
Hatfield, Charles. *Alternative Comics: An Emerging Literature*. Mississippi UP, 2005.
"Johnny Ramone Grades the Ramones." *New York Mag*, 18 Mar 2012, http://nymag.com/arts/popmusic/features/johnny-ramone-grades/. Accessed 2 Dec 2014.
Kahn-Egan, Seth. "Pedagogy of the Pissed: Punk Pedagogy in the First-Year Writing Classroom." *College Composition and Communication*, vol. 49, no. 1, 1998, pp. 99–104. *JSTOR*, http://www.jstor.org/stable/35856327. Accessed 28 Mar. 2018.
Kunzle, David. *The History of the Comic Strip*. vol. 1, California UP, 1973.
Kurlansky, Mark. *1968: The Year That Rocked the World*. Random House, 2005.
"Longest Running Animated TV Series." *Guinness World Records*, http://www.guinnessworldrecords.com/world-records/longest-running-animated-tv-series. Accessed 28 Mar. 2018.
Marcus, Greil. "Anarchy in the U.K." *The Rolling Stone: Illustrated History of Rock & Roll*, edited by Jim Miller, Random House, 1980, pp. 451–7.
Marsh, Dave. *Louie Louie: the History & Mythology of the World's Most Famous Rock 'n' Roll Song*. Michigan UP, 2004.
McCarthy, Jim, and Brian Williamson. *Gabba Gabba Hey: The Graphic Story of the Ramones*. Omnibus Press, 2013.
McCloud, Scott. *Understanding Comics*. Harper Perennial, 1994.
Melnick, Monte A., and Frank Meyer. *On the Road with the Ramones*. Bobcat Books, 2007.
Nagai, Gō. *Devilman* (デビルマン). Kodansha Comics, 1994. 5 vols.
Napier, Susan J. "*Akira* and *Ranma 1/2*: The Monstrous Adolescent." *Anime from Akira to Howl's Moving Castle: Experiencing Contemporary Japanese Animation*. 2nd ed., Palgrave MacMillan, 2005, pp. 39–62.
Ohara, T., translator. "Celebrating Its 30th Anniversary, Interview with the Artist of *Kochi-Kame*." *ComiPress*. 19 Sept. 2006, http://comipress.com/news/2006/09/19/759.html. Accessed 28 Mar. 2018.
Perry, Mark. *Sniffin' Glue ... and Other Rock 'n' Roll Habits*. Omnibus Press, 2009.
Poletti, Anna. "Auto/Assemblage: Reading the Zine." *Biography*, vol. 31, no. 1, 2008, pp. 85–102. *Project Muse*. Accessed 10 May 2013.
"Punk." *Oxford English Dictionary*, http://www.oed.com/view/Entry/154685?rskey=ShmSYo&result=1#eid. Accessed 28 Mar. 2018.
Ramone, Dee Dee. *Poison Heart: Surviving the Ramones*. Firefly Publishing, 1997.
_____, and Veronica Kofman. *Lobotomy: Surviving the Ramones*. Thunder's Mouth Press, 2000.
Ramone, Johnny. *Commando: The Autobiography of Johnny Ramone*. Abrams, 2012.
Reynolds, Simon. *Rip It Up and Start Again: Postpunk 1978–1984*. Faber and Faber, 2005.
Rockwell, John. "The Sound of Manhattan." *The Rolling Stone: Illustrated History of Rock & Roll*, edited by Jim Miller, Random House, 1980, pp. 415–23.
Rosenkranz, Patrick. "The ABCs of Autobio Comix." *The Comics Journal*, 6 Mar. 2011, http://www.tcj.com/the-abcs-of-auto-bio-comix-2/. Accessed 28 Mar. 2018.
Sanders, Ed. *Fug You: An Informal History of the Peace Eye Bookstore, the Fuck You Press, the Fugs, and Counterculture in the Lower East Side*. Da Capo Press, 2011.

———. "Liner Notes for The Fugs First Album." *The Fugs*, Fantasy Records, 1994.
Shannon, Edward. "Shameful, Impure Art: Robert Crumb's Autographical Comics and the Confessional Poets." *Biography*, vol. 35, no. 4, 2012, pp. 627–49. *Project Muse*. Accessed 2 May 2013.
Sirc, Geoffrey. "Never Mind the Tagmemics, Where's the Sex Pistols?" *College Composition and Communication*, vol. 48, no. 1, 1997, pp. 9–29. *JSTOR*. Accessed 2 May 2013.
Skinn, Dez. *Comix: The Underground Revolution*. Thunder's Mouth Press, 2004.
Spiegelman, Art. "Those Dirty Little Comics." *Tijuana Bibles: Art and Wit in America's Forbidden Funnies, 1930s-1950s*, edited by Bob Adelman, Simon & Schuster, 1997, pp. 5–10.
Tezuka, Osamu. *Black Jack*. Translated by Camellia Nieh, Vertical, Inc, 2009. 17 vols.
True, Everett. *Hey Ho Let's Go: The Story of the Ramones*. Omnibus Press, 2005.
Tucker, Ken. "New Wave: America." *The Rolling Stone: Illustrated History of Rock & Roll*, edited by Jim Miller, Random House, 1980, pp. 440-4.
Whitlock, Gillian, and Anna Poletti. "Self-Regarding Art." *Biography*, vol. 31, no. 1, 2008, pp. v–xxiii. *Project Muse*. Accessed 7 May 2013.
Wright, Bradford W. *Comic Book Nation*. John Hopkins UP, 2001.
York, Chris, and Rafiel York, editors. *Comic Books and the Cold War*. McFarland, 2012.

PART I: PUNK SUPERHERO COMICS

One Man Artistic Corps
Jack Kirby's OMAC as Punk Precursor

CHRISTOPHER B. FIELD

One of the titles DC Comics included when they rebooted the DC universe as part of their New 52 campaign in 2011 revived one of the characters that Jack Kirby first created for DC back in 1974, *OMAC*. It is interesting to note that the 2011 *OMAC* series appeared to be poised for a prominent position in the New 52 universe upon the relaunch, as the new series was written by DC Comics Co-Publisher, Dan DiDio.[1] With the sleeker metallic look of the mohawk and the bluish skin, the OMAC of 2011 looks strikingly different from the one Kirby created in 1974 and it looks more like an analogue for Marvel's Hulk character. This, of course, was not DC's only attempt to revive the OMAC concept, but this new series, even with the updated secret identity of Cambodian-American Kevin Kho and the bluish tint to OMAC's skin, still looks dated due to the titular character's obscenely tall mohawk, which is more reminiscent of and influenced by the liberty spikes mohawk haircuts of the punk movement than the shorter mohawk in the original series. The decision to place the new *OMAC* series in a prominent position in DC's new continuity is especially complicated by critical reactions to the original series. For instance, in his brilliant book on Kirby's stylistic achievements, *Hand of Fire: The Comics Art of Jack Kirby*, Charles Hatfield describes Kirby's *OMAC* series as "fitfully inspired and often bizarre," and he refers to the "disturbing superheroics" of the series (30). This type of recognition is common among Kirby critics, as the commentary on *OMAC* mostly focuses on it being an afterthought in the wake of the cancellation of his critically celebrated Fourth World work. In his introduction to *Jack Kirby's OMAC: One Man Army Corps*, a compilation of Kirby's original *OMAC* series, Kirby's former assistant Mark Evanier admits that even though he knew Kirby well—by this point, Evanier was no longer working as Kirby's assistant, but they were still close friends—

that even Evanier "didn't fully 'get' *OMAC* on first reading" (5). While Evanier's admission that he "didn't 'get'" the series at first is hardly damning criticism, it does speak to the fact that the series is a weirdly disjointed view of near future society. These critiques of the original series show that this is not a beloved Kirby property that DC decided to revive. Thus, the dated look of the material coupled with the fact that most critics have considered the original series a failure, when they have even bothered to consider it at all, certainly makes DC's decision to revisit this character and provide it with a prominent position a puzzling one. However, in order to see why the original *OMAC* series was so important as to inspire a longstanding legacy within the DC universe, it is necessary to view this series as a possible precursor to punk comics that followed it. Kirby's *OMAC* series, with a strong combination of vivid anti-authoritarian imagery and themes, can be seen as Kirby's powerful response to his feelings of alienation from the characters that he created while he was working at Marvel in the 1960s, and his incorporation of aesthetics that are later taken up by the punk movement situate this series as a valuable precursor to the punk comics movement. To clarify, I do not believe that Jack Kirby had direct influences from the punk movement while he was working on his 1974 DC Comics series *OMAC*. However, I will posit that the punk elements in *OMAC*, such as the punk aesthetics that would become synonymous with the movement, the distrust of capitalist authority figures, and the do-it-yourself (hereafter referred to as DIY) mentality that Kirby adopted in his work demonstrates that *OMAC* is a valuable precursor for later punk comics series.

The first thing that must be acknowledged about Jack Kirby's *OMAC* series is that it is incomplete. *OMAC* is an eight issue series that was first published with a cover date of October 1974, and which concluded with issue #8 sporting a cover date of December 1975. Issue #1 features OMAC's origin story, with two agents from the "Global Peace Agency" (GPA) explaining to Professor Myron Forest that they have found a candidate to receive "fantastic power" (12). As Professor Forest explains, this power will come from a satellite he has positioned in space and dubbed Brother Eye that "shall always help [OMAC] ... Give him the power he needs" (14). Brother Eye responds to his mission by declaring "[OMAC] and I shall become as brothers" (14). In the first issue, Buddy Blank, a low-level employee of Pseudo-People, Inc, is transformed into OMAC—a muscular character who wears blue tights over his torso and red tights over his legs, wears gold boots, gloves, and a belt, and who sports an approximately eight to ten inch black mohawk—just as Buddy is captured by armed security guards from his company as he is trying to figure out where his "girlfriend" Lila has disappeared to. As it turns out, Lila is a "programmed automaton for the amusement and business markets" (20) that the company has been testing out on Buddy. By transforming, OMAC now has the power to escape from the guards and to destroy the androids that Buddy never would have had. At the end of the issue, Brother Eye explains to OMAC how the powers that he now has have been transmitted to him from Brother Eye through "beams…. Some of them bring you my voice…. Others feed you instant information" (26). Some of these "beams" give OMAC the information that he was created by Professor Forest and that he must find Professor Forest before he turns his attention to the kingpin behind Pseudo-People, Inc, Mister Big.

In issue #2, OMAC meets the person responsible for his transformation, Professor Forest, who explains to OMAC that in this world "nations dare not use large armies. Large armies lead to large wars," and that OMAC's job is to "contain conflict before it grows" (35), right before two assassins hired by Mister Big rush into the room and kill Professor Forest. With Brother Eye's guidance, OMAC pursues the assassins and Mister Big while Brother Eye destroys Professor Forest's laboratory to prevent his research from falling into anyone else's hands. OMAC then finds the two assassins and fakes his own death so that he can gain access to Mister Big when the assassins take his body to Mister Big to prove that they have fulfilled their mission, and OMAC and the GPA reveal the plan and arrest Mister Big.

Issue #3 starts with Mister Big, the villain that was responsible for the action in the first two issues, now apprehended, and the series veers in a different direction, as agents from the GPA present OMAC with "official credentials" which give OMAC the authority to "stop the 'flare-ups which endanger world peace'" (55). This is followed by a surreal scene where OMAC is introduced to Mr. and Mrs. Barker, his "test parents" (57), who are chosen by the GPA to give OMAC the "ideal [family]" (56). The GPA then sends OMAC on a mission to hunt down "Kafka…. The bandit marshal and his army of hired mercenaries" because he is "on the march" with dreams of "becoming a Caesar" (58–59). OMAC then spends the rest of the issue fighting through Kafka's army before confronting the tank that holds Kafka at the end of the issue.

Issue #4 picks up on the cliffhanger of the Kafka story, with Brother Eye providing OMAC with the extra strength that he needs to overturn the tank and apprehend Kafka. OMAC then delivers Kafka to the GPA's "court of justice on top of Mount Everest" for Kafka to be booked and held in jail (82). However, Kafka's "avenger" (82)—a biological experiment that "moves like a flying octopus" (86) and which "eats matter and spits energy" (90) that gives it the power of a "hydrogen bomb" (91)—arrives to destroy itself and the prison holding Kafka so that Kafka can "die like Hitler in his bunker" (91), and OMAC is able to defeat the creature by breaking off one of the creature's horns, which sends the creature spiraling off into the atmosphere where it detonates harmlessly.

In issue #5, OMAC confronts the "crime cabal" (96) and Fancy Freddy Sparga, the broker for the cabal that sells opportunities for brain transplants for wealthy clients who want younger bodies, ultimately defeating the cabal and capturing the "Medi-Mind" computer that allows them to perform the transplants in issue #6.

Issue #7 introduces the villain Doctor Skuba, who attempts to steal the world's water reserves to force governments to pay a ransom to retrieve their water. At the end of issue #7, Doctor Skuba hits OMAC with an "electromagnetic shock wave" that transforms OMAC back to Buddy Blank. This is the final appearance of OMAC in the series, as issue #8 focuses on Brother Eye's efforts to intervene in Doctor Skuba's plans. When Doctor Skuba learns that Brother Eye is a satellite that is trying to stop him from space, Doctor Skuba sends three beams into space to magnetize Brother Eye and collect rocky debris from meteors on the satellite's surface so that it is unable to see and transmit beams to earth. The penultimate panel of the series—the last panel that is actually Kirby's—shows the fate of Brother Eye, as "It finally cools.... Brother Eye is now helpless and silent. In a prison of slag" (176). The final panel summarizes that "the effort has caused an overload in Dr. Skuba's equipment" and that the "island explodes in a gigantic fireball.... And his very success brings destruction to the evil Skuba" (176). In his introduction to *Jack Kirby's OMAC: One Man Army Corps*, Evanier clarifies that "this was the final issue of *OMAC*," because "Jack had left DC to return to Marvel, and DC Management decided *OMAC* sales weren't so phenomenal that they had to stick some poor soul with figuring out how to follow Kirby on this one" (5) According to Evanier, this is why the "last issue comes to a whiplash-inducing stop" (5). Evanier claims that "Jack had been setting up something big for [issue] #9, but since he was gone and there wasn't going to be a #9, a new panel (not by Kirby) was inserted to remove the immediate cliffhanger" (5). The result, according to Evanier, was that "Many other story points were left unresolved" (5). Indeed, the ending to issue #8—and by default the series— leaves Buddy Blank's fate unresolved. The last the reader sees of Buddy, he is being pursued by Doctor Skuba's son-in-law, Apollo, as Buddy tries to flee. It is left unresolved if Buddy is able to escape the island by the time it explodes or if he has somehow transformed again into OMAC. Thus, the end of the series leaves the reader unsatisfied, as the fate of the hero is left ambiguous.

When examining this series for punk aesthetics, one of the first things that many readers are likely to notice about Kirby's OMAC is the mohawk. While the mohawk of Kirby's OMAC is significantly more modest than the one found on the 2011 incarnation of the character, it is still prominently featured as one of the traits of the character. Many people might immediately interpret this hairstyle as a direct reference to the punk aesthetics of the 1970s; however, in Sharon M. Hannon's *Punks: A Guide to an American Subculture*, she clarifies that "The most extreme and easily recognized punk hairstyle, called the Mohawk or Mohican, came into fashion in the early 1980s" (53). This would mean that this theory as to OMAC's mohawk would be off by at least six years. However, it is also necessary to recall Mark Evanier's characterization of Kirby in the introduction to the collection of *Jack Kirby's OMAC: One Man Army Corps*, where Evanier marvels at "the number of accurate predictions Jack made about how things would be in ten, twenty, thirty years down the line" before referring to Kirby as "Man of the future" (4). Indeed, Kirby even invokes this type of verbiage in a 1969 interview with Mark Herbert when he claims, "Life moves on and even while we're talking here; you're growing old and your kid brother's ideas might prevail. Whatever you say your kid brother won't listen to because he's going to think that it's old hat; he won't accept it. I have to follow that kid because he's going to buy my comics" (5). He further explains in the same interview that this impulse to follow new trends leads him to think about "what people saw everyday and what they might see five or ten years from now" (7). While it is possible that Kirby's ability to "see five or ten years from now" could have led him to see a punk with a mohawk when he was designing the OMAC character and to incorporate the mohawk into his design due to his nearly supernatural ability to forecast trends, we can lay aside this speculation and instead concentrate on the use of the mohawk in both the punk movement and in the *OMAC* series in order to see that each is borrowing the hairstyle for the same symbolic statement: to shock the viewer through rejection of social conventions. The mohawk hairstyle, named for the Mohawk Indians due to an approximately three inch wide strip of hair worn along the crown of the head, and possibly mistakenly attributed to the Mohawk Indians even though the mohawk as we commonly identify it is closer to the pariki worn by the Pawnee Indians,[2] was meant to part with the traditional Native American hairstyles for men in order to make it more difficult for enemies to scalp them during battle. The mohawk worn by punks is meant to part with the typical hairstyle of another youth subculture, the hippies, who wore their hair long, and it also rejects the social conventions for short hair among men in the general society. In the comic series *OMAC*, OMAC's mohawk is also inspired by the horsehair crests that were worn on the top of Greek combat helmets. This can be seen through several overt references to OMAC as resembling Ares, the Greek god of war. For example, when OMAC is created by Brother Eye in *OMAC* #1 to halt the automaton-building efforts of "Pseudo-People, Inc.," one of the security staff tasked with protecting their manufacturing interests refers to OMAC as "some god of war" (22). This reference to OMAC as a "god of war" stands in stark contrast to the agents of the Global Peace Agency, who must "hide [their] faces with cosmetic spray" (13) in order to "represent every nation" (12). OMAC, or the One Man Army Corps, is developed as a way of "keeping the peace in a world that can't afford violence" (13) because this global peace is so tenuous that it cannot tolerate the use of armed forces. Therefore, OMAC is in direct violation of the mores of his society; the mohawk indicates that he is an agent of war in a society dedicated to peace.

The rejection of cultural mores through the use of the mohawk as a symbol fits with the other uses of mohawks discussed previously, as each of these cases portrays the mohawk as a marker of opposition to social customs, and the rejection of social conventions is one of the traits of the punk movement. As Sharon M. Hannon reminds us, one of the most commonly identified definitions of the punk movement calls for a "rebellion against conformity or against parents, school, work, and society at large" (2). Furthermore, Hannon argues, "Punks' disregard for authority and capitalism led them to reject the dominant culture as hypocritical, shallow, and false" (2). Thus, while OMAC is a superhero, ostensibly charged with the protection of people according to social conventions, he realizes in the first issue of the series that his enemy is not some sort of super villain who is attempting to subvert the laws he must observe; rather, OMAC understands that his enemy is "man's own capacity for self-destruction," and that he is a force to protect society from itself (25) in a fashion that is similar to the punk movement's rejection of capitalist authority figures.

While the *OMAC* series employs a cadre of villains that draw from well-established archetypes of comic book villains, OMAC's true goal in defeating each of his foes in this series is to subdue opponents who have gone too far in pursuit of capitalist aims. The developers of automatons, the "racket" run by "Pseudo People, Inc.," are the villains in issue #1. The owner of this corporation, Mr. Big, one of the "Super-Rich" (30), is the villain in issue #2. Marshal Kafka, the "bandit" (58) and his "army of mercenaries," (58) who is described as wanting "it all ... if he can get it" (59) occupies the position as the villain in issues #3 and #4. Fancy Freddie Sparga, the "Crime Cabal's Regional Manager" (98), who runs the "nightmarish racket" (96) of selling brain transplants to members of the Crime Cabal who want younger and more physically fit bodies is the major villain in issue #5, and in issue #6 OMAC captures and disables the computer that the Cabal uses to perform the transplants. And the "Atomic blackmail" (139) in issues #7 and #8, is the work of the villainous Doctor Skuba, who wants to steal the world's water supply in order to get them to "pay to get it back," promising that his "price will be high!" (149). In each of these cases, Kirby frames not just the villain but the villain's capitalist aims as OMAC's target. The first issue of the series makes this struggle against capitalist pursuits explicit when the powerful OMAC is created by transforming the corporate drone Buddy Blank, who is described as "the timid type" who "never bucks company rules" (18). Kirby even indicates Buddy's alienation from the capitalist system he works for through his last name, "Blank," which illustrates that he is blank, or lacking identity, in a system like this until he is transformed into OMAC. While the transformation into OMAC contains some undoubtedly un-punk elements—for instance, Kirby avoids the complications of portraying this transformation as something that Buddy does not get to decide to do for himself—it does allow OMAC to redress some of the wrongs that his alter ego experienced as part of the capitalist system. This struggle between the villain who abuses the capitalist system and OMAC as the avenger who addresses capitalist excess—while admittedly not as extreme of a critique of capitalism as most of those found within the punk movement—indicates that OMAC, who Evanier recounts was originally conceived of by Kirby as a "Captain America set in the future" (3), is not the one-dimensional representation of a capitalist American system that Captain America personifies; rather, OMAC is a character who allows Kirby to critique capitalist excess and to show the dangers inherent in pursuing this path.

The impulse to protect society from itself is apparent in the *OMAC* series right from the beginning. The series starts with the cryptic warning that the setting for this comic is in "the world that's coming!!" (7). As if the double exclamation points were not strong enough indicators of the urgency of the setting, this "world that's coming" tagline is also repeated multiple times in each of the issues of the series. This continuous string of references to a "world that's coming" imbues the series with a sense of dread and urgency at the fate that awaits the reader. Referring back to Kirby's preoccupation with attempting to forecast in his comics in the present what readers in the future "might see five or ten years from now," it is possible to see this series as a warning to readers of what Kirby sees as a possible—albeit an exaggerated—outcome of an unchecked pursuit of capitalist aims.

It is important to keep in mind that despite the criticism of the capitalist system that he provides in *OMAC*, that Kirby was at heart a believer in the capitalist system, using a DIY mentality not only because he preferred to have creative control over his creations but also because it allowed him to work at his own frenetic pace so that he could do more work for more money; however, at this point in his career, having left Marvel several years earlier because he felt he was not being fairly compensated for his input into the creation of many of Marvel's most successful characters, it is possible to see that Kirby's critique in *OMAC* is not focused on capitalism itself but on capitalist excess. In defining the punk movement, Hannon describes it as "From the beginning, punks embraced the do-it-yourself (DIY) ethos, disregarded authority, and rejected corporate commercialism" (2). Similarly, in her article "Misfit Lit: 'Punk Writing,' and Representations of Punk Through Writing and Publishing," Miriam Rivett describes the DIY ethos among the punk movement as that in which "producing is as crucial as *what is being produced*"

(43). As we have already seen, *OMAC* (or what is being produced) carries a strong critique of capitalist excesses, but we must also look at Kirby's method for constructing this series. The credits on the first issue of the series clarifies Kirby's role, as it claims it is "Edited.... Written, and Drawn by Jack Kirby" (8). Issues #5 and #6 would make much bolder claims about Kirby's role, with the credits to issue #5 being modified to "Produced by Jack Kirby" (97) and issue #6 proclaiming "The works by Jack Kirby" (119). While the credits are clear in attributing the bulk of the work in the series to Kirby, it must also be noted that the credits also include inking and lettering credits for D. Bruce Berry and Mike Royer. Mark Evanier's *Kirby: King of Comics* provides a relatively simple explanation for why this division of labor was necessary for Kirby, claiming that "Jack didn't like to ink" (45). Thus, Kirby chose not to ink his own books in order to focus on the portions of the book he was better suited for, which meant that the inking duties had to be assigned to someone else. Kirby, though, understood the value of such a collaboration, as in his interview with Mike Herbert he claims, "Nobody does anything by themself. When a guy comes out and makes a statement like, 'I did this,' you can be sure that 50 people helped him" (8). In these comments, Kirby points out a fundamental flaw in the DIY model: namely, that DIY often means to produce a work with little help from others, but it rarely means that the production and distribution was accomplished solely by one individual. Rather, a DIY mentality means to produce a work according to one's own artistic vision. This was, of course, one of the more difficult aspects of creating a comic for Kirby, as for most of his career he was working under corporate supervision. However, the opportunity for Kirby to move from Marvel to DC in 1970 brought with it more creative control, which in his now infamous 1989 interview with Gary Groth, Kirby describes as "like a heaven because I was an individual there. I was able to do something under my own name. In other words, if I wrote, 'Jack Kirby' wrote it. If I drew, 'Jack Kirby' drew it. And the truth was there ... and I felt at last a sense of freedom" (46). This sense of artistic freedom was important for Kirby because of his belief that he was given inadequate recognition—both verbal and monetary—for his role in creating and shaping many of Marvel's major characters. In his interview with Groth, Kirby recalls:

> I came in [to the Marvel offices] and they were moving out the furniture, they were taking desks out—and I needed the work! I had a family and a house, and all of a sudden Marvel is coming apart. Stan Lee is sitting on a chair crying. He didn't know what to do, he's sitting in a chair crying—he was just still out of his adolescence. I told him to stop crying. I says, 'Go in to Martin [Goodman, the publisher] and tell him to stop moving the furniture out, and I'll see that the books make money.' And I came up with a raft of new books and all these books began to make money.... I came up with the Fantastic Four. I came up with Thor. Whatever it took to sell a

book, I came up with. Stan Lee had never been editorial-minded. It wasn't possible for Stan to come up with new things—or old things for that matter. Stan Lee wasn't a guy that read or that told stories. Stan Lee was a guy that knew where the papers were or who was coming to visit that day. Stan Lee is essentially an office worker, OK? I'm essentially something else: I'm a storyteller. My job is to sell my stories [38].

Kirby's comments as to Stan Lee's involvement of the creation of these properties are most probably due to his frustration for not being given what he thought was fair compensation for his role in developing these properties, as most comics critics and historians will generally concede that Stan Lee at least had some role in creating these characters; however, the feelings of a worker that is alienated from the product he created are the crucial portions of this passage. This passage easily evokes a sense of the alienated Buddy Blank as he uncovers the schemes of the "Pseudo People, Inc." right before he is transformed into OMAC and he is given the power to stop them. Kirby's transition to DC, then, is echoed by his character's transformation, and his DIY methods at DC, a role which gave him a newfound creative and financial freedom because he was better compensated for his efforts, allow him to expose the capitalist abuses of his former employer. Evanier sheds some light into the creative freedoms that Kirby enjoyed at DC in his introduction to *Jack Kirby's OMAC: One Man Army Corps*, when Evanier recounts a story of an unnamed interviewer who, confused by the series, asked Kirby "Did you know what you were doing, where you were going with it?" (5). According to Evanier, Kirby responded, "I knew where I was going. If I'd known you wanted to come along, I'd have taken you with me" (5). This response, which Evanier characterizes as "silly" (5), also contains a kernel of truth. While the series is at its core a capitalist pursuit—meant to fulfill Kirby's page count quota for DC and to make money for himself and the company—it also comes with enough artistic freedom that allows Kirby to develop the series as he chooses. While this reading of the *OMAC* series is not a perfect punk parable, as the passage from the Groth interview clearly shows that Kirby had capitalist pursuits of his own, it does demonstrate that Kirby was able to draw from his experiences at Marvel on either a conscious or subconscious level in order to express themes that seem eerily prescient in light of the punk movement, such as the dangers of capitalist authority figures and anxieties over a dystopian future in the "world that's coming!"

Tying Jack Kirby's 1974 series for DC Comics, *OMAC*, to punk themes is admittedly speculative. There is not one piece of evidence that points to Jack Kirby having an affinity for early Ramones records and predicting the onset of the punk movement or an interview where he describes seeing early liberty spikes mohawks on punks and decides to coopt the look for his brand new superhero. However, some of the same traits that became synonymous with the punk movement, such as a DIY mentality and a distrust of capitalist structures, are a major theme in this work, and when those themes are connected with punk aesthetics like the use of a mohawk haircut to depict the main character as the warrior antithesis to a peace-obsessed society, it is possible to see Kirby's *OMAC* series as an early punk precursor which is deserving of a prominent place within modern comics due to its influence on subsequent punk comics.

NOTES

1. It is also important to note that the prominence of OMAC within the relaunched DC lineup is not a coincidence. The specter of Jack Kirby looms large over the New 52, as DC revived Kirby characters such as OMAC and The Demon and either gave them their own series or made them prominent parts of other series, and Darkseid is used as the villain in the first arc of the new Justice League title that leads to the formation of the league in order to protect earth from Darkseid and his forces.

2. See, for example, the description that Mark van de Logt provides in "'The Powers of the Heavens Shall Eat of My Smoke': The Significance of Scalping in Pawnee Warfare": "[Pawnee men] adorned the scalp hair, especially the scalp lock, with feathers, jewelry, and other objects. Although some men wore their hair in two braids that hung over their shoulders, the roach hairstyle was more common. This roach consisted of a small strip of hair on the top of the head. The Pawnees used animal fat to make it stand up" (83).

WORKS CITED

Evanier, Mark. "Introduction." *Jack Kirby's OMAC: One Man Army Corps*, DC Comics, 2008, pp. 3–5.
_____. *Kirby: King of Comics*. Abrams, 2008.
Groth, Gary. "I've Never Done Anything Halfheartedly." *The Comics Journal Library, Volume One: Jack Kirby*, Fantagraphics, 2002, pp. 20–49.
Hannon, Sharon M. *Punks: A Guide to an American Subculture*. Greenwood, 2010.
Hatfield, Charles. *Hand of Fire: The Comics Art of Jack Kirby*. Univ. Press of Mississippi, 2012.
Herbert, Mark. "There Is Something Stupid in Violence as Violence." *The Comics Journal Library, Volume One: Jack Kirby*, Fantagraphics, 2002, pp. 3–13.
[Kirby, Jack (w, p), and Mike Royer and D. Bruce Berry (i,l).] *Jack Kirby's OMAC: One Man Army Corps*. DC Comics, 2008.
Lawley, Guy. "'I Like Hate and I Hate Everything Else': The Influence of Punk on Comics." *Punk Rock: So What?*, edited by Roger Sabin, Routledge, 1999, pp. 100–119.
McAllister, Murray J. "Mohawks and Combat Boots: The Schizoid Dilemma of Punks." *Bulletin of The Menninger Clinic*, vol. 63, no. 1, 1999, pp. 89–102. EBSCOhost, search.ebscohost.com/login.aspx?direct=true&db=psyh&AN=1999-00963-007&site=ehost-live.
Rivett, Miriam. "Misfit Lit: 'Punk Writing,' and Representations of Punk Through Writing and Publishing." *Punk Rock: So What?*, edited by Roger Sabin, Routledge, 1999, pp. 31–48.
Sabin, Roger. "Introduction." *Punk Rock: So What?*, edited by Roger Sabin, Routledge, 1999, pp. 1–13.
Skeely, Tim. "I Created an Army of Characters, and Now My Connection with Them Is Lost." *The Comics Journal Library, Volume One: Jack Kirby*, Fantagraphics, 2002, pp. 15–17.

Captain America
All-American Punk
Jill Dahlman

When thinking of the term "punk," Captain America is not the first comic book hero who comes to mind. However, if the term "punk" itself is examined, a plethora of meanings is discovered from "inferior" ("punk") to "criminal" ("punk") to a basic understanding of punk music, which is identified by the lyrics being political or anti-establishment. Thus, when applying any of the definitions noted earlier to superheroes, Captain America is not the first that comes to mind. However, Captain America does have a revolutionary, subversive punk side. From the Silver Age representation of Captain America as "Nomad," to his appearance in *Civil War* when the character goes against the United States' government and its call for superhero registration, the attitude of being anti-establishment is considered punk. Even when considering the fashion of punk, Captain America's uniform is a rendition of the American flag, an item frequently appropriated for fashion in the punk movement. Thus, Captain America can be considered punk. A patriotic punk, but a punk, nonetheless. An examination of Captain America through the Silver era and contemporary publications demonstrates that this all–American good guy character is far more of a rebel with a cause—the cause of portraying and defending America and its ideals as Captain America believes they should be.

The use of the comic book as a means of portraying this patriotic revolutionary punk attitude is proper. The term "polysemy" is used to describe how comic books use text and image to convey a message and contributes to Dick Hebdige's meaning in the classic *Subculture: The Meaning of Style*, where Hebdige states that "each text is seen to generate a potentially infinite range of meanings" (117). What better place to discuss multiple texts and multiple meanings than through the messages embedded in a single bubble, in a single panel, in a single comic? Thus, it is through polysemy that the rhetoric of Captain America, in all of his patriotic punk renditions, lives. Within the pages, the panels, the bubbles, the gutters, language can take on multiple meanings. Action is shown through movement in different panels, but it is only in the space between the panels, the gutters, where the action takes place—where the reader determines how much and what kind of action takes place, and determines whether that action, especially in the case of Captain America, is for good or for revolutionary purposes—to determine whether Captain America is a perfect patriot or a perfect punk, or a combination of the two.

By all accounts, Captain America (a.k.a. Steve Rogers) comes from a lower-class background. This is not a person of lineage. This is evident from the description of Rogers wherein Rogers is described as sickly-looking, a "scrawny, 4-F weakling ... who participates in a secret government experiment ..." (Ross and Dini n.p.), which depicts the condition that Steve Rogers is in when he reports to Abraham Erskine's laboratory to take part in the Super Soldier experiment.

The graphic compilation *Captain America: Red, White & Blue* sets forth (in the character's words) why the character is the way he is. The character notes that upon injection of the serum, his "[B]ody radically grew and changed, the simple man that was Steve Rogers died. In his new place was born a new being, less a man than an ideal. An inspirational symbol of the glory that is America" (Ross and Dini 1). What's important to note is that as a sickly-looking (and according to the back cover of *Captain America: Sentinel of Liberty*, a mere ninety pounds) Rogers did not fit the ideal of the American soldier. He had signed up to be a soldier, was rejected, and then chose to be altered to fit the American ideal. While some may state that this is the personification of the American Dream, the message that it sends is that the "true" or real person is not sufficient or good enough to be a representative of America without some form of alteration.

This idea of being not good enough is reinforced when considering Hebdige's definition of *homology*, which is "to describe the symbolic fit between the values and lifestyles of a group, its subjective experience and the musical forms it uses to express or reinforce its focal concerns" (113). While music is not a strong part of the Captain America lore, unless considering the songs that evoke the image, such as Guns N' Roses' "Paradise City," among others, the remainder of the definition fits Captain America. He starts out as not being a *symbolic* fit of the values of America. America is the home of the free and the brave, but it is also a home of physically fit soldiers—Steve Rogers does not fit that image. Somehow, this iconic image that does not fit America's ideals in its original form becomes an embodiment of America in its altered form.

Figure 1: This image depicts the condition that Steve Rogers is in when he reports to the scientist's laboratory to take part in the Super Soldier experiment (Lee 12) © MARVEL.

This alteration of the person to fit American ideals, especially military ideals, is significant. Military personnel, former and current, claim that the military's purpose is to break down the person upon entering the military and transform that person during boot camp to become an American fighting machine. The poverty that Steve Rogers no doubt came from is best demonstrated in the inaugural issue of *Captain America* where, as noted earlier, Steve Rogers, a "sickly" man, attempts to enlist, and that background fits in well as an example of how the military could choose a second-rate citizen to be transformed into a military fighting machine. It is, however, important to note that the background of the individual is what shapes that individual into making judgment calls, morals, ethics, even perception of events. As Geoff Klock, quoting Richard Rorty, points out in *How to Read Superhero Comics and Why*:

> Getting somebody to deny a belief [or an upbringing] for no reason is a first step toward making her incapable of having a self because she becomes incapable of weaving a coherent web of belief and desire. ... She is unable to give a reason for her belief that fits together with her other beliefs. She becomes irrational not in the sense that she has lost contact with reality but in the sense that she can no longer rationalize—no longer justify herself to herself [110].

What Steve Rogers is created to be is a form of physical resurrection, and the death of the old is apparent when Captain America claims that the "old" Steve Rogers has died as noted in *Captain America: Red, White & Blue*. This metaphorical death only serves to demonstrate that the ideals of Captain America have sublimated any ideals of Steve Rogers. Furthermore, as Hebdige points out, when considering subculture, "...by the same token, nothing, not even these forbidden signifiers (bondage, safety pins, chains, hair-dye, etc.) is sacred and fixed" (115). Captain America in costume has the freedom to act or to perform a specific way that is befitting of an image. It's as if wearing a specific pair of Chucks will give the wearer a new attitude. As Danny Fingeroth points out in the book *Superman on the Couch: What Superheroes Really Tell Us about Ourselves and Our Society*:

> The superhero's answers to these questions are generally: "I will be who I must be in order to fulfill my mission of doing good works. Whatever serves that purpose is who I will be both in and out of my costume." ... This may be the key to the societal identity crises the heroes reflect. For the superhero, the answer to the contradictory needs is: "Don't be selfish. Serve the community and the rest will fall into place. Who am I? I am the mechanism for perfecting and serving society. *And I know exactly what actions I must take to do that*" [58; emphasis in original].

The cover of Captain America's debut issue, perhaps the busiest cover in the history of comics, demonstrates how revolutionary this character is. The first issue is dated March 1941, but oftentimes comic books of that era were released several months prior to the date reflected on the cover. This issue could have been released as early as December 1940—nearly one year prior to America's official declaration of war following the bombing of Pearl Harbor on December 7, 1941.[1] On that front cover, Captain America is shown punching Hitler in the jaw. Even before Congress had declared war, Captain America's patriotic punk is showing through. This character is not happy with Hitler, and he has no qualms about showing it. This image, as noted by David Zimmerman in his book *Comic Book Character: Unleashing the Hero in Us All*, "sold the very message that the idealistic reading audience wanted to buy—American soldiers were the best in the world, and each of them would submit himself to whatever the government could cook up to secure victory," (87) even if it meant better living through chemistry: injecting its waifs with the Super Soldier serum.

Captain America stood by the ideology of the American government as he taught children to abide by wartime practices such as material conservation and recycling, thus allowing children to actively participate in the war effort. For example, for a dime, children could join Captain America's Sentinels of Liberty. Kids got a membership card that stated, "I solemnly pledge to uphold the principles of the Sentinels of Liberty and assist Captain America in his war against spies in the U.S.A." (Mallory 56–57). Children believed that they were taking an active part in the war effort (even if this does ring frighteningly close to the junior spies of Orwell's *1984*)—and this pledge provided that illusion. The Sentinels of Liberty was so effective that children began notifying local authorities of suspicious behavior of neighbors and relatives, leading to the arrests of numerous spies. As a result, German sympathizers threatened the offices of Marvel Comics in New York City, and the mayor of New York City ordered extra police protection for the employees of Marvel Comics.

It wasn't just the Sentinels of Liberty that was revolutionary; Captain America's costume spoke legions. Showing his punk fashion way before the Sex Pistols brandished the Union Jack, Captain America wore a blue skull cap with an "A" emblazoned on it, a blue, chain-mail top with white sleeves, red and white vertical stripes around his middle, red boots, red gloves: he was draped in the American flag. And he carried a shield. (See Figure 2, a reprint of cover art [Lee 9].) (The shield was originally triangular with three large stars and red, white, and blue stripes, which later morphed into a sphere.) The spherical shield looked as if it were a giant bullseye (circular with red and white concentric stripes), and is more than a protector: it exemplifies Captain America's greatness. Wolverine of the X-Men (himself the epitome of punk-ness) commented, "I like the suit. Just the thing for playing it sly and sneaky," to which Captain America replies, "That's not my style. I'm supposed to be a symbol" (Duin and Richardson 72).

Following World War II, Captain America continues his career into the Korean War, but eventually America runs out of wars to sustain the character, and the character is retired along with the Golden Age of comic books. It doesn't take long for America to enter into another war, however: Vietnam. To reintroduce the character, Captain America is found by the Avengers in a block of melting ice. Things are different with the Avengers—the name alone suggests that. On the back cover of the *Avengers Masterworks* compilation, the definitions of "avenge" and "avenger" work together to enhance the notion of what is revolutionary or punk: "avenge" is defined as "to set right what has gone wrong; to correct an imbalance; to effect justice." Whereas "avenger" is defined as "a person who corrects imbalances, especially in the justice system; one who avenges." To be punk means to recognize the inconsistencies of the current government, to call attention to those inconsistencies,

Figure 2: This image depicts Captain America's "punk" uniform (Lee 9) © MARVEL.

and to attempt to effectuate a change. The Avengers are a group of street-fighting superheroes that decides to work together to fight "what has gone wrong; to correct an imbalance; to effect justice." What is important to note, though, is that in the Silver Age of comics, these "avengers" don't conform to the ideals affixed to superheroes in the Golden Age. Sometimes the individual superheroes stay with the group; sometimes they don't. In other words, they are punk or embody the qualities of punk.

Captain America's cohorts in the Avengers are atypical of the previous superheroes. They include Daredevil, a blind superhero, who relies on his heightened senses to fight crime, and the Black Panther, the first black superhero, who is an African king turned superhero, among others. All is not always sunny and rosy, and the issues are not always black and white for the Avengers. This group sometimes gets along and sometimes doesn't—it isn't always "one big happy family." It is a team with real emotions and real problems—typical of Marvel's characters of the Silver Age.

When revived in March 1964, nine years into the Vietnam War, Captain America is a changed superhero as he remembers that his kid sidekick, Bucky, died during World War II. One could call this a case of post-traumatic stress disorder. Captain America is grief-stricken and struggling with his emotions, as seen in *Avengers* #4 when he awakens from being entombed in a block of ice frantically screaming "Who am I?? For a moment, I had almost forgotten myself! But *I am not lucky enough to forget forever*! … to forget that I was once the man the world called—Captain America!" (Lee and Kirby 78). This is a changed, cynical Captain America, who cannot remain steadfast in the ideals of the character Captain America. He is missing twenty years of his life, and he watched his sidekick die. Furthermore, there's a war going on, and Captain America isn't certain the government is right.

The question of whether Captain America is going to go to war with the Vietnam contingency rises to the forefront, but with Captain America's mental status, his presence with the soldiers is not clearly defined. After an initial physical fight with the Avengers, the narrator tells the reader that "a veil of sadness comes over his [Captain America's] eyes…" (Lee and Kirby 79). This motif is repeated as his eyes are referred to as "tragedy-haunted" (Lee and Kirby 80) (or similar), and he states, "I didn't care if I lived or died…" (Lee and Kirby 80) when describing the loss of Bucky, arguably his best friend. The writers of this series understood the emotional impact losing a best friend would have upon an individual and wrote it into the storyline. Captain America faces people who recognize the iconic figure and treat him as if he were the same person, uttering words upon his return such as, "…But you've come back—just when the world has **need** of such a man—just like **fate** planned it this way!" (Lee and Kirby 83; emphasis in original). But this Captain America is unlike the Captain America of the Golden Age of comics.

This Captain America *has* changed. He muses, "What happens next?? Can't return to my career as Captain America—it would be meaningless without Bucky! I don't belong in this age—in this year—no place for me—if only Bucky were here—if only—..." (Lee and Kirby 83). Eventually, Captain America regains composure and sets out to solve a crime, stating, "This is what I was **meant** to do! This is the destiny I can never escape!" (Lee and Kirby 85; emphasis in original). While still able to perform his job, Captain America is nonetheless a changed person after watching Bucky die. This Captain America is unlikely to blindly follow orders. When there is a threat to himself or his friends, he answers the call. The enemy must be certain, though, for without a clear enemy, twenty years is too long for Captain America to gloss over.

When the enemy is not clearly defined, as was the case in the Vietnam War, Captain America has no clear enemy, and his patriotic role is called into question. Stan Lee provides insight:

> Cap felt that he was in the wrong time, living in the 1960s but with a 1930s outlook on everything, and he was aware of that. I had a line—I can't remember what the story was—but he was thinking that the establishment isn't always right, and sometimes you have to think twice before going along blindly with what the establishment says or does. And he was thinking of himself in the past, he said: "Maybe I should have acted less and questioned more." And that sort of set the tone for him when we brought him back [Mallory 61].[2]

This Captain America reflects the cynicism with the government in much the same way as the punk movement that succeeded Captain America's establishment as a superhero; the iconic symbol that is Captain America, a flag from a symbol of freedom and democracy, becomes a symbol of the unrest of that time period.

It is important to note that the ideology of Captain America is the American Dream. The American Dream, however, has failed Captain America. It is nearly impossible to conjure up all of the aspects of the American Dream that go unfulfilled. American patriotism isn't so much an allegiance to a nation, but rather, to a belief system—to a specific value code. Contained within that ideology is an atmosphere of ideological conformity as a condition for being a good citizen. As such, it is an ideology that fails most individuals in America today—and certainly many of the young citizens of the 1960s reading the *Avengers* comic books. At this juncture, Captain America questions not only his ideologies in the role as Captain America, but also the ideologies of the government—just as punk musicians question the government through its music lyrics, striving for purity in sound.

Captain America is not alone in questioning ideologies. Not too surprisingly, the superheroes had changed their way of life not only to conform to the rules of the Comics Code Authority necessary for publication in the Silver Age of comics, but also to reflect the changes in attitude towards the war(s). Gone were the Golden Age days of the super-confident patriotic superhero beating the obvious enemy to a pulp. In walked a new superhero: one with emotions, problems, and hang-ups—much like the human audience reading the pages of the comic.

The audience, too, had changed. While the primary audience in the Golden Age had been pre-adolescent children with a secondary market of mature adults,[3] teenagers and young adults traditionally were not included in the comic book audience. After the Silver Age began, comic book companies addressed this forgotten audience. To address this new audience, Marvel started a fan club, the Merry Marvel Marching Society, and a "Letters to the Editor" section—none of which had been done before in comic book history. It is within these "Letters to the Editor" that Captain America's decision of whether or not to join American soldiers in the battlefields of Vietnam is discussed by the fans. The Captain America of the Golden Age would not have hesitated to go off to war, but the Captain America of the Silver Age was a different story.

As noted earlier, Captain America was created specifically as a wartime patriot for World War II. Although he is not the first "superpatriot," he is the most enduring and one of the most-widely recognized superheroes. The character is known best for its patriotism. This sentiment is echoed by one of Captain America's creators, Joe Simon. In Mike Benton's *The Comic Book in America: An Illustrated History*, Simon, co-creator of Captain America, says: "Captain America was very much a reflection of his time. He was patriotic when the country was patriotic. ... We saw him as a political statement fleshed out to be an active force" (34). This quote by Simon is important because by the time of the Vietnam War and Captain America's clear questioning of his own position in the world noted earlier, things are about to change. As Mark Gruenwald (a Marvel Editor) puts it, "Captain America was all revved up to defend America against her enemies but 'there wasn't a clear enemy out there'" (qtd. in Duin and Richardson 72). This lack of a clear enemy is problematic for both Captain America the hero and Steve Rogers. Jim Steranko states, "[Captain America] was a great concept, ... but he's a character out of his time. He was and still is the American ideal. Of course, the American ideal has changed. It isn't easy to represent all the things the country has been through since Kennedy" (qtd. in Duin and Richardson 72-73). It is difficult to defend a country in indefensible times. It is especially difficult for an icon— a superhero—that is the very embodiment of patriotism.

Captain America faces a crisis unlike any he faced within the Avengers when it comes to his stance over the Vietnam War. As a patriotic superhero, where exactly is Captain America going to take a position? Would he support the troops and go to Vietnam? Would he buck the establishment altogether and stay out of the war? It is significant that the most patriotic superhero in the business, the superhero created for the sole purpose of promoting patriotism in a time of war, chooses to stay on the home front and say very little about Vietnam. Captain America's stance reflects the uncertainty of the times—this "no position" reinforced the "no position" or "get us out of Vietnam" position that many Americans were taking over the War. And how many young citizens at the time were celebrating the draft or running out to enlist? Few, if any. Captain America questions more and obeys less as time progresses. The reason therefor is noted by Nomad (Captain America) in *Captain America and the Falcon* issue #183:

> C.A. [Captain America] lived in a **dream** world! He was born in **1941**, at a time when the **American** dream filled **all our hearts**! We **willingly** went to war against the Red Skull's kind, because they wanted to destroy that dream! But now, with the **White House suicide** ... and everything **since**...! From the moment I returned back to life in **1964**, at the beginning of our Viet Nam War, I felt out of my time—but it took Number One [Leader of the Secret Empire] to make me see just **how** wrong things had gone while I'd been away! The people who had **custody** of the American Dream had **abused** both it and us! There was **no way** I could keep calling myself "Captain America," because the others who acted in America's name were every bit as bad ... as ... the ... Red ... Skull...! ... Oh **Lord**.... If I wasn't prepared for any and **all** threats to the American Dream, then what was I **doing** as Captain America? [Englehart 30–31].

This change in Captain America in the Bronze Age brings a new depth to the character. His purpose and resolve as a superhero upholding the American ideology seem to ebb away in the late 1960s, especially concerning his own emotional problems over the loss of Bucky and as a patriotic superhero *not* joining the troops in Vietnam. This all causes the character to slip into a major identity crisis and leaves him to temporarily abandon his superhero persona altogether. Rather than fighting Cold War adventures, Captain America tackles social problems with the Falcon, an African-American superhero. Together they battle for social justice issues, such as "poverty, racism, pollution, and political corruption" (Wright 245), which although not punk-like in its altruism, nonetheless is rebellious, especially considering how rebellious the entire idea of civil rights is, even to (and especially) this day.

By the mid–1970s, the cynicism of Watergate has changed not only Captain America, but the citizens of the United States. The 1950s version of Captain America finds himself reunited with his pal Bucky.[4] Bradford Wright describes this story best:

> Captain America discovers that an organization called the Committee to Regain America's Principles (CRAP), led by a right-winger named Quentin Harderman (who bears a strong resemblance to H.R. Haldeman) is actually a front for the Secret Empire, a fascist organization bent upon taking control of the U.S. government. The hero follows a labyrinth of political conspiracies, assassinations, and cover-ups that ultimately leads him to the White House and the Oval Office itself. Although the

lanky villain's face is obscured by shadows, there is little doubt as to his identity. Captain America gasps, "Good lord! You!" From the shadows, the villain answers, "Exactly! But high political office didn't satisfy me! My power was still too constrained by legalities!" Then, in what may have been a bit of wishful thinking on [the author's] part, the crook commits suicide, leaving Captain America in silent disillusionment. "This man trusted the country of his birth," reads the caption. Now, "Like millions of Americans each in his own way, he has seen his trust mocked! And this man is Captain America" [245].

Clearly, much to Captain America's dismay, the government has not always been truthful with him. This realization, along with other factors, including the discovery of his (and Bucky's) government-created doppelganger, causes the character to quit the superhero "business" altogether. To further this idea, in issue #177 (originally published in 1974) of *Captain America and the Falcon*, the Falcon states, "He had his faith in **America** shattered..." (9; emphasis in original). The Captain America of the Golden Age comics would neither have questioned the government nor have quit his position. The Captain America of the Silver Age would have stood by his principles. Giving up on either his position or his government would have rendered him a punk in the eyes of both the government and his audience. More important, when his friend the Falcon asks Captain America to accompany him on patrol, Steve Rogers states angrily, "**Captain America doesn't exist any more!** He's a **legend** of **World War II**—no longer living!" (Englehart and Warner 10; emphasis in original). The bigger question becomes "why," and Steve Rogers answers that when Rogers states:

> I gave up being **Captain America** because America's no longer the place I set out to **represent** in 1941. I **slept** through the '50's frozen in **ice**—and when I was **thawed** in the '60's, I guess I **needed** to believe that nothing had **changed**—to **prove** to myself that I hadn't **missed** anything! Well, it took a **long time comin'** but I **finally discovered** an **obvious fact**: Nothing's what it was in 1941" [Englehart and Warner 30; emphasis in original].

This statement is followed when Nomad states that Captain America died "the day his **ideals** did!" (30; emphasis in original). Indeed, the narrator of issue #179 reminds the readers that Rogers is "a man *twenty years out of his time.* Since that day, Captain America has sought his destiny in this brave new world. ... Now, deeply troubled by current **political events**, he has **abandoned** the role of Captain America to become, once again, plain **Steve Rogers**" (Englehart and Warner 1; emphasis in original). The abandonment causes him to reassess himself and his role in the world. The twenty-year sleep reminds Captain America that this is not the America he supported so long ago. In *Captain America and the Falcon* issue #183 he thinks to himself, "**Blast**! Why can't I ever remember how **complex** life is today? One action can spark a **hundred** reactions—a **thousand**! Everything **grows**—**mutates**...

" (12; emphasis in original). This is reiterated in the Marvel Comics Event, *Civil War: Casualties of War*, when Captain America and Iron Man Tony Stark discuss the government request for superhero registration. Captain America tells Tony Stark, "...Governments change. Administrations come and go. I had to become Nomad and Later the Captain when certain politicians decided they didn't like the way I operated," (Millar n.p.) adding more information to the background of Captain America and the political issues that caused him to turn his back on the government, essentially becoming more punk, more rebellious.

Reflecting upon his decision to leave Captain America behind, Rogers states in *Captain America and the Falcon* issue #179:

> I don't think I've **ever** felt as **free** as I have these past weeks. I've had no **master** but **myself**, and no **cause** but my own! I don't mean that **selfishly**, now—just that I've been able to live **entirely** as myself and not at **all** as a piece of **public property**! Captain America has a **legend** to live up to, and legends have a habit of **growing** as they **spread**. I was like the **President**: an **institution** instead of a **man** [2; emphasis in original].

This realization is significant. Up to this point, Rogers blindly follows orders. He is going through a reassessment of his life, his purpose, and determines that there is more. Much like punk musicians took a reassessment of the music scene and the establishment and then formulated a new sound and lyric, one that was closer to the simpler (and arguably more pure) sound of the early days of rock 'n' roll, Captain America is doing the same. What he becomes is solely dependent upon his own personal reassessment of how to reconcile the legend, the institution, with the changed person. It isn't until a fight with the Golden Archer in *Captain America and the Falcon* issue #179 that the narrator notes that Steve Rogers is put "in touch with **himself**, past and present!" (16; emphasis in original). It is the Golden Arrow, who turns out to be Hawkeye of the Avengers in disguise, who persuades Steve Rogers to not "waste" his powers "because of the craziness in **Washington**" (18; emphasis in original). Thus, Captain America becomes Nomad, the man without a country. The character has not given up on America, but because the ideals of America changed and are no longer in conformance with the ideals of Captain America, Steve Rogers, the alter ego, also changes, in essence going back to his roots from a simpler more pure time.

True to 1970's lore, as Nomad, Captain America *needs* to get away, to reinvent himself much as the punk rockers reinvent the music scene. He searches for a way to get back to his roots. As an embodiment of the ideals of America, which governmental ideals have gone astray, it makes sense that he'd have a crisis of personal ideals until he could figure out a way to reconcile with the problem of betrayal by the very government he had sworn to uphold and defend. In this case, Captain America would need to disappear in order to figure this whole mess out. Captain America is gone until his patriotism takes over, and he once again becomes part of the nation.

Thereafter, Captain America's inner revolutionary punk stays relatively under the radar until 9/11. Shortly after 9/11, Marvel Comics releases the *Civil War* series, pitting superheroes against superheroes, in response to the government's request for superhero registration. While on the surface this series appears to have nothing to do with the ideals of the United States government, or Steve Rogers, there are indeed some connections.

Civil War begins with a superhero-created disaster outside of a schoolyard in Stamford, Connecticut. The New Warriors, Speedball, Night Thrasher, Namorita (Prince Namor's cousin), and Microbe, stars of a reality television show, attempt to take down four supervillains, Cobalt Man, Coldheart, Speedfreak, and Nitro, all escapees of Rykers prison. The younger superheroes, punks themselves as represented by Hebdige in *Subculture: The Meaning of Style*, not only in attitude but also in dress style, are seriously out of their league by starting the attack. The supervillains have nearly taken out far more experienced superheroes, such as Spider-Man, and lived to tell the tale. The young superheroes do not call in for reinforcements from more experienced superheroes, but opt to take down the supervillains themselves across the street from a schoolyard.

The principal idea behind this desire to take out the villains rests with media ratings. The young superheroes decide to take on this chore not because they think they are capable of defeating these villains (in fact they question the leader, Speedball, about their ability to do so), but rather because if they succeed in defeating them, they believe it will achieve high ratings for their reality show. While three of the young superheroes do manage to take down three supervillains, Namorita and the supervillain Nitro manage to not only take down each other (Namorita is killed, whereas Nitro escapes when he is blown into another state), but because they are totally oblivious to their fight taking place outside of a schoolyard where innocent children are playing, they predictably kill 600 people in what later becomes known as The Stamford Incident.[5]

Understandably, from here, the American citizens begin clamoring for a superhero registration, one that has been in the works in the past and originally opposed by Tony Stark. With the citizens likening the superheroes to lethal weapons and demanding governmental accountability by making superheroes agents of the government who have undergone training and subjecting them to the same kind of scrutiny as other law enforcement and military officials, Iron Man believes that the superheroes' required registration is inevitable. This begins the "real" story of those superheroes in favor of registration and those who are opposed to registering their real identity with the government, seeing it as a violation of their civil rights, even though the X-Men have already been forced to register.

Not unexpectedly, the American citizens are outraged by the Stamford Incident. Citizens expect certain areas of their lives to be safe from attack. The workplace and education venues are among them. One does not expect that he or she will be mugged or attacked at the coffee pot at work, and when parents drop their children off at school, they do so believing that their children are relatively safe from attack. When attacks happen in either of these locations, it goes beyond a "that's a shame" response—people clamor for security. The protests against the superheroes take an ugly turn: people start physically attacking the superheroes, at one point putting Johnny Storm in the hospital. Goliath notes, "This is the start of the witch hunts, honey," (Millar n.p.) and this is clear from the storyline of the book. With that, the witch hunts so reminiscent of the Salem witch hunts or the McCarthy era begin anew, only this time, against those superheroes who refuse to register. If a superhero opposes the government or registration, then the individual must be "the other."

For the superheroes, superhero registration means losing civil liberties and the freedom to live an alter ego life in peace. Not unexpectedly, this is not met with great enthusiasm by all of the superheroes. Some of the superheroes have no problem registering their real identity with the government. They believe it is their civic duty. The mutants from X-Men had already been forced to register and were essentially confined to the Xavier School for Gifted and Talented Children, so they believe it is about time that the superheroes (mutants with masks) also got a taste of what registration is like. Furthermore, because some superheroes have no secret identity, it isn't a problem for them to register. (Think Dr. Reed Richards of the Fantastic Four as one such example.) Those who align themselves with registration follow the lead of Tony Stark. Those who are unwilling to register align themselves with Captain America. As Captain America points out in *Civil War: Casualties of War*, "The Registration Act takes away any freedom we have, any autonomy. You don't know who could get elected, how public sentiment might change. I'm old enough to remember Japanese-Americans being put in camps because they were judged potential threats to national security" (Gage n.p.). Captain America has lived through changes in government, ideas that had gone wrong, and ideals swept aside. His attitude reflects issues that arise when people of good conscience, attempting to do something they feel is right in the name of "national security," watch those ideas and ideals turn out to hurt innocent people, and he's not about to let it happen again.

Captain America is, technically, "old school." He is far more ideological than many of the other superheroes, and as stated in *Red, White & Blue*, he believes that the person who was Steve Rogers is dead (Ross and Dini n.p.). If any of the superheroes represents the ideals that the United States was founded on, it's Captain America. In many ways, silencing Captain America means the silencing of America's ideals. It is easy to see why Captain America is not interested in the Superhero Registration Act. As he notes, first the superhero registration and then what's next?

With the Superhero Registration Act, the rules are simple: agree to the act, register, get training, and become part of the 50-State Initiative (where superhero teams are assigned to states and cities), or go underground and enter into various battles in order to retain or, in some cases, regain, civil liberties. What's different about the Superhero Registration Act, though, is that many not-so-regular people oppose it. Villains are opposed because superheroes are going to be law enforcement agents, and that essentially makes the superheroes lethal weapons. But because the Superhero Registration Act requires resorting to spying through unknown tactics (such as Spider-Man's "new and improved" suit designed by Tony Stark), when superheroes discover they are pawns of the government, they abandon previously-held beliefs and move over to "the other side." There are defectors on both sides, including those who leave Captain America saying that registration is the act of the future, and Captain America is simply behind the times.

Battles ensue, and both sides have "tricks" up their sleeves. Nick Fury, who has been underground hiding, gives Captain America a safe house for his troops and an electronic descrambler for Iron Man's suit. Iron Man and Reed Richards create a clone of Thor, who goes severely awry and kills Bill Foster (a.k.a. Goliath). The death of Goliath is a pivotal turning point for many of the superheroes. While some choose to abandon Captain America, believing that this kind of death is not what they have signed up for, others leave Iron Man's ranks and join Captain America because creating the clone of Thor has gone too far. This includes Sue Storm (Reed Richard's wife) and Johnny Storm, both of the Fantastic Four. Ben Grimm, the remaining member of the Fantastic Four, has gone to Canada to wait out the results of the battles, especially after Iron Man's team mistakenly kills one of the members of Grimm's beloved Yancey Street Gang in the heat of a battle.

Class issues rear their head in *Civil War* as well. In many ways, this is a war between the upper class superhero Iron Man and the street class Steve Rogers acting as Captain America. Tony Stark is a millionaire who has spent little to no time struggling with the day-to-day drudgery of living, in contrast with Captain America, who as Steve Rogers, certainly has seen his fair share of poverty. At one point during the initial battle, Captain America grits his teeth and says to Iron Man, "You really think I'm going down ... to some *pampered punk* like you?" (Millar n.p.; emphasis mine) (see Figure 3). In the *Civil War* script to issue #3, Mark Millar, the author of the series, states, "Cap sees a rich guy just ripping apart everything he believes in and he's a passionate guy" (Millar n.p.). It's possible that Iron Man simply doesn't get what this fight is all about for Captain America. It isn't merely rich versus poor;

44   Part I: Punk Superhero Comics

it's ideals of freedom for the underdog, something that the punk movement associates with since they are, by very definition, rebelling against authority. In the script to *Civil War* issue #1, Joe Quesada, Editor in Chief for the *Civil War* series, states that:

> Cap is about the American ideal, not the American way. As a nation, as the greatest nation in the world, we are still a work in progress. By no stretch of the imagination are we perfect, but it's that pursuit for the ideals that America is set up on that make our nation great. Cap understands that, he sees it every day; and he above everyone else sees all the possibilities within that ideal. So, with that in mind, Cap has had a history of a character of not always being locked in step with the government. He is neither Democrat nor Republican, he's not a conservative or a liberal, he is the ideal [Millar n.p.].

As the ideal, then, Captain America's duty is to be true to the ideal, not necessarily the government, as one would expect. Captain America's job is to ensure that the ideal of America is upheld. This is very much what many members of the punk movement are aiming for: progress and change. And sometimes, that progress and that change cannot come without radical confrontation.

Figure 3: Captain America grits his teeth and says to Iron Man, "You really think I'm going down … to some *pampered punk* like you?" (Millar, *Civil War* #4, n.p.) © MARVEL.

At the final battle, Captain America has managed to get Namor to become involved with the superhero registration fight on the side of no registration. This is partly because of the death of Namorita, and partly because Captain America asks him (many of the people fighting on Captain America's side are there simply because it is Captain America). With the Atlantians helping Captain America's team, the team is clearly winning the battle, and casualties are high, including the cloned Thor who is killed by Hercules. In a particularly harrowing scene, an angry Captain America looks as if he is going to kill Iron Man, when Captain America is taken down by a group of ordinary citizens. Captain America looks up and says "Oh my God" (Millar n.p.). He realizes that he is no longer fighting "for the people," (Millar n.p.) but rather the superheroes are simply fighting. His teammates beg him to reconsider because they are winning the battle. His reply is that the team is winning everything but "the argument" (Millar n.p.). He takes his mask off and asks that *Steve Rogers* be arrested and orders his troops to stand down. A "general hero amnesty" (Millar n.p.) is given to everyone but Steve Rogers (who is later put on trial), and the 50-state initiative is put into play. Reed Richards notes in a letter to his wife (where he is asking her to come back to him) that "working with the government our remit has moved beyond simply law and order and we're now tackling everything from the environment to global poverty" (Millar n.p.). Tony Stark becomes the next director of S.H.I.E.L.D. Those who could not bear to register go to Canada in the hopes of keeping the old school alive, and there still exists a small group of underground superheroes led by Spider-Man, which neither registers nor flees the country.

Reed Richards' comments to Sue Storm are telling. Although he paints a rosy picture of everyone working together, a happy family, his words are chilling. The side that fought for and won the Superhero Registration Act wonders how superheroes were tolerated for as long as they were. Reed Richards says, "I'm sure you can appreciate the pressure we were under creating new heroes, revamping old ones… decentralizing this community from a single coast and building a super-power for the twenty-first century" (Millar n.p.). Richards says in his letter that, "What once seemed like our darkest hour has been transformed into our greatest opportunity" (Millar n.p.). Whether Captain America or Steve Rogers would agree with that statement is difficult to determine. In subsequent issues following *Civil War*, it should be noted that Steve Rogers in his capacity as Captain America is killed by a sniper en route to his trial. The character that Marvel chose in 1941 to most represent the ideals of America is dead. One cannot help but wonder if his death did not in some way symbolically represent the ideals of America dying with the Superhero Registration Act.

The idea of Captain America being "punk" is oftentimes a difficult pill to swallow. By the creators' own accounts, this character was built to be patriotic. But underneath all of the flag-waving and fighting lies a revolutionary punk. An immensely popular, patriotic punk. And just as the punk musicians changed the music scene, so too does this punk patriot, who oftentimes questions and does not always blindly follow orders. The examples noted throughout this essay demonstrate that when the revolutionary punk rears its head, the character inevitably does the "right thing"—the thing that holds true to political ideals that stay true to the Constitution. It's important to note this because this is, by all accounts, an insanely popular comic book series, and Captain America is creating a new hegemony—a new rhetoric. The character's ideas are bound to influence its readers. As Geoff Klock notes, "A successful rebel is a new hegemony, ... Because comic book superheroes are produced serially and always take place in contemporary America, it is possible (if not necessary) for characters to be rebels forever" (43)—to be punks. Thus, as Hebdige points out, "...rhetoric is not self-explanatory; it may say what it means but it does not necessarily 'mean' what it 'says'" (115). Captain America fits that bill. He looks patriotic, but he is not allegiant to the government, especially when the character believes that the government is wrong. And that sends a powerful message to the readers: they, too, can be revolutionary, rebellious punks.

Notes

1. The creation date and first publication release dates are very much in contention. While there is no definitive date as to when the first publication was released, most scholars will agree that it was approximately nine months to a year before America's entry into World War II. For the purposes of this essay, I am going with the March 1941, release date, which is the date reflected in the book: *Marvel: The Characters and their Universe.*

2. Bradford Wright reprints this page in his book *Comic Book Nation.* The frames show Cap wandering the streets deep in thought: "I'm like a dinosaur—in the Cro-Magnon Age! An anachronism—who's outlived his time! This is the day of the anti-hero—the age of the rebel—and the dissenter! It isn't hip—to defend the establishment!—only to tear it down! And in a world rife with injustice, greed, and endless war—who's to say the rebels are wrong? But I've never learned to play by today's new rules! I've spent a lifetime defending the flag—and the law! Perhaps I should have battled less—and questioned more!" (246).

3. Recall that comic books had been shipped to GIs stationed overseas during World War II. Many of those GIs returned with a desire to continue reading a favorite storyline, and many publishers catered to that audience with more mature themes.

4. Bucky was revived "(literally!) and he and the Captain are revealed to have been government doppelgangers who had themselves been put into suspended animation after the government claims that the super soldier serum has made them mentally unstable based upon their overzealous red-baiting (see Issue 155 of *Captain America and The Falcon* "The Secret Origin of Captain America," by Steve Englehart et al.) Apparently, Captain America and Bucky have unwittingly been a member of the group "Campaign to Rejoin America's Principles" (C.R.A.P.) that not so coincidentally is formed right at the time Watergate broke out.

5. Notably, in *Civil War*, the citizens do not attack the media, which is culpable in this disaster as well. Had it not been for the clamoring for ratings, Speedball might have thought twice, but no one is addressing that issue in this series.

Works Cited

Benton, Mike. *The Comic Book in America: An Illustrated History*. Taylor, 1989.
_____. *Superhero Comics of the Golden Age: The Illustrated History*. Taylor, 1992.
_____. *Superhero Comics of the Silver Age: The Illustrated History*. Taylor, 1991.
Duin, Steve, and Mike Richardson. *Comics: Between the Panels*. Dark Horse, 1998.
Englehart, Steve (w), John Romita Jr. (p), Sal Buscema (p), Frank McLaughlin (i), and Jean Izzo (l). "The Secret Origin of Captain America." *Captain America and the Falcon* #155 (Nov. 1972), Marvel Comics.
Englehart, Steve (w), Sal Buscema (p), Frank McLaughlin (i), and Sam Rosen (l). "Two Into One Won't Go." *Captain America and the Falcon* #156 (Dec. 1972), Marvel Comics.
Englehart, Steve (w), Sal Buscema (p), Vince Colletta (i), Linda Lessman (c), and Artie Simek (l). "The Falcon Fights Alone." *Captain America and the Falcon* #177 (Sept. 1974), Marvel Comics.
Englehart, Steve (w), Frank Robbins (p), Frank Giaccoia (i), Stan Goldberg (c), and Tom Orzechowski (l). "Death of a Hero." *Captain America and the Falcon* #183 (March 1975), Marvel Comics.
Eury, Michael. "Golden Age of Superheroes (1938–1954): Superheroes Help Fight World War II." *The Superhero Book: The Ultimate Encyclopedia of Comic-Book Icons and Hollywood Heroes*, edited by Gina Misiroglu and David A. Roach, Visible Ink Press, 2004, pp. 231–233.
Fingeroth, Danny. *Superman on the Couch: What Superheroes Really Tell Us about Ourselves and Our Society*. Continuum, 2004.
Gage, Christos N., et al. *Civil War: Casualties of War: Iron Man and Captain America*. Marvel Publishing, 2007.
Hebdige, Dick. *Subculture: The Meaning of Style*. Routledge, 1991.
Klock, Geoff. *How to Read Superhero Comics and Why*. Continuum, 2006.
Lee, Stan. *Captain America: Sentinel of Liberty*. Simon and Schuster, 1979.
_____, and Jack Kirby. *Avengers Masterworks. Vol. 1*. Marvel Comics, 1993.
Mallory, Michael. *Marvel: The Characters and Their Universe*. Barnes & Noble Books, 2002.
Millar, Mark, et al. *Civil War*. Marvel Publishing, 2008.
"punk." *OED Online*, www.oed.com/view/Entry/154685?rskey=0s7tZL&result=1#eid. Accessed 16 September 2016.
Roach, David. "Captain America." *The Superhero Book: The Ultimate Encyclopedia of Comic-Book Icons and Hollywood Heroes*, edited by Gina Misiroglu and David A. Roach, Visible Ink Press, 2004, pp. 111–114.
Ross, Alex, and Paul Dini. "Letters." *Captain America: Red, White & Blue*. Marvel, 2002.
Wright, Bradford. *Comic Book Nation*. Johns Hopkins UP, 2001.
Wright, Nicky. *The Classic Era of American Comics*. Contemporary, 2000.
Zimmerman, David A. *Comic Book Character: Unleashing the Hero in Us All*. InterVarsity, 2004.
Zizek, Slavoj. *The Fragile Absolute—or, Why Is the Christian Legacy Worth Fighting For?* Verso, 2000.

PART II : VERTIGO PUNK COMICS

No Future
John Constantine, Hellblazer and the '70s Punk Rocker in the 21st Century

SPENCER CHALIFOUR

Introduction

Imagine a pounding bass line, shrieking guitars, and vulgar, anarchist lyrics assaulting you, as channeled through the speakers of a brand new iPhone 6. As time progresses, once revolutionary artistic movements can become part of a mass culture. In *Sells Like Teen Spirit*, Ryan Moore writes, "a new kind of halo would later be thrown around punk in the form of legends about its outrageous acts and larger-than-life personalities, which are now glorified in [...] repackaged musical collections designed to capitalize on people's hunger for the authenticity of the original. Ironically but perhaps predictably, the punk movement [...] has been absorbed into the very rock establishment that it opposed" (211–212). What Moore highlights here is the essential paradox of punk as it exists in the 21st century: a musical movement based upon rebellion has become commodified as part of the musical establishment. Does the commodification of punk in the 21st century emasculate the surviving punk rockers of the 1970s? Must they confront the reality that the Sex Pistols foretold of "no future?"

These are the questions that writers Jason Aaron and Peter Milligan confront in the DC/Vertigo comic book series *Hellblazer*. The series focuses on the occult detective and confidence man John Constantine. In Aaron's "Newcastle Calling" (issues #245–246), Constantine must help when a documentary crew making a film about Constantine's old punk band unleashes a terror elemental, while in "No Future" (issues #265–266) Constantine aids an old punk friend who claims his shrine to Sid Vicious is actually inhabited by the spirit of the deceased punk star. In these issues, Aaron and Milligan use Constantine to examine the changes in punk culture and the punk aesthetic through the eyes of someone who witnessed punk's birth and to illuminate the consequences of Constantine revisiting his (and punk's) past. Furthermore, each writer also examines the paradoxical dichotomies of punk culture in the 21st century: as something nostalgic yet relevant, dangerous yet commodified, and belonging to both the counterculture and the mainstream.

John Constantine and Punk

John Constantine has a long association with the punk movement. He first appeared in *The Saga of the Swamp Thing* #37 (June 1985) by Alan Moore, Rick Veitch, and John Totleben, where he was introduced as a mysterious, trench-coated figure (drawn to look like Police frontman Sting) who led Swamp Thing on several adventures around America. The character proved popular enough that he gained his own spin-off series, *Hellblazer*, which was originally written by Jamie Delano and drawn by John Ridgway. Delano used *Hellblazer* to return Constantine to his native England and focus on stories that drew heavily on British politics and culture. Delano also established one of Constantine's defining features that differentiates him from other comic book characters: the fact that he ages in real time in the series. Delano began this practice in *Hellblazer* issue #9 (September 1988), where John Constantine explicitly states it is his 35th birthday when he sees a newspaper dated May 10, making his official birthday 10 May 1953. This practice was continued by the subsequent writers on *Hellblazer*, most notably Delano's successor, Garth Ennis, who devoted the entire story of *Hellblazer* issue #63 (March 1993) to the celebration of Constantine's 40th birthday.

This real-time aging means that John Constantine was roughly 24 years old when punk rock exploded onto the music scene in 1977, and thus he came of age amidst the birth of punk rock in the UK. Constantine's fictional biography was slowly revealed over the course of the series, and readers eventually learned that Constantine left his native Liverpool to move to London in the late 1970s, where he formed his own punk band, Mucous Membrane, with friend Gary Lester after being inspired by seeing the Sex Pistols perform. Constantine sang lead vocals for the band, and they made their debut at the Casanova Club in Newcastle. The group recorded a single, "Venus of the Hardsell," which was apparently popular enough to warrant the band creating their own music video for the song, which was presented in *Hellblazer Annual* #1 as a series of images from the video with the lyrics overlaid on the frames.

Roughly at the same time his interest in punk began, so did Constantine's interest in the occult. After Mucous Membrane broke up, Constantine began his career as an occult detective and eventually returned to the Casanova Club with a crew of friends who, like him, were also practitioners of the occult. There, Constantine attempted an exorcism on the young daughter of the sadistic magician who ran the club, but ended up condemning her to Hell. This event traumatized Constantine, and he spent two years in Ravenscar Secure Facility, a mental asylum, where he faced constant abuse by the people running the facility. After leaving the asylum, Constantine had transformed from the cocky, rebellious punk rocker of his youth to the disillusioned, cynical magician seen in *Hellblazer*.

Despite his career change from musician to occultist, Constantine's roots in '70s punk have been an integral part of his character throughout *Hellblazer*'s 300-issue run, and the series' writers regularly return to Constantine's punk origins. In "The Bloody Saint," a story from *Hellblazer Annual #1*, Constantine is released from Ravenscar in 1982. He meets Martin Peters, an old punk friend who used to be in a band called the Hopeless Heroins and who has since turned to "management and promotions" (Delano 6). Upon realizing Peters has gone from punk to conservative, Constantine asks, "What happened to the good old anarchic revolution, then?" (Delano 7). Peters responds, "Thatcher and Reagan hijacked it and turned it into a libertarian free-for-all. Great, eh?" (Delano 7). Peters then attempts to persuade Constantine to give him the tape of the "Venus of the Hardsell" music video, and when Constantine responds that he does not know where it is, he replies, "What you mean is, you don't want to sell out" (Delano 8). Even in this early story, Delano has established Constantine's main fear regarding his relationship to punk: he still somewhat idealizes that moment and is skeptical of a world that is slowly transforming punk's original message. His description of the emergence of punk as a "good old anarchist revolution" reveals a self-knowing nostalgia for punk's early days, whereas his bombardment with early '80s Britain after being removed for so long initiates his weariness with the treatment of punk by mainstream culture. Later in the story, when Constantine finds the tape, his friend Chas asks whether he will finally release the video, to which Constantine responds, "It goes against the grain a bit, but these days it feels like all anyone can do is shout a bit—and there's no point shouting where no one can hear you, is there?" (Delano 48). This reveals the root of Constantine's cynicism. Since he lost the years 1979 to 1982 in a mental asylum, the impact of the world he finds in the 1980s is too much for him, and he loses faith in punk as a means of creating change.

Throughout the series, Constantine's political disillusionment repeatedly comes up as the root of his cynicism. In "Haunted, Part 1" by Warren Ellis and John Higgins (*Hellblazer* issue #134, February 1999), a shop owner friend of Constantine's asks him about his resentment toward New Labour, and he replies, "This ain't Labour how I bleedin' remember it, Sanjay. More like bleedin' Thatcher how I remember it" (Ellis 11). The repetition of the word "remember" emphasizes how Constantine relates to current politics through his past and his inability to accept the current regime changes. Similarly, in "Son of Man, Part 2" by Garth Ennis and John Higgins (*Hellblazer* #130, October 1998), Constantine attempts to raise a demon but instead raises the ghost of Sid Vicious. Sid's ghost moans, "Aw, why won't iss fackin,' fackin,' fackin' bass worrrrrkk?!!" and Constantine replies, "'cos you dunno how to play it, Sid" before sending him away (Ennis 19). Constantine does not hide his contempt for Sid, yet this scene still hints at Constantine's inability to distance himself from the punk movement. Although each *Hellblazer* writer handles Constantine's occultism slightly differently, the coincidence that Constantine raises a key figure from punk suggests that in attempting to resurrect a demon he is resurrecting his punk past. It is this problem with resurrection, or more specifically Constantine's struggle to stop himself from resurrecting the past, that forms the main conflict of Aaron and Milligan's stories.

"Newcastle Calling"

With continued popularity, many bands with revolutionary roots confront the question of whether they have "sold out" in order to continue their popularity. In *The Triumph of Vulgarity*, Robert Pattison describes the Sex Pistols' response to the concept of "selling out": "In the version of the swindle myth adopted by the Pistols, when the rocker learns that the cash nexus is fundamentally dishonest, he should not waste his righteous indignation on it [...] Since the disease of money cannot be cured, it should be nurtured as a means of mortifying the world" (150). Thus, according to the Pistols, selling out is inevitable and should be embraced in all its negativity in order to reveal to the masses the shamefulness of this system, and wasting "righteous indignation" on it becomes a self-destructive maneuver. In "Newcastle Calling" (issues #245–246) by Jason Aaron and Sean Murphy, the characters struggle with being "authentic" punks and avoiding selling out, and yet in attempting to remain authentic they try to hold on to the past, which eventually leads to how long they survive in the story before meeting a gruesome end. In this section, I'll examine how each character's perceived punk authenticity and devotion to the past influences their deaths or survivals.

In this arc, a documentary crew films an episode of "The Best Bands You've Never Heard Of" which features Mucous Membrane, and the crew attempts to shoot part of the episode at the now-defunct and condemned Casanova Club. As they film the episode, one by one the crew and presenter begin to go insane before all but one of them die in gruesome circumstances. In an earlier story, Constantine responded to the events at the Casanova Club in 1979 and he discovered Astra Logue had conjured a terror element called Norfulthing to kill her depraved father, and it was in attempting to call a stronger demon to destroy Norfulthing that Constantine accidentally condemned Astra to Hell. The documentary crew, then, unknowingly disrupts Norfulthing, and after a wave of horrific crimes by people possessed by the terror elemental occur in Newcastle, Constantine arrives to investigate. In his narration, he reveals to the reader that conjuring a demon did not kill Norfulthing, but Constantine did devise a way of placating the demon by feeding it a soul every year in exchange for the demon staying caged in the defunct club. By the story's end, Constantine has caged the demon once again, although all the members of the documentary crew are now either dead or deranged.

Here, Aaron divides the story into two parts: the first part centers on the documentary crew with Constantine not appearing until the final page, and the second part centers on Constantine and his reflections upon being forced to face his past. The thematic focus of each part is also revealed by Lee Bermejo's cover art. The cover for *Hellblazer* issue #245 features a tattered poster on a brick wall showing a young John Constantine in the center, dressed in a leather jacket and padlock necklace similar to the kind worn by Sid Vicious as he snarls into a microphone. He is flanked on either side by images of his guitarists, and underneath the words "Mucous Membrane" are spelled out in the cut-out letter style popularized by the cover of Sex Pistols' *Never Mind the Bollocks Here's the Sex Pistols*. The cover of issue #246 shows John Constantine and his bandmates, now considerably older although still sporting punk fashions like spiky hairstyles and studded belts, standing against an even more tattered poster that has become unreadable. The bandmate to the far left is cut off by the edge of the cover to issue #246, but his right arm appears to the far right of the issue #245 cover, thus indicating that the two covers are in fact one single image that can be created by placing the comic book issues side-by-side. In this manner, Bermejo creates an explicit juxtaposition between the rebellion of youth and the dilapidation of age.

In the first part of "Newcastle Calling" (issue #245), Aaron focuses on the question of authenticity versus fraud as it relates to punk rock. The cover depicts a 1970s-era poster for Mucous Membrane, and thus seemingly represents the "authentic" punk rock of this era. However, its juxtaposition with the following issue's cover reveals the poster to be merely an artifact of the past, and its power has been replaced with nostalgia. The documentary crew that part one of "Newcastle Calling" follows is obsessed with regaining punk authenticity through the past. This question of validity appears in the first page, when Randy says to Corey, the cameraman, "Dude, that is seriously the worst British accent I've ever heard." Corey responds, "Bollocks! Shut yer gob, ya wanker!" to which Randy says, "Dude, c'mon, you're from fuckin' Ohio" ("Newcastle Calling Part One" 1). This moment illustrates how even though these characters strive for authenticity, their inherent weakness is they do so through essentially inauthentic methods. Corey adopts a British accent presumably because he feels this is more conducive to the punk atmosphere he hopes to create.

The dangers of trying to uncover the past are also revealed early in the story. Ivan, one of the crew, cuts his hand when he breaks the lock on the fence surrounding the Casanova Club. As he sits in the crew's van with Randy, he begins to scratch at the cut on his hand. Aaron portrays the dialogue between Ivan and Randy in one panel as occurring over a frame showing a young John Constantine singing "Venus of the Hardsell." Randy asks, "Ivan, what the fuck are you doing? Don't scratch it like that!" and Ivan responds, "I can't help it, it's like there's something down in there, and if I could just get it out..." ("Newcastle Calling Part One" 6). The juxtaposition of this dialogue over the frame of a young Constantine emphasizes the similarities between Ivan scratching at his wound and the crew's attempt to dig up Constantine's punk past. Ivan eventually hallucinates that he sees a "Pull Me" tab emerging from his hand, and when Constantine finds him in the next issue he has literally pulled his own body apart. When he asks Constantine "Maybe I should stop?" he tells him, "Ya ask me, mate ... there's no point in stopping now. Might as well see it through" ("Newcastle Calling Part Two" 7). Constantine says this as he's about to enter the Casanova Club for the first time in presumably years, and thus his words reflect Constantine's emotions as he is forced to revisit his past. Aaron thus illustrates the attempt to achieve the authentic through the past as ultimately self-destructive, although in Constantine's case he has no desire to regain his past punk glory, but merely to confront it.

The question of authenticity arises again when Corey, Dana (a producer on the documentary), and Travis (the documentary's host) debate what is the "perfect" punk song. Corey and Dana name songs like "Blank Generation" by Richard Hell, "Neat Neat Neat" by the Damned, and "We Vibrate" by the Vibrators, while Travis' sole contribution is "Basket Case" by Green Day, which draws a "Oh, for fucksake" from Corey ("Newcastle Calling Part One" 8). Dana and Corey associate punk "perfection" with the past, as all the songs they list are from the late 1970s or early 1980s, while Travis offers a song from 1994. Additionally, the bands listed by Dana and Corey never received the amount of mainstream success as Green Day, and thus Travis is, in their eyes, on the side of the sell-out. However, Travis is also the only member of the crew who survives the ordeal, although he is hopelessly deranged afterward, as evidenced by his carrying around a dead dog thinking it is Dana. Several characters comment that the only reason Travis becomes involved in going to Newcastle is because of his crush on Dana, and he is the only character to express fear about entering the Casanova Club. Thus, Travis is the one character who is not motivated by a need to reclaim the past. However, his revelation of liking Green Day means he lacks the authenticity of the other characters whose knowledge of punk goes much deeper, and thus Aaron chooses to punish him in some way for this lack of authenticity. Only John Constantine can survive unscathed, since he is an "authentic" punk from the '70s, yet he resists looking backward as a means of reclaiming his authenticity.

At the end of part one, when Dana confronts Norfulthing, she tells it, "I've been looking for him too.... We all have" ("Newcastle Calling Part One" 17). The "him" is clearly John Constantine, and her revelation that they are "looking" for him illustrates that, while it might not be the physical John Constantine they hoped to find, they still are drawn to Constantine as a figure of the punk movement. The use of the word "looking" implies that the crew hoped to find something, and this something could be the revolutionary, anarchic, and anti-mainstream spirit that Constantine in his youth channeled as a punk rocker. When this story takes place, Constantine would be roughly 55 years old, whereas the members of the documentary crew are all drawn to look considerably younger than him; indeed, Constantine refers to them as "kids" during part two. Constantine thus represents a link to punk's past that the rest of the characters crave. Corey is the only member to survive long enough to meet Constantine, although by this point he has become ensnared in the van and by his camera due to Norfulthing's effect. As he dies he asks Constantine, "There's something I have to know, Constantine.... Something you have to tell me before I die.... About the band.... Mucous Membrane..." Constantine, anticipating his question, cuts him off: "We were shite, kid. We were bloody awful. But then again, no worse than a lot of others back then." Corey says, "Heh, I knew it," before dying ("Newcastle Calling Part Two" 21). Constantine's quote reflects the thematic focus of the cover of part two: he realizes the reality of his past and has come to terms with moving beyond his past. Noticeably, on the cover Constantine is the one band member who is not dressed in typical punk wear, instead wearing his usual trench coat and shirt and tie. Thus, he has come to terms with aging and no longer needs to look like the punk he was in youth.

Aaron uses Constantine's encounter with Corey to continue exploring the question of authenticity. His admission that Mucous Membrane were "shite" would seem to go against the documentary's title that they were one of "the best bands you've never heard of," and Corey's admission that he knew this suggests that despite his obsession with punk authenticity, he has some recognition of the truth behind his romanticization of the past, and thus

Aaron allows him to live long enough to confirm this belief. At the end, Constantine also gives Corey a twig, claiming it is the "finger bone of St. Cavartigan" and that it will ease his pain. Corey believes him and holds the twig, remarking, "I can feel it working" ("Newcastle Calling Part Two" 21). Although Corey could see through Mucous Membrane's veneer, he accepts Constantine's story about the twig, and thus allows himself to accept the inauthentic as authentic. Aaron ends the story with Constantine singing "Venus of the Hardsell" as he leaves the grounds around the Casanova Club. Even Constantine allows himself to be swept away by the memory of his "shite" band despite himself, and thus Aaron suggests the comfort of the authentic that can be found in the inauthentic.

"No Future"

The question of punk authenticity leads to another question: how will the passage of time affect even the most authentic punk rockers from the '70s? In Dick Hebdige's *Subculture: The Meaning of Style*, he states, "The various stylistic ensembles adopted by the punks were undoubtedly expressive of genuine aggression, frustration and anxiety. But these statements, no matter how strangely constructed, were cast in a language which was generally available—a language which was current" (87). Hebdige's emphasis on punk style as "current" raises the question of whether punk style from the 1970s can still exist in the 21st century and still be considered "punk," or if the change in what is "current" thereby changes the definition of punk's style. In Peter Milligan and Simon Bisley's "No Future" (issues #265–266), John Constantine must once again revisit his punk roots, although this time he is no longer an observer as he was in "Newcastle Calling" and instead he fully recreates himself as an aged punk rocker. As he goes through this drastic transformation, Milligan and Bisley explore what 70s punk style means in a different era.

In "No Future," Constantine comes to the aid of an old punk friend named Faeces McCartney, who was in a band called, appropriately, No Future. Faeces believes an effigy he's made of Sid Vicious is inhabited by Vicious' spirit, and he thinks that Sid's power over his anarcho-punk collective is weakening as young punks in his group keep disappearing. Constantine investigates and eventually learns that the punks are being poached by James, a representative who works for two undead Conservative party members, who uses the punks to enact violence against leftists and others the Conservatives want to attack. Constantine, with the help of his young assistant Epiphany Graves, gives himself a punk makeover and is eventually approached by James to work for the Conservatives. Constantine tricks the Conservatives into travelling to the effigy of Sid, where it is revealed that both Sid and the Conservatives are in fact possessed by ancient spirits. Sid destroys the Conservatives and kills James, destroying himself in the process, and Constantine decides to leave Faeces and his old punk life behind.

As with Aaron and Murphy, Milligan and Bisley incorporate the concept of "selling out" into their depiction of Faeces McCartney and his collective, the Vicious. Faeces tells Constantine, "A lot of them fell by the wayside. Got jobs. Did a Sham 69 and sold out. Or sold butter to the nation like Lydon. Guess that's what happened to you, eh, John?" Constantine only replies with "Well, no one's thought of using me in a national advertising campaign yet," yet Faeces' insinuation that John has "sold out" reveals how even though Constantine's means of making a living is less than mainstream, the simple act of abandoning '70s punk culture is enough to have him labeled a sell-out ("No Future Part One" 8). This could even be a meta-fictional acknowledgment that Constantine's stories are published by an imprint of DC Comics, and therefore are part of the "mainstream" in comics culture. Faeces insists that "the Vicious are keeping it punk," thereby associating himself with the punk ethos of the '70s and distancing himself from other figures from the same era he holds in contempt, such as Sham 69 for changing their sound from harder punk to a more classic rock sound or John Lydon for appearing in commercials for Country Life butter ("No Future Part One" 8). Despite his insistence that "Never mind the bollocks, we're still here," Bisley draws the collective in a cramped panel, with most of the members lying around on couches, drinking or taking drugs ("No Future Part One" 8). In the large panel illustrating the collective, Bisley also includes an insert that takes up about a third of the panel space, which depicts a 1979-era poster promoting "No Future—Playing Sat 13 Aug." The cramped placement of the member of the collective in the lower right of the panel suggests that these punks are part of their own small bubble, with little care or influence on the outside world. The inclusion of the "No Future" poster implies that, for '70s punks like Faeces, there really was no future by remaining true to the punk ethos, and they must remain in their own world while the outside world changes and adapts.

This implication becomes clear when Faeces shows Constantine his effigy to Sid. Constantine's narration boxes state, "What has Faeces become? A punk warrior who refuses to bow down to a clapped-out society? Or a deluded has-been, clinging to youth that vanished three decades back?" ("No Future Part One" 10). As Constantine tries to convince Faeces there's nothing in the effigy, Faeces gradually from panel to panel assumes a praying position in front of Sid. Faeces literally worships his punk past, and unlike Constantine cannot let it go. Constantine attempts to show Faeces that there's nothing in his shrine to Sid, but immediately feels the impact of "The three-chord shriek of Thatcher's little monsters" ("No Future Part One" 12). After the initial impact, Bisley draws a panel depicting Constantine hunched over as the vision of a young, punk version of himself looms over him, with a caption box reading, "This is fucking great.... I was young again" ("No Future Part One" 12). Thus for Milligan, the appeal of punk for Constantine and Faeces is not a need to regain some lost authenticity, but rather to get to re-experience the excesses of their youth.

Constantine attempts to regain his youth through several methods throughout the story. He begins to show affection for Epiphany, who is roughly thirty years his junior, although she had shown interest in a romantic relationship with him in past issues (and they eventually married). He even starts to shed his normally self-interested outlook. After Epiphany gives him a punk makeover, Constantine tells Faeces, "Maybe it's time I started getting angry again. Maybe it's time I started fighting again" ("No Future Part Two" 7). This dialogue marks a dramatic shift in thinking for the usually cynical and disillusioned Constantine from earlier *Hellblazer* issues. In the center panel on the following page, Bisley even draws Constantine as looking considerably younger than the 57 years he would chronologically be when this story takes place. However, by the end of the story, after Constantine has beaten the Conservatives and released the spirit that thought it was Sid Vicious, he admits, "I'm just too tired and cynical to care much anymore. I tried.... This haircut, Epiphany, fighting the Conservatives, fuck me, I really tried" ("No Future Part Two" 21). The final image shows Constantine once again in his trench coat and tie with his back turned to the younger, punk version of himself. This image reflects Constantine's realization that punk can either become righteous rebellion or a pathetic attempt at recapturing youth, depending on one's age. Even in this final image, Constantine still sports the green-colored Mohawk Epiphany gave him, only now the haircut appears disjointed with the rest of him. Bisley emphasizes the wrinkles and cracks in Constantine's face, which become all the more apparent when juxtaposed with the smooth features of the young Constantine, and thus Constantine's punk haircut looks all the more ridiculous on the old version of John.

Milligan's use of the undead Conservatives as a sort of mirror to the punks in the Vicious further emphasizes the absorption of punk into the mainstream. At the end of part one, one of the Conservatives states "God bless the Queen. God Bless the Conservative Party," saying the second sentence in a panel where he is in shadow and the second in the final panel where his rotting corpse appears in the light for the first time ("No Future Part One" 22). Like the punks, the Conservatives are relics from a bygone era attempting to find a place for themselves in the modern world. However, the use of the phrase "God bless the Queen" in a story so steeped in references to the Sex Pistols echoes the Pistols' 1977 song "God Save the Queen." Indeed, as with the Pistols, the Conservatives do not express much allegiance with the Royal Family, and are instead merely out for themselves and use the phrase as a hollow signifier of their false British loyalty. Constantine later confronts the Conservatives and asks why they use punks, and they explain, "There is a philosophical correlation. Just a short conceptual leap from Anarchy in the UK to the kind of extreme laissez-faire capitalism that our wing of the party espouses" ("No Future Part Two" 14). The punks' affiliation with the Conservatives thus echoes Constantine's 1982 encounter with Martin Peters and furthermore suggests that punk style and the punk ethos of anarchy and anti-establishmentarianism has truly been bastardized and utilized by the ruling establishment. The imagery of the Conservatives as rotten corpses also parallels the metaphorical "corpse" of '70s punk that the characters in "No Future" seem determined to re-animate. Their aged, decayed appearance contrasts with the youthful appearance Constantine hopes to regain, yet their presence in the story highlights how the youthful rebellion of early punk has become just as decayed as the undead Conservatives.

Constantine discovers that, as an aging '70s punk in the 21st century, he can find a place in neither the old punk rebellion nor as part of the establishment. The cynical loneliness that has become integral to Constantine's character becomes representative of the state of punk style in the contemporary world, and thus Milligan illustrates how a style that was current in the '70s has become nostalgic by the 21st century.

Tomorrow's a Fiction, Yesterday a Lie

The concept of having no future appears explicitly in both Aaron's and Milligan's stories. The final page of "Newcastle Calling" ends with a text box stating, "End" and underneath in smaller letters "(no future)." The phrase appears numerous times in Milligan's story, including carved onto Sid Vicious' chest on the cover to issue #265. Both stories suggest that Constantine must make his own way in a world that has no future for him. Aaron's use of the phrase at the end of his story suggests that the idea of "no future" does not necessarily mean an "end," but rather Constantine must continue to live in the shadow of his past. Bisley's use of the phrase in blood on the cover to issue #265 echoes the inherent self-destruction that attempting to reclaim punk's past has, and thus Constantine is stuck between abandoning part of himself and destroying himself through regaining it.

Both stories also feature the lyrics to "Venus of the Hardsell," and the song's last verse states, "They're winning momma and it's getting dark/D'you think there's time to build an ark?/Tomorrow's a fiction yesterday a lie/Had a friend stuck his works in his eye perhaps he'll die?" The song's apocalyptic finale reveals that even the young punk Constantine knew that his anger and rebellion could not be sustained. When Constantine sings the song in both stories, the lyrics reflect a bygone era yet also encapsulate the contemporary feelings that each story explores. The use of the phrase "yesterday a lie" particularly resists the desire to romanticize the past, and Constantine attempts to resist this romanticization in both stories. By continuing with his current life and resisting his punk past, Constantine does stay true to his punk roots and make his own way by resisting any sort of outside influence.

Despite the deep-rooted cynicism in both stories, each also has some degree of hope to it. Although Constantine was condemned from his very beginning as a punk to have "no future," he continues to exist in the contemporary world and has enough agency to have an impact on those around him. Though disillusioned, Constantine has not become part of the establishment, and thus even though he has lost his punk style and desire to express himself through music, he has successfully avoided the pitfalls of other punks his age. Although Aaron and Milligan are skeptical of the continuation of the '70s punk aesthetic into the 21st century, both emphasize the influence this aesthetic has had and provide a glimpse into the future of someone with "no future."

Works Cited

Aaron, Jason (w), Sean Gordon Murphy (a). "Newcastle Calling." *Hellblazer* v1 #245–246 (Aug.-Sept. 2008), Vertigo Comics.
Delano, Jamie (w), Bryan Talbot (a), Dean Motter (a). "The Bloody Saint." *Hellblazer Annual* #1 (1989), Vertigo Comics.
Ellis, Warren (w), John Higgins (a). "Haunted, Part One." *Hellblazer* v1 #134 (Feb. 1999), Vertigo Comics.
Ennis, Garth (w), John Higgins (a). "Son of Man, Part Two." *Hellblazer* v1 #130 (Oct. 1998), Vertigo Comics.
Hebdige, Dick. *Subculture: The Meaning of Style.* Routledge, 1988.
Milligan, Peter (w), Simon Bisley (a). "No Future." *Hellblazer* v1 #265–266 (May-June 2010), Vertigo Comics.
Moore, Ryan. *Sells Like Teen Spirit: Music, Youth Culture, and Social Crisis.* New York UP, 2010.
Pattison, Robert. *The Triumph of Vulgarity: Rock Music in the Mirror of Romanticism.* Oxford UP, 1987.

"I Hate It Here"
Spider Jerusalem as Punk Anti-Hero
Jodie Childers

In issue #26 of *Transmetropolitan*, a cyberpunk satire published in monthly installments from September 1997 to November 2002 by writer Warren Ellis and artist Darick Robertson, the protagonist Spider Jerusalem introduces himself and his disdain for everything: "I am a journalist. I write a column for a newspaper called *The WORD* entitled 'I HATE IT HERE.' Because I do. I hate it and I hate you" (Ellis and Robertson, *Lonely City* page 32, panel 1). Later in the same issue, his reflections take a different tenor, expressing his sense of purpose in his journalistic work and a euphoric, even spiritual connection with his surroundings: "And when the sun falls down on this city it's transformed; it blooms again.... It wakes me, shakes me from the grey I'd been living in, reminding me why I'm alive, why I'm here, why I do what I do" (page 38, panel 1). Between panels and across issues of *Transmetropolitan*, Spider Jerusalem's personality fluctuates wildly between anger and ecstasy; apathy and empathy; and violence and benevolence. I read Spider's inconsistent character traits as expressions of the political and philosophical tensions as expressed in the various punk ideologies (between anarchism and socialism and nihilism and humanism) while also paralleling Spider's fears of commodification or "selling out" to the punk movement's ambivalent relationship with mainstream media. Ultimately, these complications originate from an abstract desire for liberty, political and artistic, which I argue is the predominant utopian impulse in Spider's journalistic work and in the punk movement as a whole.

Spider Jerusalem seeks an anarchic state that ensures liberty for all without imposing any social controls and limits on any individuals, which is unfeasible within the unfettered capitalist system in The City, the dystopian setting of the story where Spider engages in his journalistic work. Through his dissident writing, Spider asserts and demands political and artistic autonomy. Yet the text also expresses anxiety about the commodification of dissident impulses. The City is a monoculture in which all subversive subcultures and counter cultures (including punk music and the punk aesthetic) are depoliticized and weakened, disconnected from their iconoclastic origins and, instead, recuperated as what Louis Althusser calls "ideological state apparatuses" (n.p.) that support the totalitarian government of The Smiler, who is the president of the country and Spider's primary nemesis in the series. *Transmetropolitan* then can also be read as a speculative cyberpunk[1] work that speculates on punk's aesthetic and ideological futures. Stripped of its proletariat sensibility, the punk aesthetic as commodity is not social or even artistic rebellion, but instead self-consciousness at best and self-indulgence at worst, both of which support the status quo. Through his writing, Spider rebels against this political and artistic hegemony by creating a journalism of spectacle and by playing the punk aesthetic against itself as détournement to return it to its radical roots. Spider Jerusalem can then be classified as a punk anti-hero[2] who resists his own nihilistic impulses and restores order as disorder.

According to Tricia Henry, the "paradox" of the punk mentality expresses "a hatred of apathy and a sense of urgency concerning everything related to punk culture" juxtaposed against "an acute awareness of sociopolitical impotence, a belief that actions were inconsequential, that improvement either of self or society was at best elusive and at worst utterly elusive" (97). Across the genre and even within individual songs, punk expresses an authentic desire to change the existing social order and a totalizing disillusionment in all systems and structures; a utopian impulse to build something new and a nihilistic desire to tear it all down. These political and philosophical tensions play across the various punk ideologies from the socialist leanings expressed in the music of The Clash to the anarchy of Crass, from the nihilism of Richard Hell's haunting lyrics to the humanism espoused by Bad Religion. Foregrounding the materiality of punk, Stacy Thompson notes another significant anxiety concerning punk's understanding of artistic production within a capitalist system: "Punk is structured around a fundamental contradiction between an anticommercial impulse constitutive of punk and punks' necessary trafficking in the commodity market" (81). Though not self-consciously punk in name or identification, Spider Jerusalem as journalist grapples with these abstract paradoxes and problems at the core of the punk movement.

In *Transmetropolitan*, the contrasting images of the mountain and The City serve as visual counterforces in the text that spatially define Spider's conflict between self-indulgent apathy, even misanthropy, and purposeful, humanistic engagement with society. In the first issue, Spider is living outside of the monoculture of The City in a cabin on a remote mountain where he has secluded himself from his fans and his fame. On the first page of the series, there are two books on the floor of Spider's cabin, located prominently in the front left corner of the third panel, *Fear and Loathing in Las Vegas* by Hunter S. Thompson and John Kennedy Toole's *A Confederacy of Dunces*. These titles give us visual and intertextual clues on how to read the tensions in Spider's character. The most obvious model for Spider is Hunter S. Thompson, the notorious "gonzo journalist" who described journalism in *Fear and Loathing in Las Vegas* as "a cheap catch-all for fuckoffs and misfits—a false doorway to the backside of life" which aligns with Spider's cynical and self-deprecating perspective on the craft (200). However, Spider's antiauthoritarian and confrontational external demeanor conceals an acute inner sensitivity much like John Kennedy Toole, whose Pulitzer Prize–winning novel was only recognized posthumously after he committed suicide at 31. These tensions within Spider's character are also apparent in the title of one of the books authored by Spider himself, *Waving and Drowning*, a clever take on Stevie Smith's poem, "Not Waving but Drowning." In Spider Jerusalem, the bravado of waving and the helplessness of drowning are collapsed into a complex portrait of a writer whose internal tensions express contradictory impulses between a nihilistic desire to passively disappear or to actively self-destruct, and a humanistic longing to be saved and to save others.

The series begins at a moment of transition for Spider, from the mountain to The City, from apathy to action, from nihilism to the beginnings of humanism. Living off of the grid has become financially unfeasible for the increasingly paranoid Spider, but, in The City, Spider must confront the inequalities and injustices that cannot be ignored. After receiving a call from his editor Mitchell Royce, Spider is forced to return to The City to fulfill his contract to write two new books for his publisher. While the mountain takes on idyllic, even mythical connotations in Spider's mind, his ability to exist there is ultimately dependent on the capitalist system and his own personal wealth and fame which allows him to purchase his peace by working for periods of time before each retreat. Though he leaves the mountain reluctantly, as he enters The City he is drawn into its chaos and his words take on a poetic panache, one of the signature aspects of his gonzo journalistic style:

> The City never allowed itself to decay or degrade. It's wildly intensely growing. It's a loud bright stinking mess. It takes strength from its thousands of cultures and the thousands more that grow anew each day. It isn't perfect. It lies and cheats. It's no utopia and it ain't the mountain by a long shot—But it's alive. I can't argue that [Ellis and Robertson, *Back on the Stree*t page 18, panel 3].

The dynamism of the urban landscape invigorates and inspires Spider, but he is quickly reminded of the forces that work to contain and control that energy as he works on his first story, an exposé of police brutality against transients, a group of humans who modify their bodies with alien genomes. Thus begins Spider's friction with the state as both a physical entity (controlled by the presidents, first The Beast and then The Smiler) and as an abstract impediment to personal and collective liberty.

In The City, the state's power is hidden in everyday surveillance and made visible through force. The written word reinforces these power dynamics, forcing the people to internalize their own oppression. The City Police Department's shields read, SUBMIT NOW. Screens are built into the sidewalks and dominate the public air space, appearing as if they are suspended from the sky, surrounding the people with phrases that advertise products and broadcast the most sensational headlines. Propaganda posters promote candidates with slogans and simple imperatives like "Trust Me." Scott Bukatman observes that "comics superimpose text on the space of the city. In signs, labels, captions, word balloons and sound effects, words become a fundamental aspect of space" (176). The text that is superimposed on The City in *Transmetropolitan* codes consumption and subordination into the concrete. Yet, the writing on the wall also reflects the power to potentially subvert or even directly change the system. Graffiti, for instance, is a way in which the people can talk back to the surveillance state and confront the power structures that circumscribe their daily lives. When Spider hides himself in a portable toilet to write one of his stories, a sign on the wall reads: "Warning: Writing Graffiti on these walls will induce a chemical spray causing blindness. City Board of Health" (Ellis and Robertson, *Lust for Life* page 102, panel 4). Scrawled next to the warning is the simple response, "FUCK." In this instance and throughout the text, graffiti marks territory and expresses resistance, giving the underground a voice. Dick Hebdige notes that the usage of graffiti as a graphic style on punk records and zines is indicative of punk's "subterranean and anarchic style" (112). This message of subterranean resistance is also encoded in *Transmetropolitan*, most saliently in the message "Free Steve Chung," which pops up on city walls and on the streets throughout the series. In the final issue, the front page headline of *The Word* reads: "Steve Chung Set Free: Massive Graffiti Campaign Succeeds" (Ellis and Robertson, *One More Thing* page 130, panel 2). While this is an inside joke for the perceptive reader, it also expresses the potential for language to evince change. In The City, the word is a means of social control but can also serve as a potential site for resistance and even emancipation.

For Spider, this act of subverting power structures through defacing private and public property extends beyond the written word. One of Spider's preferred methods of traversing urban space is to stride along the tops and hoods of cars as they are packed tightly together in traffic jams. By doing this, Spider forces commuters to rethink what constitutes public and private space and refuses to let them insulate themselves from what Debord calls the "psychogeography" of the city. In one of the few articles that explore *Transmetropolitan* in depth, Scott Bukatman reads Spider Jerusalem in the context of other "urban superheroes" comparing the megapolis in the series to Superman's Metropolis, Batman's Gotham, and Spider-Man's New York. He argues that "superheroes preserve the order of the city but need not submit to it. What he must do, however, is take part of its movement" (176). This motion and dynamism is what attracts Spider to The City, and he inhabits urban space, according to Steven Shaviro, like "a postmodern flaneur" (76), existing both in and outside of its action. But he is not simply a flaneur, idly strolling through the streets, but for how he inhabits space and often provokes and incites, which puts him more in line with Debord than Baudelaire. His walks are akin to Debord's concept of the dérive, or drift, "a technique of rapid passage through varied ambiences" ("Theory of the Dérive," n.p.). Unlike the apolitical flaneur whose act of walking is predominately an aesthetic experience, Spider's confrontational style of passage through The City exposes the visible and invisible power structures that constrict mobility.

In fact in this "prank" and in others like it throughout the series, Spider acts as a sort of Situationist.[3] Like the Sex Pistols, he strategically creates "situations" that garner public outcry but also call in to question the existing social order. In The City, we see the society of the spectacle made visible in all aspects of life, both exterior and interior: "The spectacle cannot be understood as a mere visual excess produced by mass-media technologies. It is a worldview that has actually been materialized, a view of a world that has become objective" (Debord, *Society of the Spectacle*, n.p.). For the inhabitants of The City, the spectacle has become their only mode of perception, infiltrating consciousness itself, even infecting the brain at rest through "buy-bombs" that "load your brain with compressed ads that unreel into your dreams" (Ellis and Robertson, *Back on the Street* page 119, panel 7). Spider responds to this by creating his own spectacles, devising media content that shocks in style and content while also revealing truth to the people. These situations create chaos, and like the Sex Pistols, who according to Stacy Thompson "employed hyper-spectacle to piece through the façade of the industry" (40), Spider uses this anarchic potential to challenge the mainstream media's hold over the peoples' minds. By using "détournement," Spider uses the language and tools of the system against itself. Religion is one of his primary targets in this respect, especially predatory prophets who prey on the people. In one stunt, Spider disrupts a religious convention, where zealots advertise their belief systems as miracle products. Donning a white robe made out of a sheet stolen from Hotel Barabbas (a reference to the political prisoner pardoned by Pontius Pilate) and his new Air Jesus shoes, Spider reenacts the gospel narrative of the cleansing of the temple, overthrowing the tables at the conference and destroying religious propaganda as he shouts, "Thieves, the goddamn lot of you! Thieves and Leeches!" (Ellis and Robertson, *Back on the Street* page 142, panel 3).

These stunts disrupt the social order, exposing the power structures that underpin everyday life in The City. This humane human chaos (as opposed to state or media produced spectacle) reintroduces anarchy into The City, infusing it with life, even if only for a brief moment. It can then be compared to Bakhtin's description of the Medieval "carnival" for it is in the "carnivalesque" that hierarchies of power can be temporarily subverted:

> Man experiences this flow of time in the festive marketplace, in the carnival crowd, as he comes into contact with other bodies of varying age and social caste. He is aware of being a member of a continually growing and renewed people. This is why festive folk laughter presents an element of victory not only over supernatural awe, over the sacred, over death; it also means the defeat of power, of earthly kings, of the earthly upper classes, of all that oppresses and restricts [92].

In contrast to the archetypal urban superhero, Spider is not interested in imposing order, but in protecting spaces and moments of disorder. Interestingly, punk performance also encouraged the shifting of proscribed social roles between audience and performer. For instance, Thompson notes how the performance space in CBGB's made visible "the desire to erode the difference between performer and audience member, to allow those roles to become interchangeable so that any audience member could also be a performer and vice versa" (11).

Yet in *Transmetropolitan*, the spectacle is always in danger of blowing itself up, the carnival in cannibalizing itself. The spectacle must disrupt the people and wake them up, but what if it only increases the society's insatiable need for more stimulation? These tensions are reflected in Spider's ambivalent relationship with the masses. At points in the series, he identifies with the people, expressing his own hedonistic and human excesses for drugs and pleasure, and at other moments, he becomes a self-righteous prophet angrily railing against their complacency and conformity. Enforcing liberty is inherently contradictory, and thus, Spider exists in an impossible dialectic.

This inability to resolve the tension between liberty and equality is reflected in Spider's seemingly paradoxical character. Consistently, what most enrages him are affronts to his own personal liberty and the liberty of others. Yet, inequality thwarts liberty *en masse*, and this is made visible to Spider in a palpable way when he is living and working in The City. In some moments, he connects with the subterranean aspects of The City and finds communion there, but at other times, he expresses a libertarian apathy or even misanthropy, imagining the transients as self-indulgent narcissists and the masses as weak and lumpen. Taken as a whole, Spider's political position appears to be a form of anarchism, but Spider understands that anarchy cannot simply exist as a state of mind when the state imposes its will on the bodies and minds of the people. His socialist leanings then come out in the stories he composes that explore the lives of the unheard and downtrodden: child prostitutes, the disenfranchised cryogenic revivals, and the marginalized transients. Above all else, Spider prizes individual liberty, but inequalities in the system threaten the realization of that liberty for all, especially in The City. This leads him to espouse a political vision as complex and contradictory as the political ideologies that underpin the punk movement, but that holds an internal consistency as an abstract utopian ideal.

From its inception, punk culture has also expressed ambivalence about mass media and its potential to disseminate content to audiences. While mainstream radio and television provide access to audiences outside of the local or underground scene, they also can potentially control, contain, and commodify artistic expression. Derek Jarman's 1978 film *Jubilee* helped make visible these themes and established a distinctive visual punk aesthetic tied to the British scene formed around Malcolm McLaren and Vivienne Westwood's SEX shop on King's Road in London. Jarman's England, however, unlike *Transmetropolitan's* America, is situated in the dystopia of the present, highlighting and hyperbolizing the economic desolation of 1970's London, merging a gritty realism with future speculation, all set within the frame story of Queen Elizabeth I visiting from the past only to discover that the current queen has been killed in a random act of violence. Jarman's film not only captures punk as an expression of style but also as an interior condition by foregrounding the boredom, nihilism, and apathy in the central characters, whose deterioration and deviance reflects and enacts a "postmodern schizo-fragmentation" (Jameson 372). The characters alternate between playfulness and violence, embodying in exaggerated form Richard Hell's "blank generation," and ultimately become blank commodities themselves as the nefarious producer Borgia Ginz states in the film, "They all sign up in one way or another." While some, including Westwood, criticized Jarman's vision when the movie first screened, it was undoubtedly prescient in its argument that commodification would play a key role in punk's incorporation into mainstream society.

The tension between the artist and the media industrial complex has been a salient feature of the punk narrative. Some punk artists on major labels explored these issues by using détournement, subverting media tropes through their lyrics and performance. "Know Your Rights" by The Clash, for instance, begins as a public service announcement and then questions the way that hegemony manifests in the everyday life of the masses. More playful than overtly political, The Talking Heads' band name refers to a particular shot often used in news and documentary of a disembodied head, which calls attention to the absurdity of a media trope that most audiences have come to accept as authoritative. The Sex Pistols took a more confrontational approach, garnering the notorious epithet the "filth and the fury" after cursing on *Today* with Bill Grundy in 1976. Similarly, the MC5 faced continual scrutiny because of their language and the political content in their lyrics. Other bands were kept entirely on the outside. Suicide (named after an issue of the *Ghost Rider* comic book) was never able to go mainstream and frequently encountered backlash even by the underground audiences at CBGB's due to provocative performances and controversial songs like "Frankie Teardrop." Yet media also holds power, and punk musicians have shown a particular interest in creating independent content in a DIY style that has been a salient feature of the movement. In 1974, Patti Smith released her single "Hey Joe" independently, and the punk movement has continued in that trajectory, creating labels (Crass Records, Dischord, Kill Rock Stars, etc.) and independent media content from zines to films and even television shows such as Glenn O'Brien's cable access *TV Party*, which O'Brien frequently described as "a cocktail party that could also be a political party" in his introduction to the show.

Transmetropolitan explores this tension between media as a means of social control and media as a potential avenue for independent and dissident expression. In the universe of *Transmetropolitan*, punk culture aligns with Jarman's cynical vision as it is entirely stripped of political and cultural power and is represented as a reflection of commercial style dictated to the people rather than created by them. In this "supermarket of style" in a post-subcultural and counter-cultural economy, the distinction between "subordinate" and "dominant" cultures is not easy to identify on aesthetic signification alone. In The City, punk is not dead; instead it suffers from what Dylan Clark terms "hyper-inflation" (229) and punk rebellion, including Spider's own brand, is incorporated into the market as fast as it is created—or, in most cases, is imposed on the people by the media in collusion with the government. Within the marketplace, consumers engage in the exchange of cultural and aesthetic products, buying and selling "hipness as a form of subcultural capital" (Thornton 202). In the cultural marketplace of The City, consumers have the agency to choose from a veritable bazaar of products and ideologies, from religious cults to alternative lifestyles, and these choices produce the illusion of freedom, but these seemingly subversive aesthetics become so quickly absorbed into the monoculture that it is difficult to even discern the difference between those who are resisting and those who are conforming. Countercultural ideologies become mere gimmicks to sell products: even Ken Kesey's Kool-Aid is for sale in The City.

Similarly, Spider Jerusalem's dissident columns become commodities almost as quickly as he writes them. Even Spider's persona is a brand that can be used to market goods. For instance, in issue #16, as Spider walks through The City, he notices that the walls of buildings are covered with posters marketing his book. As he continues his walk, he sees people all over the streets wearing replicas of his own signature asymmetrical red and green sunglasses. When he turns the corner, he discovers the reason: the bookstore is offering a "Promotional Giveaway Today Only. Spider Shades!" (Ellis and Robertson, *Year of the Bastard* page 79, panel 2). Spider's style and even his body become visual signs that publicists can use to package him and his ideas into a distinctive, recognizable brand.

Punk music as genre is of little cultural and political import in The City and is frequently satirized within the text. Spider's first antagonist, Fred Christ, is a leader of a spurious religious cult, but was formerly a music producer who was "managing bands," and had "passed over CFC," a popular band frequently referenced in the series (Ellis and Robertson, *Back on the Street* page 36, panel 3). Fred is cowardly, degenerate, and most of all, predatory. In another jab at the music industry, we discover later in the series that Fred also "manages" transient prostitutes. In *Transmetropolitan,* the band CFC is most often a pejorative label, and this becomes even more evident when Spider's assistant Channon introduces her trendy, narcissistic boyfriend whose CFC tattoo is prominently featured on his bicep. It is also significant to note that the acronym CFC can be rearranged as FCC, a coded reference to the Federal Communications Commission, the body in charge of regulating television and radio. CFC, while not directly attacking free expression, serves as an equally dangerous regulatory instrument by occupying the cultural position of punk while attenuating its more revolutionary impulses.

As Spider writes content that calls the system into the question, he also gains widespread acclaim from the masses who buy, sell, and trade rebellion as commodities. Spider's desire to remain pure from these corrupting influences and to focus on the pursuit of truth is one of his most fascinating internal conflicts in the series. In the midst of this dark series, Ellis offers a surprisingly optimistic perspective on the individual's ability to resist capitalist impulses and nihilistic descent, at least if those impulses are countered by another force, in this case, Spider's quest for truth. Another way that Spider maintains his integrity is by using the trappings of capitalism: media, celebrity, and consumerism against the system in acts of détournement. As noted previously, parallels can be drawn to the Sex Pistols who tactically sought and used media attention to challenge power structures, for instance, releasing their subversive song "God Save the Queen" during Queen Elizabeth II's Silver Jubilee.

However, Spider does not like being a celebrity. Spider's contempt for his fame and for fame in general is made evident in the series as early as the first issue, but it is only in later issues that we begin to understand the specific ways in which the media colludes with the government to incorporate and recuperate dissident voices like Spider's by commodifying them and rebranding them in fetishized packages. In fact, all strains of rebellion are essentially commodified in a culture in which thoughts and ideas can be marketed to the masses, enacting a continuous cycle of ideological rebellion and commodification akin to what Henri Lefebvre outlines in *Everyday Life in the Modern World*: "Has not this society, glutted with aestheticism, already integrated former romanticisms, surrealism, existentialism, and even Marxism to a point? ... That which yesterday was reviled today becomes cultural consumer-goods, consumption thus engulfs what was intended to give meaning and direction" (95). In the issue "What Spider Watches on Television," Spider spends an afternoon in front of the television to understand this process and to investigate firsthand "how TV works on the minds of the people in this city" (Ellis and Robertson, *Back on the Street* page 100, panel 3). The shows he watches range from the absurd to the profane (*Anthrax Cat, Republican Party Reservation Compound, JFK's Magic Penis*). Tired of being a passive observer, he initiates a media stunt, calling into several interactive call-in talk shows and interrogating the hosts and harassing the guests on topics from politics to cooking. These are some of his earliest Situationist pranks that disrupt the media culture, culminating when he becomes recuperated by the media as his own image appears on the news site AMFeed: "Oh my God, I have become television" (Ellis and Robertson, *Back on the Street* page 115, panel 4). Spider's relationship to his own fame is a complicated one. While he is dependent upon it financially, he is also disgusted by the culture of narcissism surrounding it, and his fear of "becoming television" expresses a fear of his own reification and of being consumed as a cultural commodity.

This fear becomes more pronounced as his stardom increases over the course of the series. As Spider is descending into paranoia after the president's office orders a D-notice (a total form of censorship) on his work, he watches television again, encountering various versions of his own image, simulacra all created by the media to capitalize on his notoriety. In the first show, a cartoon entitled *Magical Truthsaying Bastard Spidey!* Spider watches himself portrayed as a wacky teenager, engaging in pointless acts of rebellion and sexual conquest. Graphics and textual effects hit the viewers with irreverent maxims called "Truth Bombs!" that package his personality into consumable bites. He changes the channel in frustration only to find a melodramatic rendering of his life story in the television film, *From the Mountain to the City*. He even has a pornographic double in *I Hump It Here*. These representations of Spider differ in their approaches; however, they all flatten his character, recuperating his dangerous and dissident impulses and actions. While this operates as a containment strategy to control Spider, it also appeases the people, providing virtual outlets for the rising anger and agitation triggered by Spider's columns. By drawing out rebellious impulses and desires, these shows permit the expression of dissident strains of thought within the television universe, attenuating them at their origins before they can mature into action.

Spider understands the risk in the reification of his work and image and realizes he must fight against both, but he is stuck between the hard power of governmental censorship and the soft power of media commodification:

> This is how it's become. They all know me. Familiarity breeding contempt. Celebrity hack. Merchandise line. Column that everyone pretends to read, après the inevitable backlash. Column that's been made meaningless by the quiet censorship apparatus turned on it ... the media have made me a defanged, tamed thing they can pet on television and on toy store shelves... [Ellis and Robertson, *Gouge Away* page 30, panels 1–2].

Interestingly, what revives Spider from these particular feelings of powerlessness is to walk through the streets of the city again, to actively seek out the people and places that draw out both his nihilism and his humanism to "get the city under [his] feet. Become alive again" (Ellis and Robertson, *Gouge Away* page 33, panel 1). Walking through The City is simultaneously an act of power and an act of submission. As Spider moves upon The City, the City moves upon him. This dialogical encounter with The City hinges upon listening: "I only ever experience this City properly on the street. It only speaks to me here. The TV is too managed" (page 33, panel 2). For Spider, the "dérive" is then not only a means of confronting the masses as expressed in his more aggressive walks but also an act of listening to The City and connecting with the people in a human encounter that is not mediated through technology but situated in and experienced through the body. By listening to The City's "chatter and music" as well as its "dissonance," Spider steps outside of his own myopia and solipsism and gains power over his nihilism.

Ultimately, however, Spider must move from manipulating the mainstream media to discovering alternative sources and forums for his work in a DIY punk journalistic style. After being fired from *The Word*, Spider teams up with independent media sources to disseminate his work. In the issue "Back to Basics," he meets with John Nkrumah and Lau Qui who run the independent feedsite, *The Hole* and asks if they'd be willing to run a "completely free" column. What draws him to *The Hole* is its independence, autonomy, and flexibility: "And that's the beauty of it. It's mobile. It's difficult to track down. And it's outside the mainstream. The Word has to adhere to the rule of shareholders and corporate peers and the politicians it ate with and fed off" (Ellis and Robertson, *Spider's Thrash* page 22, panel 4). In this independent space, free from the market and from governmental control and censorship, Spider can "say what I want to say, unedited and uncontrolled" (Ellis and Robertson, *Spider's Thrash* page 23, panel 1).

Once he is outside of the mainstream and freed from his affiliations with

The Word, Spider becomes simultaneously a more empathetic and dangerous writer, which is perhaps also a reaction against his commodified image popularized in the mainstream media. While working for *The Hole* he takes emotional and investigative risks and engages in ethically questionable behaviors to get his stories. When explaining his reason for pursuing a story on the topic of child prostitution to the director of a children's home in The City, he explains that when he worked for *The Word* this type of story got "spiked." As a freelancer, literarily working for free, Spider "can say what I want, when I want, now" (Ellis and Robertson, *Spider's Thrash* page 93, panel 3). Having no authoritative entity to scrutinize his work, Spider is essentially emancipated from the constraints of the mainstream press, but he goes on to point out that this new freedom must be balanced against his own personal accountability: "So I have to make even more certain than before—I have to make sure I'm saying something worth saying. Otherwise I'm just jerking off" (Ellis and Robertson, *Spider's Thrash* page 93, panel 3). The market, then, is not the only deterrent to truth and authenticity, but also the capitalist impulses inside the self that steer the artist towards complacency, narcissism, and self-indulgence. Ultimately, Spider espouses a self-moderated anarchic vision of journalism that involves risk and self-reflection, courage and compassion, and a combination of exterior and interior work.

In *Transmetropolitan*, Warren Ellis imagines a postpunk universe where all expressions of aesthetic and ideological dissidence are recuperated by the state and used as hegemonic tools to produce the appearance of freedom in a totalitarian media industrial complex. How can the dissident artist/journalist/musician counter the counterculture as commodity? *Transmetropolitan* does not provide an easy solution to this question, but in his internal victory over his own nihilism and self-commodification, Spider Jerusalem succeeds in expressing his own artistic liberty, though he must return to the mountain at the end of the series to preserve it. And in regards to his work, Ellis refuses to succumb entirely to nihilism as well. When asked in an interview, "What do you think we need to learn in order to survive this world we have created?" Ellis responded, "There is such a thing as truth. Non-relative, unassailable, valuable truth. Do not let people relativise the concept of truth into vapour" (McBride n.p.).

Notes

1. Arguably, *Transmetropolitan* has as much in common with Jonathan Swift and George Orwell as J. G. Ballard and William Gibson, but the visual aesthetic is distinctly cyberpunk in its juxtaposition of the "high tech" and "low life." While many scholars have discussed the ways in which punk music has informed cyberpunk as a literary genre, Larry McCaffery perceptively articulates their shared ideological and iconoclastic origins and impulses:

what unites all of these artists is what might be termed a shared "attitude"—an attitude of defiance towards cultural and aesthetic norms; an attitude of distrust towards rationalist language and all other forms of discourse required by legal, political, and consumer capitalism ... an attitude that artists need not only to disrupt the usual modes of communication but to find a means of self-expression that is more "authentic"... [288]. With his preoccupation with authenticity, his antiauthoritarian personality and a DIY approach to journalism, Spider Jerusalem then shares traits not only with the punk musician but the quintessential cyberpunk protagonist.

2. I use the term "antihero" as a reference to Spider's similarities to the prototypical cyberpunk protagonist and to Spider's classically Byronic disposition.

3. In *Lipstick Traces*, Greil Marcus notes the influence of the Situationist International on Malcolm McLaren and the Sex Pistols and reads the band as part of and a culmination of a larger radical history.

Works Cited

Althusser, Louis. *On the Reproduction of Capitalism: Ideology and Ideological State Apparatuses*. Translated by G.M. Goshgarian, Verso, 2014.
Bakhtin, Mikhail. *Rabelais and His World*. Translated by Iswolsky Hélène, Indiana UP, 1984.
Baudrillard, Jean. *Simulacra and Simulation*. U of Michigan, 1994.
Bentham, Jeremy, and Miran Božovič. *The Panopticon Writings*. Verso, 2010.
Bukatman, Scott. "A Song of the Urban Superhero." 2003. *The Superhero Reader*, edited by Charles Hatfield, Jeet Heer, and Kent Worcester, U of Mississippi, 2013, pp. 170–198.
Clark, Dylan. "The Death and Life of Punk, the Last Subculture." *The Post Subcultures Reader*, edited by David Muggleton, Berg, 2003, pp. 223–238.
Debord, Guy. *Society of the Spectacle: With New Introduction*. Soul Bay, 2012.
_____. "Theory of the Dérive." *Les Lèvres Nues* no. 9, 1956, reprinted in *Internationale Situationniste* no. 2, 1958, translated by Ken Knabb. Situationist International Online, http://www.cddc.vt.edu/sionline/si/theory.html. Accessed 18 Dec. 2014.
Ellis, Warren (p), Darick Robertson (a), and Rodney Ramos (i). *Transmetropolitan: Back on the Street*. DC Comics, 1998.
_____. *Transmetropolitan: Dirge*. DC Comics, 2010.
_____. *Transmetropolitan: Gouge Away*. DC Comics, 2009.
_____. *Transmetropolitan: Lonely City*. DC Comics, 2009.
_____. *Transmetropolitan: Lust for Life*. DC Comics, 1998.
_____. *Transmetropolitan: One More Time*. DC Comics, 2011.
_____. *Transmetropolitan: Spider's Thrash*. DC Comics, 2010.
_____. *Transmetropolitan: The Cure*. DC Comics, 2011.
_____. *Transmetropolitan: The New Scum*. DC Comics, 2009.
_____. *Transmetropolitan: Year of the Bastard*. DC Comics, 1999.
Fear and Loathing in Gonzo Vision. Directed by Nigel Finch, performances by Hunter S. Thompson and Ralph Steadman, BBC Omnibus, 1978.
Hall, Stuart, and Tony Jefferson. *Resistance through Rituals: Youth Subcultures in Post-war Britain*. Routledge, 2006.
Hebdige, Dick. *Subculture the Meaning of Style*. Routledge, 2002.
Henry, Tricia. *Break All Rules!: Punk Rock and the Making of a Style*. UMI Research, 1989.
Jameson, Fredric. *The Political Unconscious: Narrative as a Socially Symbolic Act*. Cornell UP, 1981.
_____. *Postmodernism, Or, The Cultural Logic of Late Capitalism*. Duke UP, 1991.
Jubilee. Directed by Derek Jarman, performances by Jenny Runacre, Nell Campbell, Linda Spurrier, Toyah Willcox, and Adam Ant, Whaley-Malin Productions, 1978.
Marcus, Greil. *Lipstick Traces: A Secret History of the Twentieth Century*. Harvard UP, 1989.
Marx, Karl, and Friedrich Engels. *The German Ideology. The Collected Works of Karl Marx and Friedrich Engels. General Works 1844–1895*. Volume 5. InteLex Corp, 1976.
McBride, Melanie. "The Transmetropolitan Condition: An Interview with Warren Ellis." *Mindjack*, 08 Oct. 2002, http://www.mindjack.com/interviews/ellis.html. Accessed 20 Aug. 2014.
McCaffery, Larry. "Cutting Up: Cyberpunk, Punk Music, and Urban Decontextualizations."

Storming the Reality Studio: A Casebook of Cyberpunk & Postmodern Science Fiction, edited by Larry McCaffery, Duke UP, 2012, pp. 286–307.
McHale, Brian. "Towards a Poetics of Cyberpunk." *Beyond Cyberpunk: New Critical Perspectives*, edited by Graham J. Murphy and Sherryl Vint, Routledge, 2010, pp. 3–28.
Percy, Walker. "Foreword." *A Confederacy of Dunces*, written by John Kennedy Toole, Grove, 1980, pp. Vii-Ix.
Shaviro, Steven. *Connected, Or, What It Means to Live in the Network Society*. U of Minnesota, 2003.
Smith, Stevie. "Not Waving but Drowning." *Poetry Foundation*, https://www.poetryfoundation.org/resources/learning/core-poems/detail/46479. Accessed 13 Oct. 2014.
Thompson, Hunter S. *Fear and Loathing in Las Vegas: A Savage Journey to the Heart of the American Dream*. Vintage, 1998.
Thompson, Stacy. *Punk Productions: Unfinished Business*. State U of New York, 2004.
Thornton, Sarah. *Club Cultures: Music, Media, and Subcultural Capital*. U of New England, 1996.

24-Hour Murder People
The Punk Iconography of Grant Morrison's The Invisibles

Keegan Lannon

In "Different Every Time," the introduction to Patrick Meaney's *Our Sentence Is Up*, Timothy Callahan bemoans the difficulties which arose during his own attempts to write about Grant Morrison's long-running series *The Invisibles*:

> [The] only way to fully understand *The Invisibles*, I thought, was to immerse myself in the works of literature, art, and music which inspired Morrison's work on the series. So as I reread all the issues of *The Invisibles*, I started making a list. A list of everything Morrison alluded to in the comic: from the Beatles to "Department S," from *The Prisoner* to Maya Deren, from Jerry Cornelius to the I-Ching…. It became a massive list [(1–2].

Callahan had fallen down a deep rabbit hole, watching all the shows, reading all the books, and listening to all the music to which Grant Morrison alludes in the series. Waist deep in his massive list, he felt overwhelmed by the research, and eventually abandoned his project.

Though it creates difficulties, Callahan is right: the series can be best understood by reading it through Grant Morrison's influences, as daunting a prospect as that might seem. If there is one thing that people can agree upon regarding *The Invisibles* (1994–2000), it is the autobiographical nature of the text. Some have argued that Morrison has written himself into his seminal text, and there are several obvious examples: King Mob is bald, is fashion conscious, and practices magic (or magick); Morrison is also bald, is fashion conscious, and practices a type of magic. As the series progressed, the line between the author and character dissolved further. Patrick Meaney notes:

> After giving King Mob a viral illness near the end of volume one, Morrison found himself suffering from a similar illness and on the verge of death. He decided to "make friends" with the virus by writing it into the comic as the Archons, and shortly after, he recovered.... He's also discussed giving King Mob a girlfriend in volume two to get himself laid in real life. He went to the same places that the characters did and did the same things that they did. He got high on a mesa, and he walked into the palace of the scorpion gods. The series is based on things that happened in Morrison's own life, filtered through the conspiracy theories of the time, big American action movies, books Morrison loved as a teenager, and other things that influenced his own life [*Our Sentence is Up* 11–12].

Indeed, as Meaney claims here, the series moves beyond the physical similarities. Certainly, some of the characters looks and act like Morrison, but they also share the same world view. Marc Singer, in *Grant Morrison: Combining the Worlds of Contemporary Comics*, says:

> Running for three volumes over nearly six years, [*The Invisibles*] evolves from a wide-ranging survey of Morrison's philosophy to a grueling year-long trial of initiation and rebirth, then to a violent action movie in volume two, then to a self-reflexive, self-critical text disgusted with violent action movies, and finally back to a survey of Morrison's substantially changed philosophy in volume three [98].

Morrison himself has been quite vocal about the connections between the book and himself. In 2000, speaking at Disinfo.con, Morrison gave a long talk in which he delineates the connection between *The Invisibles* and his burgeoning magic practice. He argues that the series is a way to bring his magic to life. In *Supergods*, Morrison's collection of personal anecdotes and analysis of superhero comics, he notes that the series was developed during his personal rebirth, in which, financially buffeted by earlier works, he was able to travel the world seeking his new self. Morrison says:

> I decided to do a book where I could contain and address all my interests. I already had the vague concept of a vast occult conspiracy thriller set in the real world, the present day.... The characters were all parts of me mixed with people I knew: Dane McGowan, the Liverpool street punk destined to be a bodhisattva, was the working-class cynic who still kept me in check. King Mob was the art school, fashion-conscious chaos magician. Ragged Robin was my sensible anima; Lord Fanny, my indomitable tranny witch disguise; and Boy, the practical, pragmatic voice of reason that made sure I always paid my bills and taxes and fed the cats. Even the villains, blind Gnostic forces of repression, tyranny, and cruelty, were my own self-hate and fear given form, named and tamed like demons [258].

Furthermore, the act of writing himself into his comics is a recurring trope for Morrison's comics. He famously wrote himself into his run of *Animal Man* (1988–1990), quite literally meeting with the titular character in the final issues. Whatever interest is forefront in his own mind at the time of writing tends to work itself into his comics. In a very real way, to read Morrison's comics is to read a fictionalized and figurative autobiography. What is different about *The Invisibles* is the encompassing nature of the text.

Rather than try to delineate the wide-ranging field of allusions and biographical detail, a better approach to *The Invisibles* is from a specific and well-defined angle. Of course, this method will have the personal slant of the author and will necessarily trace what the critic finds most interesting or obvious. The two compendiums to the series, Meaney's aforementioned *Our Sentence is Up* and Patrick Neighly and Kereth Cowe-Spigai's *Anarchy for the Masses*, both admit to this shortcoming. In *Anarchy for the Masses*, Neighly and Cowe-Spigai begin by saying, "Don't believe anything you read in this book.... A strange way to open, to be sure, but taking any interpretation of *The Invisibles* as definitive is to miss the point altogether. What we offer is our interpretation..." (9). Meaney begins his book with an almost identical sentiment:

> This book isn't designed to be the definitive interpretation of *The Invisibles*.... Now you may be thinking: *The Invisibles* [sic] *is so well-regarded, but so confusing, and I bought this book to understand the series! But now you're telling me that you don't have the answers?* ... Well, I do have answers. It's just that I can't claim to have the *definitive* ones. In fact, to expect a single definitive answer is to misunderstand the series. It's impossible to tell someone the "right" answers when it comes to the series, precisely because so much of it is about the interaction between the reader and text— and between fiction and reality. What the series means depends on who you are when you read it and what kind of world you read it in [*Our Sentence Is Up* 8].

With the density of the allusions and references and the play between the reader and the text, Morrison has crafted a comic that resists simple interpretation. Essentially, any attempt to interpret the series (or even a single issue) will create *an* interpretation, not *the* interpretation.[1]

To gain access, then, the reader needs to decide, consciously or otherwise, what to look for within the series, and to trace that aspect through the twisting narrative. Most focus on one of three major influences: first, some critics focus on Morrison's use of "pop magic," the author's unique brand of everyday magic which exists in the modern world and is accessible to everyone; second, others have focused on the effects of his alien abduction while he vacationed in Kathmandu, which had profound effects on his understanding of time and his relationship with the Universe; and finally, another popular focus is Morrison's philosophy of language, and how the series probes the interaction between signs and that which is signified. Exploring the traces of these elements has produced some interesting examinations of the series, including the two compendiums mentioned above. This essay will take a different tack: considering the influence of punk on Morrison's *The Invisibles*.

Before examining the punk aesthetics found in *The Invisibles*, it is worthwhile to determine how punk has influenced Morrison. There has not been much written about punk and Morrison's comics by other critics. None of the three book-length, extended analyses of Morrison's work contain much of a discussion of his punk influences. In Guy Lawley's "'I like Hate and I Hate Everything Else': The Influence of Punk on Comics," he argues that punk themes can be found in the British comic writers, including Morrison:

> The entry of British writers like Neil Gaiman, Grant Morrison, and Peter Milligan into the mainstream [US comic market] (directly following from the successes of Alan Moore and Frank Miller) brought punk-influenced subject matter like oppositional politics, alternative sexuality, and the everyday life of ordinary people into the medium more widely than ever before [117].

Speaking more directly of Morrison, Lawley writes:

> None of Morrison's work concerns itself much overtly with punk subject matter. Like Milligan and McCarthy he has an awesome array of other influences in his arsenal, and also moved on to *2000 AD* and DC Comics, where he has consistently been one of the best comics scripters published in the mainstream [109].

Lawley goes on to note how Morrison has publicly claimed that punk was very influential to his worldview. Interestingly, Morrison often discusses punk when people ask him about comics. Considering how emphatically Morrison talks about punk music (which will be discussed in more detail below), it seems strange to flippantly discount *The Invisibles*, or any of Morrison's work, as concerning itself "overtly with punk subject matter." This could be because Lawley seems to privilege comics with "crude vitality and immediacy of communication," two things which *The Invisibles*, or any mainstream comic really, lacks (100). However, that does not exclude the comic from overtly dealing with punk themes or having punk aspects.

On the subject of punk music, Morrison has been quite clear: punk had a major influence in shaping his world-view. In a long interview with Nick Hasted for the April 1995 edition of *The Comics Journal*, Morrison was directly asked about the impact punk had on him as a teenager, to which he responded: "Total. Complete. I was just utterly transformed by it" (55).[2] When asked if he still considered himself part of the movement, he responds: "Yeah, yeah. And I probably still do, which is the tragedy of it all" (55). Years later in *Supergods*, Morrison expounds on how punk shaped his life:

> One Thursday night, I was sprawled on the settee with *Top of the Pops* on the telly when Poly Styrene and her band X-Ray Spex turned up to play their latest single: an exhilarating sherbet storm of raw punk psychedelia entitled "The Day the World Turned Day-Glo." By the time the last incandescent chorus played out, I was a punk. I had always been a punk. I would always be a punk.... This music reflected my experience of teenage life as a series of brutal setbacks and disappointments that could in the end be redeemed into art and music with humor, intelligence, and a modicum of talent. This, for me, was the real punk, the genuine anticool, and I felt empowered. The losers, the rejected, and the formerly voiceless were being offered an opportunity to show what they could do to enliven a stagnant culture [171–172].

After this TV-inspired moment of clarity, Morrison went on to form a band in Glasgow, despite never having played a musical instrument before. In punk music, Morrison found a voice that would surface again in his comics: "We [his band] were being told we could do anything, so we did. I still had no girlfriend, but I was learning how to make my fantasies into reality, and that was a start" (172). When he eventually begins to write *The Invisibles*, he would find a more aptly suited vehicle for turning fantasy into reality.

When Morrison began to write comics professionally, he crafted an identity from his punk ethos: "My public persona was punk to the rotten core. Outspoken and mean spirited, I freely expressed contempt for the behind-the-scenes world of comics professionals, which seemed unglamorous and overwhelmingly masculine by comparison to the club and music scenes" (*Supergods* 213). Despite his obvious disdain for superhero comics and those writing them, Morrison has primarily and ironically worked with the larger, more-masculine oriented comic companies. His earliest successes came with DC characters, reviving a few struggling series: *Animal Man* and *Doom Patrol* (1989–1993). Even his most critically acclaimed and financially successful works, *Arkham Asylum* (1989) and *All-Star: Superman* (2005–2008), are the most quintessential mainstream titles in comics.

Pushing a counter-cultural agenda from a mainstream source is not, strictly speaking, unheard of in punk music: the Sex Pistols signed with EMI, the New York Dolls signed with Mercury Records, and the Clash signed with Columbia, just to name a few of the bands who signed major-label record deals, often early in their careers. Despite the fact that so many early punk bands signed with larger record labels, and some, like the Sex Pistols, earned massive signing bonuses, the label to which a band is signed is often a metric used to determine the authenticity of a punk band. Punk fans and scholars often use the "sellout" moniker to suggest that a punk band signing with a major label for financial stability has lost sight of the punk ethos, and thus are not authentically punk. In a column for *Noisey*, an arm of *Vice*, Dan Ozzi summed up the prevailing argument:

> The move [to sign with a major label] was never received well, and always seen [*sic*] as an affront to those who had launched the bands out of the basements in the first place. Whether the band's major label debut was a commercial success or a flop, a critical darling or panned piece of trash, many fans stuck a middle finger to the whole thing, as if to say, "We support you, but not enough for you to be able to quit your job at Whole Food!" ["Major Label Debut" n.p.].

Ozzi questions the validity of the "sellout" debasement, calling it "petty and dumb in retrospect," but the belief is often held that mainstream productions cannot be punk (see anything ever written about Green Day, for example). Morrison seems aware of this stigma and folds it in to his punk plan:

> And so we [the British Invasion artists and authors] arrived in our teens and twenties, in our leather jackets and Chelsea boots, with our crepe-soled brothel creepers and skinhead Ben Shermans, metal tattoos, and infected piercings. We brought to bear on the American superhero discourse the invigorating influence of alternative lifestyles, punk rock, fringe theater, and tight black jeans. We rolled-up in anarchist hordes, in rowdy busloads, drinking the bars dry, munching our hosts' buttocks (artist Glenn Fabry drunkenly assaulted editor Karen Berger's glutes with his molars), and swearing in a dozen or more baffling regional accents. The Americans expected us to be brilliant punks and, eager to please our masters, we sensitive, artistic boys did our best to live up to our hype. Like the Sex Pistols sneering and burning their way through "Johnny B. Goode," we took their favorite songs, rewrote all the lyrics, and played them on buzz saws through squalling distortion petals [*Supergods* 186].

Granted, had it not been for forward-thinking (or profoundly misinformed) executives, both the Sex Pistols and Grant Morrison would not have been able to preach their punk sermons to the masses using the tools of the mainstream media. Regardless of the distributor, it would be hard to say that the Sex Pistols albums are not punk. It seems a better evaluation of a work's punk authenticity would be to examine what the work does with the opportunities it has. If the Ramones signed with Sire Records and cut their hair or changed their sound to increase their sales numbers, that would be a good argument for selling out. Grant Morrison, like the Sex Pistols before him, took his opportunity on the main stage to give the readers a healthy dose of his punk ideology.

Unlike the Sex Pistols, whose very appearance oozes punk ethos, *The Invisibles* have more difficulty proving their punk credentials. Published serially by Vertigo, a DC imprint (an adult-oriented imprint, but nonetheless tied to the largest, corporate-owned publishing house at the time), there certainly is nothing "DIY" about the full-color comic, especially compared to self-published zines and mini-comics like Adrian Tomine's *Optic Nerve* (1995-present), John Porcellino's *King Cat* (1989-present), or Peter Bagge's *Hate* (1990–2011). In a very real way, this was a mainstream comic following the mainstream comic conventions: exaggerated anatomy, brightly colored characters, action-oriented stories, and so forth. Especially in the second volume, a group of costumed heroes (albeit bizarrely costumed heroes) are rendered in what could be called the typical, generic "hero" style normally found in other, more recognizable DC titles. When put against some of the underground comics mentioned above, or even compared to *Sandman* (1989–1996) which was likewise published by Vertigo, *The Invisibles* looks like any other superhero comic on the rack.[3]

But this is the punk genius of the series. It works to subvert the expectations of the art form to which it belongs. Morrison uses the tools of "the man" to push his subversive message. *The Invisibles* seeks to challenge mainstream comics from within mainstream comics. Of course, the series is long and takes some pretty wide turns in style and content over the 55 issues. There is a lot one could say about how punk influences Morrison's narrative (both in content and style), but unfortunately, this essay has limited space. Here, I will focus on the first issue of the first volume, specifically the cover and first two pages. In this story, titled "Dead Beatles," Morrison lays bare his punk ideology.

As noted above, Morrison certainly did not select the publisher for *The Invisibles* which would neatly align with his punk ideologies. That said, Vertigo did knowingly publish the anarchist, counter-cultural comic. Morrison's intention is obvious from the first issue. Consider the cover of *The Invisibles* #1. Published serially, as what is sometimes called "a floppy," the first issue would have shared rack space with several other similarly sized, shaped, and colored comics. With very few exceptions, the covers for comics from the mainstream publishers (DC/Vertigo, Marvel, Image, and Dark Horse) follow a very simple formula: show the titular character and the central villain either gearing up for a fight, mid-fight, or standing triumphant after the fight.[4] The key is to suggest action and violence. Even tie-in comics like *Barbie* #45 and *Beavis and Butthead* #7 (both Marvel) follow this convention. Team comics, such as *New Titans* #114 (DC), or *Galactic Guardians* #3 (Marvel), feature several, if not all, of the team members on the cover. There is a simple reason for this formula. According to ComicVine.com, the four mainstream comic companies above put out 2,500 individual issues in 1994, so any one of 200 or so issues which came out each month needed to attract the attention of potential buyers. Nothing sells comics better than action and excitement.

The Invisibles takes a different, decidedly more punk approach. Rian Hughes was the cover artist for the first volume, as well as the creator of the series logo. "Dead Beatles" immediately disregards the standard conventions for covers. Not only is there no action, but there are no people on the cover of the book. There is no information about the team of heroes featured in the comic. Instead, a purple (or pink, possibly) hand grenade is emblazoned on a red field with Morrison's and artist Steve Yeowell's names running across the middle in white block letters. The bright, fluorescent colors are reminiscent of those used on The Sex Pistol's debut album, *Nevermind the Bollocks*, and the typeface for the creative team resembles the lettering stencils used to spray-paint words on shipping crates. The title appears across the top of the cover, making use of the negative space on the page to give the impression it was cut from the red background.

The cover, a sort of collage made using a hyper-aggressive Warhol-style silkscreen and a can of spray-paint, pitches the punk ideology of the comic. As Neighly and Cowe-Spigai say:

> The purple grenade depicted in Warhol style tells us instantly that this series is going to subvert our assumptions, transforming weapons into art and making a statement about civilization that has turned even war into a processed consumer spectacle. The use of a fifth color in the printing process helps to further differentiate *The Invisibles* as something different, and the logo, created entirely from negative space, is a brilliant display of series as object [*Anarchy for the Masses* 15].

The decision to allude to Warhol's painting is itself a nod to the series punk intentions. Warhol, both as an artist and through his counter-cultural incubators, The Factory, has deep connections to punk. In *A Cultural Dictionary of Punk: 1974–1982*, Nicholas Rombes includes an entry for Warhol. He notes that Warhol was only "distantly associated" with punk music through his connection with The Velvet Underground, but that his art has a more immediate association (305). Ideologically, punk music and Pop Art have a lot in common. Warhol's art challenges the sacred and elevates the mundane: he painted an effeminate portrait of the controversial Chairman Mao Zedong and lionized the Campbell's soup can. The Sex Pistols had a similar visual aesthetic on their promotional material for *Anarchy in the UK* and the single *God Save the Queen*. The posters often feature manipulated versions of iconic images of British pride, like the portrait of the Queen or the Union Jack flag. These are frequently mutilated in some way: the flag is torn to ribbons, or the Queen has a safety pin through the mouth, or *God Save the Queen* and the Sex Pistols pasted over her eyes and mouth.[5]

This same visual aesthetic is intended in Hughes' cover for the first issue of *The Invisibles*. Like Warhol's *Campbell's Soup Cans* and the Sex Pistols album art, this comic seeks to challenge the reader's conceptions of war, of art, and of comic books. As Meaney notes, "the series announces itself as a day-glo grenade, in the style of pop art, set to blow up the reader ... and perhaps the medium itself" (*Our Sentence is Up* 19). The grenade is a synthesis of contradictory signs. As a tool of war, it can bring explosive destruction and acts as a faceless sign of military strength or oppression. The grenade is not a solider with personality and empathy, but a tool used to anonymously destroy things. However, bright day-glo colors have a connection with more countercultural movements. In "The Punk Paper: a Dialogue," Ester Leslie notes:

> Day-Glo was the color of choice for punk.... In the entry on the word Day-Glo, the OED quotes an article from the *Listener*, from 1968, which condemns the use of flashing Day-Glo colors as vulgar signal of an orgasm in a film by Jack Cardiff. The hippies used Day-Glo in their cultural artefacts, and even on their bodies, but theirs was an attempt to paint over the world in the colors of their hallucinogenic trips. Day-Glo was being taken into the student bedroom, the kids' blacklit den where individual meditation could hinge on the wonders of a perceptual trick that disappeared when normal electricity resumed. It took punk to fully assimilate Day-Glo without transforming it—that is vulgarity and all..." [n.p.].

Leslie goes on to say, "Fluorescence holds nothing back for later—like punk, its mode is the mode of anti-interiority, denial of the romantic self, a cheap trick, a cheap trip without innerness, an upfront, slap in the face of public taste" (n.p.). Rendered in these vulgar colors of the common people, the grenade then is not a tool of the oppressive power structure, but a tool of the counterrevolution. There will still be explosive destruction, but it will be used to tear down the status quo. Like the album art for the Sex Pistols and other punk acts, the cover for *The Invisibles* #1 promises a violent, populist rebellion just by its visual aesthetic.

It does not take long for the comic to bring this promise to fruition. The first page of "Dead Beatles" begins mysteriously with five panels in which the unnamed King Mob collects a "khephra," a beetle which "goes down into darkness and rises again, bearing the sun in his mandibles," establishing early the theme of death and rebirth which will play out across the series (9). The adjoining page is a jarring juxtaposition: a splash page with the artist information and the title of the issue splayed across an image of Dane McGowan, fist raised in the air, standing slightly turned with legs shoulder-width apart, ready to toss a lit Molotov cocktail. The fiery tail of the cocktail has created a broken hula-hoop of fire near Dane's waist. His scream, "FUUUUUUUUUCK!" is printed in red and encapsulated in a jagged speech bubble across the top of the page. It is a bold choice to open the first issue of his first creator-owned title with such a vulgar curse word. While Alan Moore and Dave Gibbons' *Watchmen* (1986) and Frank Miller and Klaus Jansen's *Batman: The Dark Knight Returns* (1986) had loosened the Comic Code Authority's censorial grip, DC was still very much concerned with getting the Comic Code's stamp of approval on most of their comics.[6] Crass language such as this was rarely seen in comics, and hardly with such immediate gusto.

Here again, it's useful to return to the Sex Pistols as a good analogy for Morrison's punk ethos in *The Invisibles*. A little more than a year after their first show at St. Martins College, the Sex Pistols, then signed to EMI, made an appearance on *Today*, a British news program. At this point in their career, the Sex Pistols were building a larger following on the heels of several successful shows, their first single, "Anarchy in the UK," and an appearance on Tony Wilson's *So It Goes*, but they were hardly household names. When Queen, another band signed to EMI, dropped out of an appearance on *Today*, the Sex Pistols were given the opportunity to play to a larger audience unfamiliar with the band. EMI probably saw this as an excellent opportunity to gain some publicity for the band, but the Sex Pistols did not quite cooperate. Lasting roughly two minutes, the whole interview is incredibly surreal. Host Bill Grundy, looking a bit drunk and somewhat uncomfortable with a stage full of punks (the Sex Pistols brought along a handful of the Bromley Contingent, most notably Siouxsie Sioux), introduces the band by saying, "They are punk rockers. The new craze they tell me. Their heroes? Not the nice clean Rolling Stones. You see they are as drunk as I am ... they are clean by comparison. They're a group called the Sex Pistols, and I am surrounded by all of them." The remaining interview is uneasy at best, as Grundy openly antagonizes the band for signing a major record deal and brazenly flirts with Siouxsie Sioux. Rising to the occasion, the Sex Pistols peppered the live taping with a flurry of profanity. This profanity, particularly near the end when guitarist Steve Jones calls Grundy a "dirty fucker" and "a fucking rotter," drew outrage in the tabloids. The next day, *The Daily Mirror* had a front-page headline written in all capital letters: "THE FILTH AND THE FURY!" accompanied by a grainy photo of the Sex Pistols smiling and reaching for the camera. In the months that followed, the Sex Pistols were banned from several counties around the UK, Bill Grundy was let go from *Today*, and EMI dropped the band.[7]

Obscenities have long been a tool of the counterculture, so it is not surprising both Morrison and the Sex Pistols shared a proclivity towards using curse words in their art. While "obscenities" can mean a lot, from suggestive metaphors, lurid images, or profane gestures—and while punk music has never shied from all the of these—I am mostly concerned with swear words, or as Melissa Mohr defines them: "[words which] vividly reveal taboo body parts, actions, and excretions that culture demands we conceal, whether by covering with clothing, shrouding in privacy, or flushing down the toilet" (*Holy Sh*t* 6). Mohr's physiological, linguistic, and historic analysis of the words and phrases loosely collected under the umbrella of swear words often discusses how class and language are intertwined in discussions of obscenities:

> Good manners and refinement of language became [in the 18th and 19th Century] a indication of social and moral worth, a sign of distinction that differentiated the middle classes from the great unwashed outside and below.... Obscene words violated class norms—they were seen as the language of the lower classes, the uneducated—and accessed the deepest taboo of Augustan and Victorian society, the human body and its embarrassing desires, which had to be absolutely hidden away in swaths of fabric and disguised in euphemisms [176].

While this quote is directly tied to Victorian sensibilities, her discussion of James Joyce's *Ulysses* (1922) and D.H. Lawrence's *Lady Chatterly's Lover* (1928) and the censorship leveled against both due to their perceived obscenity demonstrates how these attitudes were still pervasive deep into the 20th century, especially by those who held the power. In fact, Mohr notes that it was not until the British Obscenity Act of 1959 that, officially, a questionable novel or work of art could have legal protections because of the overall artistic merit of the piece (243). Mohr argues that "an era of new openness" for swear words began in the middle of the 20th century, following the obscenity trials for *Ulysses* and *Lady Chatterly's Lover* (243).

While Mohr does provide an interesting and compelling argument regarding the populist attitudes towards profanity, watching the protests following the Sex Pistols appearance on *Today*, archived in Julien Temple's *The Filth and the Fury*, one might want to qualify this statement. Certainly, those returning from wars in Germany and Vietnam might have been more amenable to swearing, but there was certainly a vocal contingent who still looked to protest and suppress the language use of the punk subculture. What undergirds the arguments made during these protests is the Victorian notion that cursing and baseness go hand-in-hand. People swearing are a lower class, and the children (and those in the lower class) need to be protected from the base influences. As Mohr notes:

> Behind the anxiety about swearing lies a fear that civilization is a thin veneer, barely covering a state of chaos. We worry that this fragile membrane can be ripped apart by swearing, which violates so many dictates of polite, rational discourse and gives voice to will [15].

For some, all that stands between a decent society and one of total chaos is unuttered swear words. Knowing this, countercultural movements have embraced obscenities as a way to push against the power structures and create disarray. The hippies "Fuck the draft" signs in the 1960s, rap music's appropriation of "nigga," and Steve Jones calling Bill Grundy a "fucking rotter" all have the same goal: demonstrate control over language and violate the prescriptions of a polite society. Mohr notes how obscenity is particularly suited for these ends:

> Obscenities are particularly useful in these contexts [the struggle to survive and resist] because they are the words with the most emotive force. They are the go-to words for expressing aggression, for putting someone else down, for resisting "the system" and the dominant culture that expects certain kinds of "good" language and behavior [247–248].

It is certainly an aggression aimed at "the system" which motivates Dane McGowan as he launches his Molotov cocktail at the school's library. With a loud curse, he sets fire to an institution portending to hold all the relevant information. This act, burning down the library, is a rejection of the assumptions that the library represents: these books are the important books, and those not cataloged within are not important. This, similarly, is the intention Morrison has for *The Invisibles*. The philosophy of the comic is lobbed like a cheap grenade into the reader's hands where Morrison, like McGowan and King Mob, will set fire to your assumptions.

Of course, this only scratches the surface of Morrison's long-running comic series and the various traces of a punk ideology that run through it. There is a lot more that could, and should, be said. For example, a close examination of the "costumes" (if they can be called that) which The Invisibles wear throughout the series and how this aligns with Dick Hebdige's conception of punk as a bricolage of influences would certainly yield some interesting finds. Likewise, an analysis of Morrison's BARBELiTH as the personification of the punk scene's sense of alienation would be well worth someone's time and effort. Of course, the shifting nature of the text would complicate some of these readings (and likely complicates the above analysis, as well). By the third volume, Morrison seems to despise all the violent revolution he built in the first two volumes, and his world view and philosophy have drastically shifted. Moreover, by the end of the series, he has worked to dissolve the culture/subculture dichotomy of The Invisibles and The Outer Church, which is a decidedly un-punk thing to do. Regardless, there is sufficient evidence detailed above to warrant further discussions about Morrison's punk influences.

Notes

1. Of course, this could be said to be true of any act of interpretation. Indeed, reader response theory is based on this idea.
2. Oddly, this quote was also referenced in Lawley's article. Knowing this, he still contends that Morrison did not deal overtly with punk themes.
3. Certainly, the use of superheroes does not instantly preclude a comic from punk influences. Daniel Clowes' *Eightball*, for example, includes a recurring story, "Death Ray" which also features superheroes, though in a more superficially subversive manner than *The Invisibles*.
4. Not surprisingly, Vertigo's *Sandman* is one of the comics which, like *The Invisibles*, constantly breaks with convention for the issue covers. To find these examples from 1994, the year *The Invisibles* was first published, I used Comic Vine, the incredible online database for everything comics. While this is likely not an exhaustive search of the comics on the shelf when *The Invisibles* went to print, the search for issues published in 1994 did provide a representative sampling.
5. The Sex Pistols official website has several examples of the art work associated with their music (http://www.sexpistolsofficial.com/sex-pistols-artwork/).
6. The Comic Book Legal Defense Fund has a great primer by Amy Kiste Nyberg on their website for those unfamiliar with the history of comic censorship. Interestingly, the Comic Code was still in use until as late as 2011, though only DC and Archie still subscribed near the end.
7. Julien Temple's *The Filth and The Fury*, a biographic film about the Sex Pistols, includes the entire Bill Grundy interview.

Works Cited

Callahan, Patrick. "'Different Every Time': An Introduction." *Our Sentence Is Up: Seeing Grant Morrison's The Invisibles*, written by Patrick Meaney, Sequart, 2010, pp. 1–7.
Callahan, Timothy. *Grant Morrison: The Early Years*. Sequart, 2011.
Disinfo.Con. Performance by Grant Morrison, Disinformation, 2007.
The Filth and the Fury. Directed by Julien Temple, Warner Bros., 2000.
Hasted, Nick. "Interview with Grant Morrison." *Comics Journal*, no. 176, Apr. 1995, pp. 52–87.
Hebdige, Dick. *Subculture: The Meaning of Style*. Routledge, 1979.
Lawley, Guy. "'I Like Hate and I Hate Everything Else': The Influence of Punk on Comics." *Punk Rock, So What?: The Cultural Legacy of Punk*, edited by Roger Sabin, Routledge, 1999, pp. 100–19.

Leslie, Esther, and Ben Watson. "The Punk Paper: A Dialogue." *Militant Esthetix*, n.d., http://www.militantesthetix.co.uk/punk/Punkcomb.html. Accessed 16 Aug. 2015.
Meaney, Patrick. *Our Sentence Is Up: Seeing Grant Morrison's The Invisibles.* Sequart, 2010.
Mohr, Melissa. *Holy Shit: A Brief History of Swearing.* Oxford UP, 2013.
Morrison, Grant. *Supergods.* Spiegel & Grau, 2012.
_____, Steve Yeowell, Jill Thompson, and Dennis Cramer. *The Invisibles: Say You Want a Revolution.* DC Comics, 1996.
Neighly, Patrick, and Kereth Cowe-Spigai. *Anarchy for the Masses: An Underground Guide to The Invisibles.* Mad Yak, 2002.
Nyberg, Amy Kiste. "Content: Selected Essays on Technology, Creativity, Copyright, and the Future of the Future." *Comic Book Legal Defense Fund*, n.d., http://cbldf.org/. Accessed 16 Aug. 2015.
Ozzi, Dan. "Major Label Debut: Punk's 'Sell Out' Albums Revisited." *Noisey: Music by Vice.* Vice, 2 Apr. 2015, https://noisey.vice.com/en_us/article/major-label-debut-punks-sell-out-albums-revisited?utm_source=noiseyfbus. Accessed 16 Aug. 2015.
Rombes, Nicholas. *A Cultural Dictionary of Punk: 1974–1982.* Continuum, 2009.
"Sex Pistols Artwork." *Sex Pistols The Official Website.* n.d., http://www.sexpistolsofficial.com/photos/?wppa-album=4&wppa-cover=0&wppa-occur=1. Accessed 16 Aug. 2015.
Singer, Marc. *Grant Morrison: Combining the Worlds of Contemporary Comics.* U of Mississippi, 2012.

Anarchy at the Alamo

The Creation of a 21st Century American Punk-Western in Garth Ennis and Steve Dillon's Preacher

RUSSELL WEBER

The Birth of a Legend—An Introduction to the American Punk-Western

The *topos* of the American Western was born through bloodshed, warfare, and death. Approximately "188 American volunteers," on the morning of March 6th, 1836, courageously fought roughly two thousand Mexican soldiers in defense of a mission in south-central Texas (Hatch 3) and, through their deaths, provided one of the central influences for the foundational ideologies of the American Western genre.[1] These volunteer soldiers, who included James Bowie and David Crockett, did not know that the exemplary bravery they embodied while fighting and dying for a politically autonomous Texas would become immortalized in the folklore and popular culture of the United States of America (61, 77–79). The deaths of these 188 rebels at the Battle of the Alamo came to represent the virtues of honor, courage, and self-sacrifice found in the archetypal hero of the American west.

The apotheosis of history into mythology serves as the essence of any nation's popular culture. The transformation of men and women into divine idols of pristine virtue through the symbolic narratives of legends, however, unavoidably convolutes the historical accuracy of ordinary people's extraordinary actions and "inflate[s] fact to fiction" (Grady 49). In Issue #59 of *Preacher*, for example, Garth Ennis demonstrates how the legend of the Battle of the Alamo ignores both the moral ambiguity of James Bowie, who participated in the slave trade and was suspected to be "a drunk" and "psychotic," and the possible cowardice of David Crockett, who may have surrendered at the Alamo and "beg[ged] for his life" prior to his execution (59.2).[2] This simplification of history to create mythology inherently disregards truth in favor of patriotism and emotional catharsis. The trade-off, however, is that these simplistic and ambiguous national mythologies are capable of not only representing different cultural values to different subsets within a society, but also serving as a nexus for the integration of seemingly conflicting and incompatible cultural ideologies.

The mythological grounds of the Alamo Mission provide one of the many settings for Garth Ennis and Steve Dillon's critically acclaimed comic book series *Preacher*, which Vertigo Comics published from 1995 to 2000. *Preacher* tells the story of a preacher from Annville, Texas, named Jesse Custer, who, at the beginning of the narrative, is experiencing a crisis of faith. After drunkenly accusing his congregation of gross immorality at Annville's local bar, gossip spreads throughout the small town and an embarrassed Jesse must give his sermon regarding the importance of forgiveness to his unusually crowded church (Ennis 1.5–8, 22). Before beginning his sermon, however, a half-angel, half-demon entity called Genesis possesses Jesse, an act which inadvertently destroys his church and slaughters his entire congregation (1.23–25). Determined to exact justice for the deaths of these innocent bystanders, Jesse, empowered with the Word of God and joined by Tulip O'Hare, his gun-toting, ex-assassin girlfriend, and Proinsias Cassidy, an anti-establishment Irish-American vampire, embarks on a revenge fueled odyssey to hunt down God himself and hold the Almighty accountable for passively allowing this senseless massacre.

While *Preacher* provides an excellent example of the morally complex narratives told through the comic book medium, it also acts as a pioneering text through which Ennis and Dillon shatter the traditional definition of the classic western archetype by creating a new, hybrid genre, the American punk-western. The ruins of the Alamo Mission, for example, although an obvious literary setting for a supernatural comic book series based in Texas, also function as one of the many gateways through which Ennis and Dillon amalgamate the "Hollywoodized" archetypes of the American West and the ideologies of the American punk subculture. Ennis and Dillon argue, through their depiction of the Alamo, that the deaths of the 188 souls who fought for Texan independence not only represent the honor and courage of the American West, but also illustrate the personal accountability, non-conformity, and do-it-yourself ethos of the American Punk subculture.

The punk-western characteristics of the Alamo Mission, however, provide only one instance of the genre amalgamation essential to the ideological, thematic, and aesthetic essence of *Preacher*. Ennis and Dillon, through their moral characterization of Jesse Custer, transform him into the living embodiment of their American punk-western. Jesse co-opts ideologies and characteristics from not only his spiritual mentor, a hallucination of John Wayne's ghost, who serves as the zenith of the archetypal western hero, but also his best friend Cassidy, who serves as the ideological manifestation of the punk subculture. Even Jesse's physical aesthetic, specifically his clothing and mannerisms, provide another rhetorical layer through which Ennis and Dillon blend the American Western mythology with American punk ideologies. Finally, Ennis and Dillon use the relationships between Jesse, Tulip, and Cassidy to develop a "punkified trigger trio," which allows them to manipulate and distort the paradigms of the American Western beyond the isolated characterization of their protagonist hero, allowing their genre amalgamation to permeate throughout the entire narrative of *Preacher*.[3]

While the act of fusing America's western mythologies and punk ideologies in *Preacher* deserves recognition, Ennis and Dillon's American punk-western goes beyond simple rhetorical and aesthetic craftsmanship. Through their development of the American punk-western genre, Ennis and Dillon skillfully illuminate to their readers the literary compatibility between the American Western mythology and American punk ideology, and in doing so, not only reinvigorate the presence and popularity of the western comic book genre, but also establish the precedence for future comic book series to amalgamate the American Western mythology with other literary genres.[4]

Oil and Water—The Unlikely Compatibility of Western and Punk

Before delving into the nuanced synthesis of America's western mythology and punk subculture in *Preacher*, one must first acquire a basic understanding of the philosophical pillars present within both of these cultural philosophies. As Devlin states, the thematic foundation of the American Western, especially in traditional Hollywood cinema, relies upon three central characteristics: "a hero who displays morally good qualities," "a villain who serves as the [hero's] antagonist," and a "confrontation" between the two in which "the hero triumphs in the end" (222). The heroes of traditional American Westerns, according to Devlin, "always [do] the right thing" and are "morally justified" through their actions, such as courageously and selflessly protecting a town for which they hold no personal or communal attachments (223–225). Uly argues that, by exemplifying this virtuous courage, western heroes are often characterized as honorable loners, "abandoned by all," (31) and, according to Skobble, even though they are occasionally compensated for their services, these loner vigilantes are considered honorable primarily because of their willingness to defend innocents who live outside the protection of civic justice (140–141).

The rise of triumphant individualism seen in the lone vigilante, however, offered an opportunity in American Western films, beginning in the late 1960s, to examine and question the complex mythology of America's frontier (Grady 42–43), specifically its "notions of honor and violent bravado" (Lenihan 124). For example, in Sergio Leone's "Dollars Trilogy," Clint Eastwood's "man with no name" represents the new, morally ambiguous protagonist who acts honorably, but only when it promotes his goals of self-preservation or personal gain (Lenihan 129–130). This shift from "white hatted" western hero to morally complex and more realistic protagonist remained a dominant trend in American Western cinema into the twenty-first century, epitomized in Ethan and Joel Coen's critically acclaimed *No Country for Old Men*, which challenged the traditional moral archetypes of both the western hero and villain (Devlin 227–229). This newfound ideological flexibility in the American Western mythology to dress even its most honorable heroes and corrupt villains in more convoluted, yet realistic, shades of gray has allowed the American Western to become more compatible with other literary and cinematic genres, such as science fiction, fantasy, and martial arts/action, ensuring its continued influence in American culture throughout the twenty-first century (Slatta 84, 88).[5]

The American punk subculture, as a late-twentieth century political and cultural movement containing multiple subsets, always should be viewed on an ideological continuum to account for varying levels of ideological commitment, including dogmatic extremism (Malott 30–31). The cohesion of the American punk subculture, therefore, must be found in the ideological similarities with which many punks viewed themselves and the movement. The ideological crux of America's punk subculture, much like the archetypal western hero, revolves around the importance of courageous actions that promote justice in one's society. Participants of the American punk movement in the 1970s constantly "embraced the do-it-yourself (DIY) ethos, disregarded authority, and rejected corporate commercialism" (Hannon 2). Emerging from this disregard for authority, the punk ideology promoted accountability only to oneself, encouraging individuals to "take full responsibility for the consequences" of their "own rules" and "beliefs" (Sinker 129). American punks also saw themselves as part of the social movement for justice and equality across all of humanity, believing that their goals could be achieved by resisting societal conventions both from within and outside of the established governmental institutions (Malott xiv, 35, 68). Above all else, the American punk subculture, according to Malott, characterized itself through its determination to revolutionize humanity and rebel against the restrictive and exclusionary "definitions" that societies force upon their citizens (117).

Punk, however, was not a uniquely American cultural movement and, therefore, it is important to acknowledge the relationship between the British and American punk subcultures. The British punk subculture, which developed concurrently with the American punk subculture, promoted and cultivated a culture of political extremism and violence, which arose from its inception as a blue-collar, working class movement (Hannon 4–5). The growth of violence within the British punk movement ultimately led to the quick transition in the late 1970s and early 1980s towards a more "hardcore punk" philosophy, signified through the dissolution of many founding British punk bands, such as the Sex Pistols (18). While violent extremism was not as noticeable at the inception of American punk, by the early 1980s it began its visible conversion into a more hardcore movement, and therefore a potentially more violent and exclusionary movement (Hannon 21–22).

Since both the British and American punk subcultures were connected to the economic plights of the white-working classes, racist, sexist, and homophobic subsets within the movements occasionally entered periods of growth and popular support (Malott 2, 12, 28–30). These ideological outliers within the British and American punk movements, however, were divergences that should not be seen as characteristic of mainstream punk culture, which consistently promoted social equity. For example, women, who were actively involved in the early years of the American punk movement, especially through their participation in early punk bands, such as the Slits and the Runaways, began to be pushed out of the American punk movement in the early 1980s as sexist beliefs contaminated the culture (Hannon 59–60). Women responded to this forced alienation by beginning the "Riot Grrrl" movement and creating their own branch of feminist punk in the 1990s, which gained popularity not only with female punks, but also members of the mainstream American punk subculture, many of whom rejected the sexist ideologies that arose in the 1980s (Hannon 10–11).

The ideological flexibility that allowed racism, sexism, and homophobia to arise in subsets of America's punk subculture also serves as one of the movement's most alluring characteristics. Sharon M. Hannon begins her analysis of America's punk subculture by simply stating that "[p]unk is personal" and "[i]t means different things to different people," illustrating that "punk" has no singular definition and, therefore, is extremely malleable to an individual's own beliefs (xi). In fact, some punks rebelled against the "endless miasma of codes, guides[,] and forbiddings" within the subculture, believing that their individualism and rebellion against the rules and regulations of mainstream punk made them more punk than those who conformed (Sinker 123). By choosing to amalgamate the inherently malleable ideology of America's punk subculture with the newfound flexibility of the western mythology in *Preacher*, Ennis and Dillon not only illustrated the inherent commonalities of honor, individual action, personal responsibility, and an obligation to rebel against injustice and corrupt authority within both the western and punk philosophies, but also demonstrated the compatibility and adaptability of these two unique ideologies, inadvertently spearheading the western-hybrid comic book movement, which culminated in the growth of both the publication and popularity of western-hybrid comic books in the early twenty-first century.

Jesse Custer—The Great Amalgamator

From the day he was born, Jesse Custer was a man who embodied two conflicting cultures. His father, John Custer, was a Texan, a Vietnam War veteran, and an independent young man who dreamed of living like the cowboys and gunslingers of the old American west; his mother, Christina L'Angelle, was a Louisianan, a Vietnam War protester, and an optimistic young woman who dreamed of escaping the captivity of her racist and religiously zealous southern plantation family (Ennis 9.2–7). While John and Christina overcame their initial differences and established the foundation of their unbreakable relationship on their shared admiration for each other, hope for the future, and desire to make the best life possible for their young son, Jesse always knew that he was the physical manifestation of his parents' unorthodox yet harmonious love.

Jesse's self-awareness of his traditionally incompatible cultural heritages allows him to discern why Genesis chose him for his human vessel. In issue #3, Jesse, who is able to begin accessing Genesis's powers and memories within days of being possessed, informs Tulip that Genesis was the offspring of an angel and a demon who, since "Heaven an' Hell're at war with each other[,] ... broke the rules when they fell in love" and, by consummating their love, symbolically initiated the first act of punk rebellion against God (Ennis 3.22). Through their forbidden union, these cosmic lovers created a child that was not only "good and evil mixed" (23.17) but also a "***new idea***" (3.22) that both Heaven and Hell considered "unnatural" (23.17).[6] The heavenly host and demonic hoard's intolerance towards the passionate love that created Genesis mirrors the bigoted opinions of Marie L'Angelle, Jesse's grandmother, who hated the union of Jesse's parents, believing that John Custer was nothing more than "Texas white trash" who polluted her family's great southern bloodline (8.22). By paralleling Jesse and Genesis's status as familial and societal pariahs, Ennis and Dillon skillfully demonstrate how being indebted to two conflicting cultures, while simultaneously belonging to neither, made Jesse the ideal choice as Genesis's vessel.

Ennis and Dillon further analyze Jesse's complicated heritage through an exploration of the power Genesis gives him to reshape himself and his world. Continuing his recollection with Tulip of Genesis's past, Jesse explains that Genesis, as the first half-angel, half-demon entity in all of creation, "was a new idea ... as powerful as either've the old ones" and, therefore, was endowed with some of the powers of the Almighty himself, which Jesse controls after his possession (3.22). While Jesse does not hold mastery over all of creation, he does control the Word of God, which compels any individual who comprehends its message to obey unconditionally, thus allowing Jesse to reshape the world as he sees fit. While scholars, such as Labarre, have argued correctly that Jesse's power to reshape his world with the Word of God metaphorically illustrates "the possibility of reinventing" (256) and reshaping the "most familiar clichés" of American southerness (248–249), such as plantation elitism and racist bigotry, by infusing them with the "values and codes of the [American] Western" (256), these arguments do not go far enough. Jesse's role within *Preacher* does not end, as Labarre argues, but rather begins with unifying the conflicting ideologies of the American south with the American west. By not only combining these conflicting cultural ideologies, but also embracing Genesis's divine power to perform virtuous miracles or commit malicious atrocities, Jesse becomes Ennis and Dillon's embodiment of ideological, societal, and cultural fusion. Jesse, serving as the great amalgamator, provides a cultural canvas on which Ennis and Dillon integrate and reconcile the ideological differences between America's western mythology and its punk subculture.

The heart and soul of Jesse Custer was nurtured on American Western mythology. In issue #9, Ennis reveals that, from the moment Jesse could walk and talk, John, to the chagrin of Christina, snuck him "into every John Wayne movie" that played in their small town, which would have helped instill in Jesse a western sense of heroic honor, courage, and justice (Ennis 9.8). In fact, even John Custer's last words to Jesse before being murdered by Jodie, a sadistic henchmen of Jesse's grandmother, compelled him to idolize the American Western hero: "You gotta be like **John Wayne**: you don't take no shit off fools, an' you judge a person by what's in 'em, not how they look. An' you do the **right thing**. You **gotta** be one of the good guys, son: 'cause there's way too many of the bad" (9.14). While it is debatable as to whether John Wayne truly lived up to the reverence and idolization that John Custer showed him, Ennis and Dillon, through John's final words, provide a logical rationalization for a young, frightened, and abandoned child to hallucinate the ghost of John Wayne, his father's own role model, as his protector and sage mentor (11.9). Haunted for the rest of his life by the nightmare of his father's unjust murder, Jesse held on to the only things that encouraged him to fight injustice and cruelty: his father's last name (8.22), his father's last words begging him to become "one of the good guys" (9.14), and his relationship with the specter of John Wayne, who remained Jesse's emotional tether to his father throughout his life (11.9, 17–18).

Attempting to live up to the memory of his father and justify John Wayne's trust in him as a "pardner," Jesse incorporates many aspects of America's western mythology into his code of ethics and personal morality (Ennis 4.1). For example, although Jesse spent much of his young adult life providing for himself as a mechanic and a part-time car thief, he held himself to a strict code of honor regarding his thievery, which included a refusal to steal horses (Ennis "Tall" 1.1). Tulip and Amy, Tulip's best friend and fellow car thief, mock Jesse's distaste for stealing horses as some kind of "***suthan thang***" ("Tall" 1.24), and even Christina, when she is reunited with Jesse in the small town of Salvation, Texas, after years of both believing the other was dead, is amazed at how closely Jesse's moral code resembles his father's, acknowledging that both men were "[l]iving a western" (Ennis 45.5). Ennis and Dillon, however, use Jesse's western paradigm regarding horses to reflect his deeper beliefs regarding honor and fairness. Jesse, finally explaining his aversion to horse thieves while hanging a horse thief for his crimes, states that in nineteenth-century Texas if "you stole a fella's horse" and "stranded him in the desert" you "all but condemned him to death," and therefore, the crime "was taken pretty damn seriously back in them days" ("Tall" 1.45). Jesse's continued practice of this antiquated yet symbolic code of the American west further allows Ennis and Dillon to illustrate the crucial influence that the American cowboy's code of honor had in shaping Jesse's own morality.

Jesse's moral code also includes the western tradition of honoring one's word to friends and enemies alike, which he exemplifies through his interaction with the Saint of Killers, a specter assassin whom two Adelphi angels order to kill Genesis (Ennis 1.20–21). In issue #23, while attempting to help Cassidy escape imprisonment from Herr Starr and the Grail, a religious organization that desires to use Genesis's powers to herald the second coming of Christ and tyrannically control the entire world, Jesse makes a deal with the Saint of Killers, agreeing to use Genesis's powers to learn how the Saint's family died in exchange for help escaping the Grail's prison (23.8). Although Jesse and Cassidy are separated from the Saint during their escape, Jesse insists on keeping his word and risks his life in issue #36 to inform the Saint of the bitter truth that the Lord ensured his family died to manipulate him into becoming the Saint of Killers (36.4–7). Through this noble deed towards the Saint of Killers, Ennis and Dillon demonstrate how Jesse, by keeping his word to others, even when it is dangerous or disadvantageous to himself, not only earns the respect of the Saint of Killers, who agrees to stop hunting him and turns his aggression towards killing God (36.7), but also maintains his self-respect by keeping his "iron," his western honor, through honorable "words and deeds" (McNarron 167).

Surprisingly, even Jodie, the man who executed John (Ennis 9.14–15) and supposedly murdered Christina (9.22–24; 43.1–3), is not exempt from Jesse's sense of western honor. Ennis reveals in issue #8 that Marie L'Angelle, in an attempt to regain control over her grandson's life, ordered Jodie to kidnap Jesse and Tulip, bring them to her plantation, Angelville (8.20–24), and emotionally torture Jesse by forcing him to watch Tulip's execution (10.24). Jesse manages to escape his captivity and confronts Jodie, seeking vengeance for the violent deaths of his parents and Tulip (12.3), unaware that God miraculously resurrected Tulip shortly after her death (11.11–14). While Jesse could have used the Word of God to order Jodie to drop dead, he refused to use Genesis's powers, believing that the only way to avenge his loved ones and finally bury the memories and trauma of his horrid past is to kill Jodie, without assistance, in an honorable, fair fight (12.7–8). Although Jesse almost loses, his indomitable spirit emerges victorious and he kills Jodie with his bare hands, finally reclaiming his self-worth by successfully conquering his demons without ever abandoning his western code of honor and justice (12.19, 22).[7]

Although it is clear that Ennis and Dillon developed the core of Jesse's morality from the traditional archetype of America's western cowboy, they also incorporate many punk ideologies into Jesse's code, illustrating the complementary nature of these two distinct philosophies. For example, while Jesse chooses not to use the Word of God against Jodie, fulfilling his western desire to win his own battles without assistance, his continual reluctance to employ the Word of God arises from his punk distrust of established authority, specifically God and his religious institutions. Although Jesse "believed in God Almighty" (Ennis 1.3) his grandmother forced him to become a preacher (10.22) and, through her example, illustrated to Jesse all of the zealous fanaticism, abuses of power, and bigoted hatred that organized religion often masks (10.2–3). This distrust of organized religion extends to a distrust of Jesse's control over the Word of God, especially after God disabled it when Jodie first kidnapped Jesse and Tulip (8.13–14), foolishly hoping that this failure of Genesis's power would persuade Jesse to abandon his quest and return to his life of religious devotion (11.13–14).

Ennis and Dillon, however, also use Jesse's fear of becoming "too reliant" on the Word of God to illustrate his growing distrust of God's morality since the Annville massacre (Ennis 15.6). While escaping the Grail's prison in issue #24, Cassidy informs Jesse that the Almighty visited him and told him that he was a "beast" and that Jesse's association with him was "against the law've God" (24.23). Ennis provides perhaps his most succinct summation of Jesse's punk-western moral code, when Jesse calmly yet assertively informs Cassidy that "[God] can shove his law up his ass, if just one word of it says I can't stand by my friend" (24.23). Through this single sentence, Ennis illustrates how Jesse's morality, by placing importance on meaningful, good actions in the present, such as loyalty to one's friends, above following arbitrary laws to gain future entrance into Heaven, combines the personal accountability to one's own morality and the do-it-yourself resistance against unjust authority of America's punk subculture with the honor and courage of America's archetypal western hero.

While Jesse does not rely on or frequently use the Word of God, he does embody a strong sense of personal responsibility regarding the knowledge and power he has received from Genesis. In accordance with his do-it-yourself ethos, Jesse believes that, as Annville's preacher and Genesis's vessel, it is his responsibility to hunt down God and exact justice for not only the death of his entire congregation, but also God's personal rejection of Genesis and overall abandonment of humanity (Ennis 4.16). Jesse unapologetically perceives the Lord's forsaking of humanity, the people whom he created, as a rejection of responsibility and "a **Goddamn betrayal**" (29.20). Knowing that only Genesis is strong enough to hold the Almighty accountable for his actions, Jesse accepts his responsibility to bring God to justice for being "just another son of a bitch" who "did wrong," "fucked people up," and "start[ed] runnin' as soon as it look[ed] like He'll be called to account" for his crimes (29.19–20).

Jesse's rationale for risking his life to exact justice upon the Almighty, however, does not fully persuade his vampire ally. In issue #35, Cassidy, who ironically embodies the physical attributes of the punk subculture yet rejects many of its moral platitudes, drunkenly challenges Jesse's do-it-yourself ethos and his willingness to sacrifice himself for humanity, whose only legacy, according to Cassidy, has only been "genocide" (Ennis 35.13). Ennis and Dillon use Cassidy's pessimistic doubts, which center on his belief that "there's not a country on this Earth wasn't born outta blood an' killin,'" to elaborate on the punk attributes of Jesse's moral code (35.13). Jesse explains to Cassidy that he believes everyone in life has "a chance to do somethin' good" and "so long as [a] chance is there" to hold God accountable by using "this damn Word ... [to] make him do right by [humanity]," he "cannot ignore it" (35.13–15). Ennis and Dillon, through Jesse's commitment to bring God to justice for his abandonment of humanity, illustrate how the punk do-it-yourself ethic and belief of personal accountability compliments Jesse's western morality, specifically his unyielding desire to act courageously and honorably by ensuring that the guilty, regardless of who they are, receive justice.[8]

Finally, Jesse firmly believes in the punk ideology that individuals must take direct action to promote societal change. In another conversation with Cassidy in issue #31, Jesse recounts the night he attended a Bill Hicks's show who, unwilling to compromise in his own life, continued performing stand-up comedy throughout his losing battle with pancreatic cancer (Ennis 31.14).

Recounting this inspirational night to Cassidy, Jesse confesses that he "hate[s] a lie ... [his] own most of all" and reveals that Hicks's courage in the face of a slow, yet inevitable death not only motivated him to end his passive ignorance of humanity's pervasive immorality, specifically in his Annville parish, but also motivated his alcohol fueled rage of honesty towards his congregation the night before Genesis possessed him (31.15).

Although Jesse's rekindled commitment to direct, honorable action and his newfound aversion to lying is commendable, Ennis and Dillon prevent Jesse's apotheosis to moral perfection, specifically through his inability to transcend his western sexism. In issue #17, shortly after Herr Starr and the Grail capture Cassidy under the false pretense that he is Jesse Custer, Tulip and Jesse discuss his plan to save Cassidy, which quickly devolves into a heated argument regarding Jesse's sexist inclination to feel responsible for protecting Tulip from danger (Ennis 17.18–21). Tulip attempts to explain to a supposedly naïve Jesse that, even though some women romanticize the idea of a man who will stand up for them and defend their honor, they still "can take care of [them]selves" and want a man who will respect that desire (17.19). Jesse, to Tulip's surprise, responds that he understands that she is not only "*empowered*" and "as smart ... an' as capable [as him]," but also a strong woman who can protect herself without his help (17.20). While Jesse explains that he developed this new perspective regarding gender equality from reading feminists scholars, such as "Germaine Greer" and that "Dworkin woman," the former of which he personally prefers, he also shamelessly admits that "all that bullshit goes right out the fuckin' window" when he thinks about his actions placing Tulip's life in jeopardy (17.20).[9] Tulip, however, informs Jesse that he will "have to learn to live with it" since she will never abandon his side during this quest, regardless of the danger in which she would be placing herself (17.21).

While Jesse's punk ethos of personal accountability compels him to attempt to achieve not only a sense of gender equality in his relationship with Tulip, but also a high degree of honesty in all his relationships, Ennis and Dillon clearly demonstrate how his emotional and irrational desire to protect Tulip, fueled with his inherent western chauvinism, directly challenges his pursuit of both gender equality and honesty. Jesse, in issue #21, consciously chooses to lie to and abandon Tulip when he goes to confront the Grail and save Cassidy (21.14), an act which he later repeats in issue #64 when he yet again abandons Tulip to confront Herr Starr and Cassidy in the series' final, climatic showdown (64.6). While Jesse acknowledges that his actions are wrong, he genuinely believes he is committing the lesser of two sins, since he believes his dishonesty will ensure Tulip's safety (21.20–21). Ironically, Jesse's plan does not work the second time since Tulip, embracing her inner strength and independence, arrives to the final battle, against Jesse's wishes, and kills Herr Starr without any aid or assistance from Jesse (65.35–36).

These acts of dishonesty alone would greatly hinder the strength of Jesse's relationship with Tulip. Jesse's greatest sin, however, both against Tulip and himself, is when he consciously tarnishes Tulip's trust and his own honor through his deceit and abandonment in issue #64, which compels him to break a promise he made to Tulip in issue #28 that he would "*always* trust [her]" and never lie to or abandon her again (28.3–4). Jesse's western courage and sense of self-sacrifice, coupled with his punk do-it-yourself ethos, validates his choice to break his promise to Tulip and battle the Grail on his own without endangering the life of the woman he loves. This betrayal of Tulip's trust, however, not only jeopardizes Jesse's honor and violates his commitment to honesty and personal accountability, but also allows Ennis and Dillon to demonstrate how easily Jesse can succumb to male chauvinism and personal detachment, two of the most common perversions of his cherished western chivalry and punk individualism.

Even though Ennis and Dillon use Jesse's internal conflict regarding his deception of Tulip to humanize their punk-western hero, this conflict also serves a rhetorical purpose within the narrative of *Preacher* by providing the setting for Jesse to succeed, finally, in amalgamating the conflicting aspects of his moral code. In the final issue of *Preacher*, Jesse sincerely and remorsefully apologizes to Tulip for his deception and dishonesty, crying for the first time since his father was murdered and catalyzing their heartfelt reconciliation (Ennis 66.15–16). Through this single act, Jesse not only redeems himself, earning Tulip's forgiveness and love, but also abandons his western male chauvinism and punk loner mentality, which in turn allows him to reconcile and unify the honor, courage, and justice of his American Western upbringing with his personal accountability, direct action, do-it-yourself American punk ethos. Jesse, finally claiming his mantle as the great amalgamator by establishing his own unique, personal moral code, completes the creation of the American punk-western genre and validates Ennis and Dillon's argument that the American Western mythology and American punk ideology, although distinct, are inherently compatible philosophies.

Clothing Makes the Man—The Punk-Western Aesthetic of Jesse Custer

Although Garth Ennis and Steve Dillon shared an equal partnership in the creation of both *Preacher* and the American punk-western comic book genre, Dillon's artistic contributions, specifically his creation of *Preacher*'s punk-western visual aesthetic, deserve their own analysis. Jesse, still serving his role as the great ideological and cultural amalgamator, blends the traditional attire and mannerism of both the western cowboy, epitomized yet again through John Wayne, and the rebellious, anti-establishment, hardcore punk, exemplified through Cassidy, into a unified punk-western aesthetic.

Ennis informs his readers that *The Searchers* was John Custer's first John Wayne film (Ennis 18.10). *The Searchers*, which was also most likely Jesse's first Wayne film, clearly influenced Jesse's understanding of the iconic western cowboy, since he adorns his specter of John Wayne in the traditional western apparel of Ethan Edwards, Wayne's character from *The Searchers* (63.23). While Ennis and Dillon tease the reveal of John Wayne in a single panel of *Preacher*'s first issue, his aesthetic introduction does not occur until the second issue, in which Dillon ensures that Wayne's appearance oozes with western bravado. Dillon dresses Wayne in a traditional wide-brimmed cowboy hat, dark denim pants and chaps, a light red, button-down wool shirt that contrasts against his dark brown vest, and finally a light blue scarf concealing his neck (2.16). Wayne's face, covered in shadows, is the only aspect of his aesthetic that Dillon purposefully obscures, signifying the psychological ambiguity regarding Jesse's hallucination of his western idol. Wayne, holding his slightly cocked gun belt, simply addresses Jesse as "Pilgrim," solidifying the American Western imagery of John Wayne as a man of pride, simplicity, and few words (2.16).

Ennis and Dillon's decision, however, to clothe Jesse's idolized depiction of John Wayne in the attire of Ethan Edwards holds a much deeper, symbolic role in both Jesse's evolution as a character and Ennis and Dillon's own critique of the American Western genre. Arthur M. Eckstein argues that the "'heroic' Ethan Edwards ... is not at all a traditional western hero," specifically since he "shoots people in the back (and robs them), disrupts funerals (and weddings), views all religions with open cynicism and sarcasm, and continually desecrates the bodies of the dead" (3–4). Adding to Eckstein's analysis, William Luhr notes that *The Searchers* does not "[glorify] ... the traditional western hero," but rather "critiques it ... in disturbing ways" (82), mostly through what Martin Winkler refers to as Edwards's "savagery and increasing obsession and madness" (152). Fascinatingly, even though one can assume that Jesse watched *The Searchers* at least once in his life and saw the dishonorable acts that Ethan Edwards commits in the film, Jesse still believes that Ethan Edwards represents the honorable John Wayne, after whom John Custer, with his last words, implored Jesse to model his life. Dillon, by implicitly contradicting the immoral Ethan Edwards with romanticized John Wayne, allows Jesse to embrace, simultaneously, the aesthetics of the former and the idealized morals of the latter. Furthermore, through Jesse's refusal to acknowledge and reject the immoral aesthetic of Ethan Edwards in his depiction of John Wayne, due to his unwavering loyalty to and love for his father's morals, and therefore his father's hero, Ennis and Dillon yet again illustrate the power of mythology, specifically within the American Western genre, to manipulate facts and truths into believable romanticized legends.

The nuanced accuracy with which Dillon's illustrations of John Wayne capture the aesthetics of the American Western is paralleled by how successfully Cassidy's own apparel embodies the aesthetics and imagery of the punk subculture. Through his short, spikey brown hair, three day shadow of facial hair, plain white t-shirt, torn denim jeans, singular golden hoop earring, sunglasses, and sleeveless blue shirt, Dillon ensures that Cassidy, through his visual conformity to Britain's punk fashion (Ennis 1.2–3; 2.24) and "total fuck-off look" (Sinker 124), could serve as an aesthetic doppelganger for any member of the Sex Pistols or the Clash (Kugelberg 160–161, 205). The "less is more" simplicity and slapdash nature of Cassidy's clothing reflects an overall apathy towards others' perception of him and his lifestyle, which was a common attitude for many American and British punks (Hannon 57). Cassidy further illustrates his complete disregard for societal courtesy when he reveals his vampirism to Jesse and Tulip by ferociously biting and ripping out the throat of an assailant (Ennis 2.22–23). Embodying, to an almost humorous extent, an extreme manifestation of punk's reckless and rebellious nature, the blood covered Cassidy, either oblivious of or apathetic to the outrageous nature of his actions, nonchalantly asks a shocked Jesse and Tulip if there is "[s]omethin' the matter" (2.24), perplexed at their horrified reaction to him simply having a decent meal with good company (3.3–4).

While Dillon successfully embodies the iconic beauty of the American Western and British punk in John Wayne and Cassidy, respectively, the true greatness of his artwork becomes apparent in his ability to use these two contrasting visual styles to create a unique punk-western aesthetic through Jesse. There are several instances throughout *Preacher* in which other characters forcibly modify Jesse's physical appearance, such as when God, in issue #49, plucks Jesse's left eye from its socket as divine penance for challenging his authority at Monument Valley, Arizona, which then compels Jesse to wear an eye patch throughout the remainder of the narrative (Ennis 49.14), or the adulteration of his long hair to a short flattop in issue #47 and issue #48 at the hands of Miss Oatlash, a neo–Nazi lawyer who becomes romantically obsessed with Jesse while he serves as sheriff of Salvation, Texas (47.23; 48.1–2).

Excluding these forced aesthetic modifications, however, Dillon chooses to keep Jesse's personal image consistent throughout the entirety of *Preacher*. By remaining in his black clerical shirt, white clerical collar, and white jeans, even after the massacre at Annville, Jesse consciously co-opts a symbol of the Christian faith and transforms it into a punk image of rebellion, visually reflecting Jesse's personal responsibility, as Annville's preacher, to ensure that God is held accountable for his crimes (4.24).[10] Through the simplicity of

Jesse's preacher attire, coupled with his semi-long, curly black hair and five o'clock shadow of facial stubble, Dillon compels his readers to recognize the aesthetic parallels between Jesse and members of American punk bands, such as the Ramones (Kugelberg 132–133). Fascinatingly, even when Jesse gives up his preacher's shirt for a black duster and sheriff's badge during his tenure as Salvation's sheriff, his black eye patch and tendency to obey his own morality instead of the law (44.6–8; 45.14) adds another layer of punk rebellion to the iconic sheriff's clothing, which, traditionally, symbolized the institutionalized authority of the American west (Ennis 44.3).

Jesse's aesthetic, while significantly punk, embodies several crucial characteristics of Wayne's archetypal cowboy that cannot be overlooked. While Jesse's dark brown cowboy boots, only dawned as a replacement to his black dress shoes after the Annville massacre, are technically the only western item of clothing that Jesse consistently wears throughout *Preacher*, it is important to note how Dillon's depiction of Jesse's physical mannerisms mirror those of John Wayne (1.29). For example, when Ennis and Dillon tease John Wayne's appearance in the first issue of *Preacher*, there is a single panel where Jesse and Wayne walk side by side, through which Dillon creates the aesthetic of his archetypal, masculine, punk-western hero (1.29). Jesse's confident, almost arrogant stride matches Wayne's step for step. Both men, shoulders squared, heads held high, walk with a purpose and a determination—a western bravado—so resolute that anyone would think twice before interfering with them or their goals. Dillon, by presenting Jesse not as an insecure punk rebel who simply defies authority for the sake of being different, but rather as a punk-cowboy who incorporates a western bravado and sense of purpose with his defiant punk attitude, symbolically illustrates that while Jesse is rebelling against the highest authority in the universe, the Lord Almighty, he does so with a western commitment to honor and justice that not only validates his actions, but also demands that he completes his quest.

While Dillon carefully blends and unifies Jesse's punk clothing with his western mannerisms to create a truly unique punk-western aesthetic, the single most amalgamated and culturally rich aspect of Jesse's aesthetic is the smallest item in his possession: his father's cigarette lighter. This plain, silver lighter, inscribed with the words "Fuck Communism," was presented to every man in John Custer's squad in the Vietnam War by John Wayne (Ennis 18.1, 6–7). This token of honor for service in defense of the United States of America quickly became one of John's most prized possessions until the day he died and Jodie stole it from his bloody corpse (8.19). Recovered by Jesse after killing Jodie at Angelville, this lighter also becomes Jesse's most cherished possession, as it is the only physical item of his father's that he ever owned (12.22). Dillon, through the simple symbolic imagery of this lighter, provides yet another physical manifestation of Jesse's amalgamated punk-western aesthetic. Not only reflecting the punk ethos of individual defiance and rebellion through its "Fuck Communism" quotation, this simple lighter also exemplifies the honor, courage, and patriotism of western cowboys, especially since it belonged to Jesse's father, the only true western hero Jesse ever personally knew.[11]

You Are What You Eat—Preacher's Punkified Trigger Trio

While Jesse Custer, both through his morality and aesthetics, clearly embodies Ennis and Dillon's amalgamated punk-western genre, it is also important to explore how Ennis and Dillon "punkify" Jesse's archetypal western relationships with both Tulip and Cassidy. In "The Good Guys Wore White Hats," Ray White examines the cultural impact of early-twentieth century American Western cinema, paying close attention to films whose heroes form a coalition called the "trigger trio" (144). According to White, the traditional trigger trio consisted of three individuals, the white-hatted, morally upright protagonist and his two partners, "a young, hot-tempered romantic cowboy and ... a crusty old codger"; all three of whom work together to bring justice to the wicked and restore order to the west (145).[12]

Ennis and Dillon waste very little time punkifying this American Western trope in *Preacher*, beginning this process in issue #1 at the Five Ages Diner, when Jesse, Tulip, and Cassidy, through the simple act of ordering their dinners, symbolically foreshadow the roles they will occupy within *Preacher*'s trigger trio (Ennis 1.1–2). Jesse, ordering a cheeseburger, perhaps one of the most iconic American meals, declares himself the central protagonist who will embody the archetypal values of the traditional western hero. Although Jesse's amalgamated punk-western morality has been thoroughly examined above, specifically his inclination to wear a morally grayer cowboy hat than his heroic western predecessors, his cowboy hat shines particularly bright regarding his courage and his code of honor and justice, specifically his constant ability to "judg[e] people by what's in them, not how they look" (41.19). In fact, the only ideological areas in which Jesse's moral authority darkens within the trigger trio is his constant disregard for the law (44.6–8) and continual struggle with his male chauvinistic belief that he must protect Tulip from danger, even at the cost of his honor and her trust (63.7–10).

Tulip, a self-proclaimed vegetarian who orders "the chicken salad... [without] the chicken," immediately problematizes the chauvinistic archetype of the hot-tempered, romantic gunslinger in *Preacher*'s trigger trio (Ennis 1.2). By eating a meal that represents the antithesis of both Jesse's cheeseburger and the hyper-masculinity of the traditional western cowboy, Tulip superficially and falsely establishes herself as the stereotypical gendered inverse of Jesse's western male chauvinistic hero and, therefore, exhibits herself as his potential damsel in distress. Tulip's initially misleading characterization (1.2), however, provides Ennis and Dillon the opportunity to challenge and subvert the inherent sexism and chauvinism in America's Western mythology, which often declares women to be naturally defenseless, "passive[,] and submissive" (White 149–150), by gradually revealing Tulip's strength of character, independence, and punk ethos of personal accountability for her own life.

Tulip, from a very young age, fought for equality with the boys, preferring to play baseball than play with dolls or wear makeup (Ennis 51.18). Tulip's "tomboy" nature, in fact, compelled her father to teach her how to shoot, which allowed her to develop excellent proficiency with firearms and establish herself as the best marksperson in *Preacher*'s trigger trio (51.15–17). Whether fighting Marie L'Angelle and her henchmen (12.4, 11–12), Herr Starr and the Grail (16.10–13; 20.4–5; 37.4–5), or the vampire obsessed cult Les Enfants du Sang (31.6–9; 33.6–9), Tulip's expertise with firearms allows her not only to hold her own in a fight, but also to save both Jesse and Cassidy's lives countless times, which further subverts the typical damsel-in-distress paradigm of the western genre. Ennis and Dillon's decision to subvert Tulip's damsel-in-distress status by having her reject her stereotypical femininity in favor of stereotypically masculine characteristics, such as dexterity with firearms and an inclination towards violence and killing, illustrates that, even though Ennis and Dillon successfully introduce a punk sense of gender equality in the narrative of *Preacher*, Tulip is only able to achieve this equality in the eyes of Jesse by embracing the masculine American western bravado which he not only reveres, but also believes is a necessity to keep oneself alive both in the American west and during their hunt to find God Almighty.

While Tulip's combat mastery, which is essential to the success of Jesse's quest, could be argued as Ennis and Dillon simply adhering to the sexism of the western by illustrating Tulip's equality to Jesse and Cassidy through hypermasculine violent tendencies, Tulip's most important characteristic and contribution to the trigger trio is her courage and indomitable spirit. Even when tragedy strikes and Tulip believes that Jesse has died at Monument Valley (37.19–21), she refuses to let her hardships "***destroy*** [***her***]" (54.17) and, after a brief bout with grief and substance abuse, decides to take control of her life and begins rebuilding it without Jesse (51.2–9). Tulip's courage in times of despair continually motivates Jesse, who obsessively "***torture*[*s*]**" himself with his troubles, to persevere on his quest to find God (54.17). Through her punk rebellion against and defiance of the sexism of the American Western's archetypal damsel-in-distress, Tulip establishes herself as both Jesse's true love and the punk heroine of *Preacher*'s trigger trio, thus allowing Ennis and Dillon to illustrate that within the punk-western genre it is acceptable and welcome for the heroine to support, protect, and even save the life of the hero.

The most ambiguously complicated member of *Preacher*'s trigger trio is Cassidy, who serves as the old curmudgeon. Cassidy was turned into a vampire as a young man on April 27, 1916 (Ennis 25.12–15) and his bitter and pessimistic "old-timer" views of the world, since he is at least ninety years old during the events of *Preacher*, are juxtaposed with an ironically youthful demeanor (2.24). Cassidy's decision to order nothing for dinner, practically explained through his vampirism and general apathy for consuming food, foreshadows his questionable past and continued moral ambiguity throughout *Preacher* (Ennis 1.2). Born to an Irish Catholic and an Irish Protestant, Cassidy, as a man of two worlds, quickly forms a friendship with the culturally amalgamated Jesse (4.3, 7), which only is strengthened through Jesse's respect for Cassidy's fierce loyalty and willingness to stick by Jesse until he finishes his quest (26.21–22). Cassidy, later admitting to Tulip that he lived a selfish life, believes that helping Jesse find God is his "last chance to do somethin' good" and earn redemption (34.20).

Cassidy's selfishness, however, is the primary source of strain within the trigger trio. Tulip, concerned with Jesse's fast-formed friendship with Cassidy, worries that Cassidy does not take her "very seriously" (Ennis 13.10) and may be a "bad influence" on Jesse (14.18). This distrust of Cassidy is validated when he confesses his love for Tulip behind Jesse's back, both accusing Tulip of hiding her own love for him and criticizing Jesse's chauvinistic readiness to deceive the woman he loves (27.22–23). Cassidy's selfishness, in fact, temporarily shatters the trigger trio when Jesse, after recovering from his injuries at Monument Valley, learns that Tulip and Cassidy, believing he was dead, entered into an intimate relationship (40.20), in which Cassidy continually manipulated and abused Tulip (54.7, 10).

While Cassidy does serve as a villain and antagonist for much of the final third of *Preacher*'s narrative, Ennis and Dillon allow Cassidy a final act of redemption. Knowing that he can never make amends for his betrayal of Jesse and Tulip, Cassidy makes a deal with God, agreeing to help him kill Genesis on the condition that both Jesse and he are resurrected if they die during the final battle at the Alamo Mission (Ennis 66.9–11). Living up to the punk ethos of direct action and personal accountability for the first time in his life, Cassidy, through his deal with God, simultaneously gives Jesse the opportunity to bring God to justice while, in the process, tricks the Almighty into saving both of their lives. While Cassidy's righteous actions symbolically atone for his sins and heal the trigger trio (65.29–31), it costs him his immortality, since, after burning to death at the Alamo, God resurrects Cassidy as a human (66.27–30). This act of self-sacrifice reflects that even though Cassidy's morality rarely coincides with the ethics of either the American Western mythology or the American punk subculture he is able to fulfill, through his friendships with Jesse and Tulip, even if only for a moment, his predestined role as a heroic member of *Preacher*'s punkified trigger trio.

Conclusion—A Return to the Alamo

Ennis begins the final arc of *Preacher*, aptly entitled "The Alamo," with a very simple, yet poignant narration, stating "[i]t ends here[, at the Alamo]... [i]t ends in the place that the legend began" (Ennis 59.1). Narrating the prologue to Jesse's final battle with God at the Alamo, Ennis and Dillon caution their readers that if they "look too close ... the legend [of the Alamo] cracks" (59.2). This, however, is not a condemnation of the cracks within this American Western legend, but rather a commendation, since it is within the cracks of the Alamo that Ennis and Dillon found the artistic space to incorporate America's western mythology with its punk ideology. Jesse's death and rebirth at the end of *Preacher*, the symbolism of "his initials," and his role as the great amalgamator and cultural peacemaker evoke a Christ-like imagery that is so obvious even Tulip feels compelled to mock Jesse for it in issue #61 (61.22). Jesse not only embodies the best of America's western mythology and punk philosophy, but also succeeds, with help from his punk-western trigger trio, at restoring justice to the universe by condemning God to death at the hands of the Saint of Killers and finally bringing punk's anarchy to the Alamo (66.20). Jesse's anarchy, however, does not represent chaos, but rather the absolute freedom that one can achieve when the corrupt or arbitrary institutions of power, such as organized religion or defined literary genres, are replaced with individual choice and personal responsibility. By ushering in a new commandment of cultural amalgamation and genre flexibility, Jesse serves as Ennis and Dillon's literary Jesus Christ, calling their readers to overcome the ideological differences between western and punk by understanding that, through his example, these two philosophies may be reconciled to achieve a greater, more profound cultural genre not simply in comic books, but potentially throughout all of literature.

Notes

1. William Grady, in "Transcending the Frontier Myth," argues that "myth lies in the boundaries of cultural history," building upon the theories of cultural history proposed by Richard Slotkin (42). Slotkin, in *Gunfighter Nation: The Myth of the Frontier in Twentieth-Century America*, argues that the three concepts required to make culture are "*ideology, myth,* and *genre*" (5). Slotkin goes on to propose that "*[i]deology* is the basic system of concepts, beliefs, and values that defines a society's way of interpreting its place in the cosmos and the meaning of its history"; "*genres* ... provide ways of articulating ideological concepts directly and explicitly"; and finally "[m]yths are stories drawn from a society's history that have acquired through persistent usage the power of symbolizing that society's ideology and of

dramatizing its moral consciousness—with all the complexities and contradictions that consciousness may contain" (5). This essay uses the terms "ideology," "genre," and "mythology" in accordance with Slotkin's definitions.

2. Thomas Hatch, in his *Encyclopedia of the Alamo and the Texas Revolution*, corroborates Ennis's claims regarding James Bowie's participation in the slave trade and drunken nature (54–55, 59–60), as well as David Crockett's possible cowardice during the Battle of the Alamo (78).

3. Ray White, in his article "The Good Guys Wore White Hats: The B Western in American Culture," uses the term "trigger trio" to refer to a common *topos* of American Western film in which there are three central heroes, each of whom plays an archetypal role within the dynamic of their relationships and the narrative as a whole (144–145).

4. Ennis and Dillon's *Preacher* pioneered the rise of western-hybrid comic book series in the twenty-first century. What follows is a brief list of some of the most critically acclaimed western-hybrid comics that began publication after *Preacher*'s conclusion in 2000. *American Vampire*, a horror-western written by Scott Snyder and penciled primarily by Rafael Albuquerque, which began publication in 2010, narrates the history of America from the 1880s through the late twentieth-century by following the life of Skinner Sweet, a notorious old west thief and murderer who is transformed, accidentally, into America's first vampire. *East of West*, a steampunk, dystopian western, written by Jonathan Hickman and penciled by Nick Dragotta, which began publication in 2013, follows Death, a western vigilante and one of the Four Horsemen of the Apocalypse, as he attempts to find his son and stop the other three horsemen from beginning Armageddon. *Pretty Deadly*, a fantasy, horror-western written by Kelly Sue DeConnick and penciled by Emma Rios, which began publication in 2013, follows Death's daughter, Ginny, as she hunts down her father in an attempt to gain retribution for his past crime against both her and her mother. *Scalped*, a crime-western written by Jason Aaron and penciled by R.M. Guéra, which began publication in 2007, explores the attempt of undercover FBI agent Dashiell Bad Horse, an Oglala Lakota, to expunge the corruption that has run rampant in his reservation over the last thirty-years. With the exception of *Scalped*, which concluded in 2012, all of these series are still on-going.

5. As with comic books, cinema saw a rise in the production of western-hybrid movies and television shows in the twenty-first century. What follows is a brief list of some of the most critically acclaimed and popular western-hybrid movies and televisions shows. *Firefly*, a twenty-sixth century space-western television show created by Joss Whedon, follows the exploits of Captain Malcom Reynolds and the crew of *Serenity*, his Firefly class spaceship, as they attempt to survive as intergalactic smugglers under the oppressive regime of the Union of Allied Planets. *Firefly*, after airing for only one season, was concluded through Joss Whedon's film, *Serenity*, in 2005. *Cowboys & Aliens*, a 2011 science-fiction western film based on Scott Mitchell Rosenberg's 2006 graphic novel *Cowboys & Aliens*, takes place in the 1870s and follows an unnamed outlaw who attempts to save the members of a small town in the New Mexico Territory who have been abducted by aliens. *Kill Bill*, a two-part martial arts, action-western film, created by Quentin Tarantino and released in 2003 and 2004, respectively, follows the revenge fueled quest of a lone female assassin, known only as "The Bride," who attempts to hunt down and kill her former employer, Bill, and her fellow assassins, who slaughtered her fiancé and attempted to kill her and her unborn child on her wedding day.

6. Please note that all quotations from the comic book series *Preacher* are exact quotations and any stylistic emphasis included, such as bolded or italicized words or phrases, occurred within the text of the comic book itself.

7. The traditional American Western cowboy has always been rooted within the virtues of honor, righteousness, and courage. For example, in *Shane*, the protagonist and hero, a cowboy named Shane, selflessly and courageously protects a group of homesteaders in Wyoming from a villainous and corrupt cattle baron named Rufus Ryker. William J. Devlin, in his article "*No Country for Old Men*: The Decline of Ethics and the West(ern)" argues that Shane's heroic nature arises not only from his ability to kill the villainous Ryker and save the homesteaders' land (223), but also from his selfless courage that compels him to "follow his [moral] duty" and protect the homesteaders and their land, even though it may result in his death (225). Another excellent example of the honor required to be a western hero can be

found in John Sturges's *The Magnificent Seven*, based on Akira Kurosawa's *The Seven Samurai*. Aeon J. Skobble, in "Order without Law: The Magnificent Seven, East and West," argues that the villagers initially ask for the help of these seven wandering gunslingers because they witness Chris and Vin, two of the gunslingers, "perform a heroic task" and, therefore, determine them to be "honorable [men] who [don't] mind taking a risk for the sake of what ... is right" (140). Chris and Vin, along with the other five gunslingers, agree to work as hired guns to protect the town in exchange for food and shelter. In the climax of this film, the seven gunmen decide to return to the town, now under the control of the villainous Calvera, in an attempt to free the townspeople, knowing full well that they might die and, therefore, showing their western honor and moral commitment to keeping their word. While four of the seven gunslingers die while freeing the village in the final battle, Skobble argues that "by keeping their honor" and serving a purpose in which they themselves believed, even in death, "they achieved [their own] victory" (146).

8. The punk do-it-yourself ethic and belief in personal responsibility are often best seen in some of the movement's most influential rock bands. For example, the British anarchist punk rock band Crass, according to Hannon in *Punks: A Guide to an American Subculture*, provided one of the movement's "first example[s] of anarchy as political and social action" and took it upon themselves to promote the DIY ethic by "engag[ing] in civil disobedience" and "actively support[ing]" causes such as "feminism, pacifism, [and] animal rights" (10). This punk commitment to DIY ethics was also the backbone for the "Riot Grrrl" movement, which, through the creation of "feminist punk zines and bands" helped successfully "empower women in punk to take charge and create their own art and cultural material" (Hannon 10–11). Finally, the creation and popularity of fanzines or zines, which were homemade magazines that "chronicl[ed]...local punk scenes," further reflects the ultimate commitment to and power that the DIY ethic held within the punk subculture (Hannon 37).

9. Germaine Greer, an academic theorist and feminist scholar, wrote *The Female Eunuch*, which examines how men can use women's sexuality as a tool to control them within society. In *The Female Eunuch*, Greer not only argues that "the female [within society] is considered as a sexual object for the use and appreciation of other sexual beings, men," but also explores how feminine characteristics praised within society often mirror the characteristics "of the castrate—timidity, plumpness, languor, delicacy, and preciosity" (Greer 17). Andrea Dworkin, another academic theorist and feminist, wrote both *Pornography: Men Possessing Women* and *Intercourse*. *Pornography: Men Possessing Women* examines how "pornography as a genre is male power" (24), specifically analyzing how, in pornography, "the degradation of women exists in order to postulate, exercise, and celebrate male power" (25), thus reinforcing the supremacy of male power and men within society. *Intercourse*, which poses the radical argument and exploration of the idea that "[i]ntercourse as an act often expresses the power men have over women" (159), and that female sexual subordination has been inherent in western society since women were "inferior in existence right from the beginning" (204), which Dworkin traces back to the creation story found in *The Book of Genesis*. Assuming that Jesse read all three of these books, one can logically assume that he would agree more with Greer's ideas than Dworkin's, especially since Jesse, when examining his sexual relationship with Tulip, which Ennis and Dillon constantly depict as healthy and enjoyable for both parties, would not perceive himself, rightly or wrongly, as using his intimate relationship with Tulip as a tool to control her actions (Ennis 13.3, 7–8). Jesse's relationship with Tulip, however, from an objective standpoint, does subscribe to some of the misogyny that Dworkin critiques, since Jesse has sexual intercourse with Tulip the night before he abandons her to fight the Grail, presumably to either tire her out or emotionally distract her so he can sneak away in the night (Ennis 21.14), and then uses sexual intercourse as a distraction to drug Tulip's water prior to abandoning her again to confront Cassidy and the Grail (63.7–10).

10. The concept of co-opting other groups' clothing or symbols was prevalent throughout the development of punk clothing and fashion. For example, Doc Marten boots, which were initially created as a durable tradesmen and working class shoe in the 1950s eventually became a staple of the punk aesthetic when English punks, such as Sid Vicious of the Sex Pistols, began wearing the classic 1460 black Doc Martens to add a working class, militaristic

flare to their attire (DeMello 98). This fashion co-opt occurred again when American punks began wearing Converse's Chuck Taylor "All Stars" shoes (Hannon 49), which were a high top sneaker designed specifically for playing basketball (DeMello 80). Perhaps one of the best examples, however, of punks appropriating a particular fashion aesthetic is their utilization and popularization of tattoos. Ian MacKaye, founding member of Minor Threat, cofounder of Dischord Records, and foundering member of the "Straight Edge" hardcore punk movement (Hannon 9, 119), discusses the evolution of tattoos in punk culture during an interview with Sharon M. Hannon. MacKaye explains that "[t]attoos were incredibly rare in the [punk] scene" when he "grew up" because tattoos were aesthetic symbols that signified stereotypically violent and dangerous individuals, such as "sailors and gang members and people in jail" (Hannon 127). Punks, by co-opting the aesthetic of the tattoo, which had come to symbolize these sordid groups, were able to empower the reputation of their movement through the implied association with this supposedly violent and dangerous subculture in America.

11. Ironically, many punks opposed capitalism, specifically "reject[ing] corporate commercialism" (Hannon 2) in favor of a more anarchical society. The "Fuck Communism" sentiment on Jesse's lighter, which implicitly supports American capitalism and therefore is in direct contradiction with a traditional punk ideology, still accurately embodies the ideals of personal accountability to one's own morality and philosophies as well as the individual, do-it-yourself, rebellious nature of the punk movement.

12. The "trigger trio," according to Ray White, first began when Republic Pictures began releasing B Western feature films based on William Colt McDonald's *Mesquiteer* novel series (144). The most popular Mesquiteer trigger trio was comprised of actors Robert Livingston, Ray Corrigan, and Max Terhune, who completed fourteen features together and, according to White, "developed a spirit and cohesion unmatched by other trios" (144). The other most famous "trigger trio" can be found in Paramount Pictures' Hopalong Cassidy series, "based on the western novels of Clarence E. Mulford" (White 145). White argues that the dominance of Hoppy's character on screen shifted the notion of a "trigger trio" from three equal personalities, as was in the *Mesquiteer* series, to a singular leader with two strong supporting sidekicks (145). Even though *Preacher* is centered around Jesse's story, Ennis and Dillon not only fully develop Tulip and Cassidy's personalities, but also give both characters their own story arcs outside of their participation in Jesse's quest to hunt down God. Ennis and Dillon's willingness to focus on all three members of *Preacher*'s "trigger trio," although primarily telling the story of Jesse Custer, places it stylistically between the archetypal "trigger trios" of the *Mesquiteer* series and the Hopalong Cassidy series, with a slightly stronger inclination towards the *Mesquiteer* series.

Works Cited

DeMello, Margo. *Feet & Footwear: A Cultural Encyclopedia*. Greenwood Press, 2009.
Devlin, William J. "*No Country for Old Men*: The Decline of Ethics and the West(ern)." *The Philosophy of Westerns*, edited by Jennifer L. McMahon and B. Steve Csaki, University of Kentucky Press, 2010, pp. 221–240.
Dworkin, Andrea. *Intercourse: Twentieth Anniversary Edition*. Basic Books, 2006.
_____. *Pornography: Men Possessing Women*. G. P. Putnam's Sons, 1981.
Eckstein, Arthur M. "Introduction: Main Critical Issues in *The Searchers*." *The Searchers: Essays and Reflections on John Ford's Classic Western*, edited by Arthur M. Eckstein and Peter Lehman, Wayne State UP, 2004, pp. 1–46.
Ennis, Garth. (w), Steve Dillon (p, i). "The Time of the Preacher." *Preacher* #1 (Apr. 1995), DC Comics/Vertigo Comics.
_____. "And Hell Followed With Him." *Preacher* #2 (May 1995), DC Comics/Vertigo Comics.
_____. "And the Horse You Rode In On." *Preacher* #3 (Jun. 1995), DC Comics/Vertigo Comics.
_____. "Standing Tall." *Preacher* #4 (Jul. 1995), DC Comics/Vertigo Comics.
_____. "All in the Family." *Preacher* #8 (Nov. 1995), DC Comics/Vertigo Comics.
_____. "When the Story Began." *Preacher* #9 (Dec. 1995), DC Comics/Vertigo Comics.

_____. "How I Learned to Love the Lord." *Preacher* #10 (Jan. 1996), DC Comics/Vertigo Comics.
_____. "Pardners." *Preacher* #11 (Feb. 1996), DC Comics/Vertigo Comics.
_____. "Until the End of the World." *Preacher* #12 (Mar. 1996), DC Comics/Vertigo Comics.
_____. "Came A Pale Rider." *Preacher* #13 (Apr. 1996), DC Comics/Vertigo Comics.
_____. "Boys Will Be Boys." *Preacher* #14 (Jun. 1996), DC Comics/Vertigo Comics.
_____. "Crashing the Party." *Preacher* #15 (Jul. 1996), DC Comics/Vertigo Comics.
_____. "Judgment Night." *Preacher* #16 (Aug. 1996), DC Comics/Vertigo Comics.
_____. "Miracle Man." *Preacher* #17 (Sept. 1996), DC Comics/Vertigo Comics.
_____. "Texas and the Spaceman." *Preacher* #18 (Oct. 1996), DC Comics/Vertigo Comics.
_____. "Too Much Gun." *Preacher* #20 (Dec. 1996), DC Comics/Vertigo Comics.
_____. "Stormbringer." *Preacher* #21 (Jan. 1997), DC Comics/Vertigo Comics.
_____. "Revelations." *Preacher* #23 (Mar. 1997), DC Comics/Vertigo Comics.
_____. "And Justice for All." *Preacher* #24 (Apr. 1997), DC Comics/Vertigo Comics.
_____. "Cry Blood, Cry Erin." *Preacher* #25 (May 1997), DC Comics/Vertigo Comics.
_____. "To the Streets of Manhattan I Wandered Away." *Preacher* #26 (Jun. 1997), DC Comics/Vertigo Comics.
_____. "Gunchicks." *Preacher* #27 (Jul. 1997), DC Comics/Vertigo Comics.
_____. "Rumors of War." *Preacher* #28 (Aug. 1997), DC Comics/Vertigo Comics.
_____. "Old Familiar Faces." *Preacher* #29 (Sept. 1997), DC Comics/Vertigo Comics.
_____. "Underworld." *Preacher* #31 (Nov. 1997), DC Comics/Vertigo Comics.
_____. "Price of Night." *Preacher* #33 (Jan. 1998), DC Comics/Vertigo Comics.
_____. "Once Upon a Time." *Preacher* #34 (Feb. 1998), DC Comics/Vertigo Comics.
_____. "You and Me Against the World." *Preacher* #35 (Mar. 1998), DC Comics/Vertigo Comics.
_____. "Come and Get It." *Preacher* #36 (Apr. 1998), DC Comics/Vertigo Comics.
_____. "The Shatterer of Worlds." *Preacher* #37 (May. 1998), DC Comics/Vertigo Comics.
_____. "Arsefaced World" *Preacher* #40 (Aug. 1998), DC Comics/Vertigo Comics.
_____. "The Man from God Knows Where." *Preacher* #41 (Sept. 1998), DC Comics/Vertigo Comics.
_____. "Christina's World." *Preacher* #43 (Nov. 1998), DC Comics/Vertigo Comics.
_____. "Custer's Law." *Preacher* #44 (Dec. 1998), DC Comics/Vertigo Comics.
_____. "Southern Cross." *Preacher* #45 (Jan. 1999), DC Comics/Vertigo Comics.
_____. "Jesse Get Your Gun." *Preacher* #47 (Mar. 1999), DC Comics/Vertigo Comics.
_____. "Good Night and God Bless." *Preacher* #48 (Apr. 1999), DC Comics/Vertigo Comics.
_____. "First Contact." *Preacher* #49 (May 1999), DC Comics/Vertigo Comics.
_____. "Freedom's Just Another Word for Nothing Left to Lose." *Preacher* #51 (Jul. 1999), DC Comics/Vertigo Comics.
_____. "I Built My Dreams Around You." *Preacher* #54 (Oct. 1999), DC Comics/Vertigo Comics.
_____. "Texas, by God." *Preacher* #59 (Mar. 2000), DC Comics/Vertigo Comics.
_____. "The Wonder of You." *Preacher* #61 (May 2000), DC Comics/Vertigo Comics.
_____. "Jesse's Girl." *Preacher* #63 (Jul. 2000), DC Comics/Vertigo Comics.
_____. "If I Knew the Way I'd Go Back Home." *Preacher* #64 (Aug. 2000), DC Comics/Vertigo Comics.
_____. "Shoot Straight You Bastards." *Preacher* #65 (Sept. 2000), DC Comics/Vertigo Comics.
_____. "A Hell of a Vision." *Preacher* #66 (Oct. 2000), DC Comics/Vertigo Comics.
Ennis, Garth. (w), Steve Dillon (p), John McCrea (i). "Tall in the Saddle." *Preacher Special: Tall in the Saddle* #1 (Feb. 2000), DC Comics/Vertigo Comics.
Grady, William. "Transcending the Frontier Myth: Dime Novel Narration and (Jesse) Custer's Last Stand in Preacher." *Comic Books and American Cultural History: An Anthology*, edited by Matthew Pustz, Continuum International Publishing Group Inc., 2012, pp. 40–58.
Greer, Germaine. *The Female Eunuch*. Farrar, Straus and Giroux, 1971.
Hatch, Thomas. *Encyclopedia of the Alamo and the Texas Revolution*. McFarland, 1999.
Hannon, Sharon M. *Punks: A Guide to an American Subculture*. Greenwood Press, 2010.

Kugelberg, Johan, and John Savage, editors. *Punk: An Aesthetic*. Rizzoli Publications, 2012.
Labarre, Nicolas. "Meat Fiction and Burning Western Light: The South in Garth Ennis and Steve Dillon's *Preacher*." *Comics and the U.S. South*, edited by Brannon Costello and Qiana J. Whitted, University of Mississippi Press, 2013, pp. 242–265.
Lenihan, John H. "Westbound: Feature Films and the American West." *Wanted Dead or Alive: The American West in Popular Culture*, edited by Richard Aquila, University of Illinois Press, 1996, pp. 109–134.
Luhr, William. "John Wayne and *The Searchers*." *The Searchers: Essays and Reflections on John Ford's Classic Western*, edited by Arthur M. Eckstein and Peter Lehman, Wayne State UP, 2004, pp. 75–92.
Malott, Curry, and Milagros Peña. *Punk Rockers' Revolution" A Pedagogy of Race, Class, and Gender*. Peter Lang Publishing, Inc., 2004.
McNarron, David L. "From Dollars to Iron: The Currency of Clint Eastwood's Westerns." *The Philosophy of Westerns*, edited by Jennifer L. McMahon and B. Steve Csaki, University of Kentucky Press, 2010, pp. 149–170.
Sinker, Mark. "Concrete. So as to Self-Destruct: The Etiquette of Punk, its Habits, Rules, Values and Dilemmas." *Punk Rock: So What?: The Cultural Legacy of Punk*, edited by Roger Sabin, Routledge, 1999, pp. 120–139.
Skobble, Aeon J. "Order Without Law: *The Magnificent Seven*, East and West." *The Philosophy of Westerns*, edited by Jennifer L. McMahon and B. Steve Csaki, University of Kentucky Press, 2010, pp. 139–148.
Slatta, Richard W. "Making and Unmaking Myths of the American Frontier." *European Journal of American Culture*, vol. 29, 2010, pp. 81–92.
Slotkin, Richard. *Gunfighter Nation: The Myth of the Frontier in Twentieth-Century America*. Atheneum, 1992.
Uly, Douglas J. Den. "Civilization and Its Discontents: The Self-Sufficient Western Hero." *The Philosophy of Westerns*, edited by Jennifer L. McMahon and B. Steve Csaki, University of Kentucky Press, 2010, pp. 31–54.
White, Ray. "The Good Guys Wore White Hats: The B Western in American Culture." *Wanted Dead or Alive: The American West in Popular Culture*, edited by Richard Aquila, University of Illinois Press, 1996, pp. 135–159.
Winkler, Martin. "Homer's *Iliad* and John Ford's *The Searchers*." *The Searchers: Essays and Reflections on John Ford's Classic Western*, edited by Arthur M. Eckstein and Peter Lehman, Wayne State UP, 2004, pp. 145–171.

PART III: UNDERGROUND PUNK COMICS

Aspiring Revolutionaries and "Petty" Conflicts
The Penis in the Punk Movement and Binky Brown

MICHAEL DAVID MACBRIDE

> *"You may deem my material as being too indulgent, morbid and obscene. I daresay many of you aspiring revolutionaries will conclude that instead of focusing on topics which would lend themselves to social issues, I have zero'ed in on the petty conflict in my crotch!"*
> —Binky Brown, "Confession to My Readers"

Nearly every academic discussion of Justin Green's 1972 comic *Binky Brown Meets the Holy Virgin Mary* begins with a discussion of the "confession to my readers" that precedes the rest of the text, because: it sets the tone of the text, it's a direct window into Green's intentionality behind the text, it is even more confessional than the confessional text that follows, it offers Green's version of the iconic image of the "tortured artist," and, well, it's the first thing a reader encounters after the cover. Why should this discussion be any different? The image, complete with a vial of "dad's blood" with which Green is inking the very comic book the reader is about to read, is of a bound and tortured Green, suggesting the suffering that went into creating his art. The artist speaks of his leaving the Catholic Church (on Halloween of 1958) and his "compulsive neurosis," and he pleads with his readers not to think of him as "an asshole." Critics have addressed nearly every aspect of this opening speech bubble and of the "tortured artist" image, but they've neglected two important ideas that Green puts forth in this introductory page: (1) the idea that his readers may be "revolutionaries," and (2) that this book spends a lot of time dealing with the "the petty conflict in [his] crotch." I will argue that not only are these two ideas essential to understanding *Binky Brown*, but that they are interconnected.

In 1972, when *Binky Brown* was first published, the punk movement was in its latency phases. The Kingsmen's loose and sloppy cover of "Louie Louie" (1963) had rocked the world, and the following year the Kinks landed with "You Really Got Me" and "All Day and All of the Night." The Peruvian band Los Saicos hit it big with six singles released between 1964 and 1966. The Sonics' *Here Are the Sonics*, with "The Witch" and "Psycho," was released in 1965. The Velvet Underground's "I'm Waiting for the Man" (1967) was its one dalliance with the "new" punk sound. The MC5 shocked the world, their record company (Elektra), and Hudson's department store, by shouting "motherfuckers" on the opening to the second track of their album *Kick Out the Jams* (1969); they were subsequently dropped from their label.[1] The band Suicide posted its 1970 band flyer using the phrase "punk music" for the first time in history. Iggy Pop and the Stooges had been unleashed on the world and were nearly "done" (their final record, before a reunion much later, would come out in 1973). The New York Dolls were formed in 1971 and would release their final album three years later. In short, punk was "in the air" when Justin Green was working on *Binky Brown*, and the Hippie movement and the Summer of Love were fading memories.

It's no accident that the punk movement grows out of opposition to the "summer of love" and the frustration felt by the lack of progress by the hippie movement against the administration, civil rights movement, and the wars in Southeast Asia. If rock 'n' roll was about sex and drugs, then punk sought to push the envelope further. Where rock 'n' roll tended towards lengthy, gratuitous guitar solos and an indulgence in groupies and drugs, punk rock was about breaking down all kinds of barriers: first the barrier between the stage and the audience that signified the difference between "us" (artists) and "them" (audience), then the barrier between the corporate machine of recording companies and average performers (smaller labels sprung up, and some bands opted to self-produce their albums), and finally the barrier of social taboos in general.

The Penis in the Punk Movement

Punk bands found that dubbing themselves something offensive was almost a sure-fire way to attract attention and gain an audience. While simple obscenity certainly worked, punk bands quickly navigated to using the penis, and its many, many euphemisms, to attract attention, shock audiences, and to assert themselves. The following is not intended to be all-inclusive, but rather a quick survey of the earliest examples: Cock Sparrer (1972, London); Sex Pistols and Throbbing Gristle (both 1975, UK), Big Balls and the Great White Idiot (1975, Germany); Buzzcocks, the Members, Penetration, and the Vibrators (all 1976, UK); The Dickies (1977, USA); Urinals (1978, USA) and Crass (1978, UK); The Dicks and Meat Puppets (both 1980, USA); The Meatmen (1981, USA), and The Hard-ons (1981, Australia).[2] In addition to the band names, song titles and song subject matter frequently attempted to shock: Throbbing Gristle's "Five Knuckle Shuffle," DEVO's "Uncontrollable Urge," and Black Flag's "Slip It In," just to name a few.

While the origins of "punk" might be hotly contested, typically falling into a UK vs. the U.S. debate, euphemistic use of the phallus is apparently universal worldwide. Some bands used the phallus as an ironic way of drawing attention to the feminist movement. By "thrusting" their penises at the audience, they forced them to confront the anxiety they felt, and similarly women would feel, when confronted with sexual violence. Some bands simply used the phallus as a marketing gimmick, challenging their fans to see what the band would do next. Regardless of intention, just as "sex sells" in advertising, the penis made people take notice in punk rock. The penis is just another in a long line of symbols which have been associated with punk: some co-opted like the anarchy symbol, the squatting sign, and the Sex Pistols wearing Nazi propaganda, and others homegrown like the band logos of Black Flag, Dead Kennedys, Misfits, and Bad Religion.

Imagery and iconography are essential elements of the punk movement, and the Museum of Contemporary Art (MOCA), Los Angeles has recently released a documentary series "The Art of Punk" (2013) to explore it. As of the writing of this essay, the series has three episodes, each featuring a prominent punk artist—Raymond Pettibon (Black Flag formed in 1976), Winston Smith (Dead Kennedys formed in 1978), and the team of Dave King and Gee Vaucher (Crass formed in 1977). Each artist, or team of artists, explores the inspiration behind the symbols and the work they created, but all express one consistent motivation: the desire to create a symbol that is unique and simplistic enough to be recreated easily (whether it be as graffiti, tattoo, or for simple screen printing purposes). Of these three, without a doubt, the most iconic logo is the one Raymond Pettibon created for Black Flag. It's simple, elegant, and one of the staples of punk iconography.

Raymond Pettibon

Pettibon is most famous for naming Black Flag and creating the band's logo—four black bars staggered to suggest a waving black flag. Though he left the band before Black Flag ever really got off the ground, he continued to create art for the band's flyers and posters for much of their career. Pettibon's art of the late 70s and early 80s typically consists of ink drawings with accompanying text. The art Black Flag used for their posters, albums, and flyers was created by Pettibon, but not necessarily created explicitly for the band. Pettibon was a prolific artist in his own right, and he was happy to share his work with almost anyone who asked.[3] Like the Black Flag logo, Pettibon's other work is bold and his messages are powerful.

Some of Pettibon's posters featured Charles Manson, Jesus, Ronald Reagan, J. Edgar Hoover, Gumby, Elvis, and nude males. The subject matter was drawn from pop culture, literary and artistic references, and events in the news of the time. For example, one famous piece depicts a police officer with a gun in his mouth—it accompanied the single for Black Flag's "Police Story"—which acts as a response to LAPD brutality and harassment of punk bands and fans. Pettibon and Black Flag were no strangers to controversy. In the MOCA series on Pettibon, Henry Rollins (Black Flag lead singer from 1981–86) states, "If you notice, there's a solid year of Black Flag flyers where there's nothing but erect penises. I swear, a good five shows. It's like nude man, another nude man, bunch of nude men. It's just relentless." However, Pettibon actually believes he's been rather consistent over the years, and, what's more, the members of Black Flag chose from his art—he didn't dictate which pieces they used. Via a conversation on Twitter between the artist and myself, Pettibon stated, "They chose them from 100's [and] The dck [sic] is like the letter 'I' to me." So, this wasn't simply a "penis period" that he went through. Furthermore, despite Rollins' claim of "erect penises" for a "solid year," the examples I found (after looking through several collections of Pettibon's work) feature primarily flaccid members. In fact, erect penises are a rarity in Pettibon's art— generally, when they do appear, they appear on fantastical creations (like devils and demons).

Whereas the erect penis could suggest aggression and one capable of assault, the flaccid penis is not only unthreatening but also suggests impotence. In the same interview, Rollins relates a story where he requested art from Pettibon of an aggressive middle finger to accompany their new single "My Rules." What Pettibon produced wasn't exactly what Rollins had in mind: "It's the most effeminate limp [middle finger]… even the middle finger's wilting… it's like salad left out in the afternoon sun." While the band might have been hoping for something to shock and offend, Pettibon's wilting middle fingers and flaccid penises undermine the notion that punk bands need be aggressive to garner attention. Pettibon's use of the penis in his work is not about demeaning women or aggressively using the penis to assert masculinity, but rather it's more in keeping with the traditional male nude.

There are many, many depictions of male nudes in sculpture, and they typically depict a "realistically" sized male member in the flaccid state. The

Aspiring Revolutionaries and "Petty" Conflicts (MacBride) 117

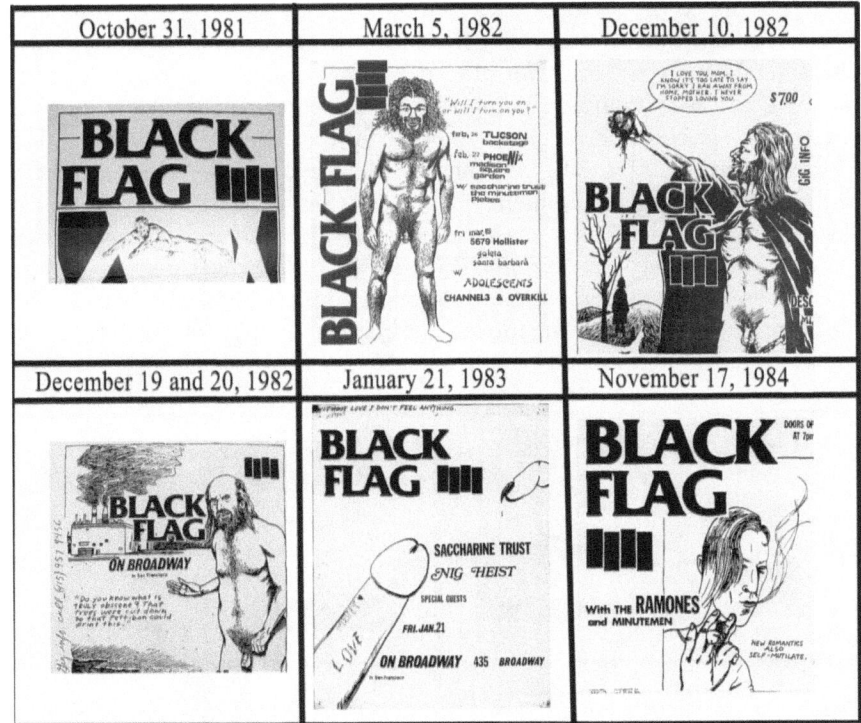

Figure 1: Various images from Raymond Pettibon's work (courtesy Raymond Pettibon).

muscles and dimensions of the men depicted might otherwise be romanticized, but the penis size is proportional or even slightly diminutive to the rest of the image.[4] Most of these more classical artists were attempting to depict reality, even if was a "perfected" (or romanticized) reality that they captured on canvas and in stone. In cartooning, features are exaggerated for effect—noses made larger, lips stretched, breasts and penises enlarged, and eyes enlarged or shrunk. Comic books walked a line somewhere in between, and in the underground comix (R. Crumb, Jack Jackson, even Art Spiegelman), the drawings aligned more closely to the style of cartoons. This is in part because of the influence of Tijuana Bibles, which challenged social norms the way that punk would in the 70s, long before the surge of punk comics in the early to mid–80s.[5]

Sometimes called eight-pagers, gray-backs, Jiggs and Maggie books, jo-jo books, Tillie and Mac books, two-by-fours, fuck books, and several other regional names, Tijuana Bibles were essentially underground comix before underground comix existed.⁶ Like comix, they were transgressive in nature. They frequently featured famous people (politicians, actors, actresses, comic characters) having sex, or performing an act uncharacteristic of their "public" persona, and were completely ungoverned and uncensored. Depending on whom you ask, these books either emerged during World War I or just after.⁷ However, certainly by the 1930s these books are common, cheap, explicit, and popular among young men. These books served as the inspiration for the next generation of great artists/writers—Crumb, Green, and Spiegelman were all born in the 40s. *Mad Magazine* (first *Mad Comics*), also frequently cited as an inspiration for the underground comix artists, was born in the 50s. The underground comix movement began in earnest in the 60s, just as the punk movement was also being born.⁸

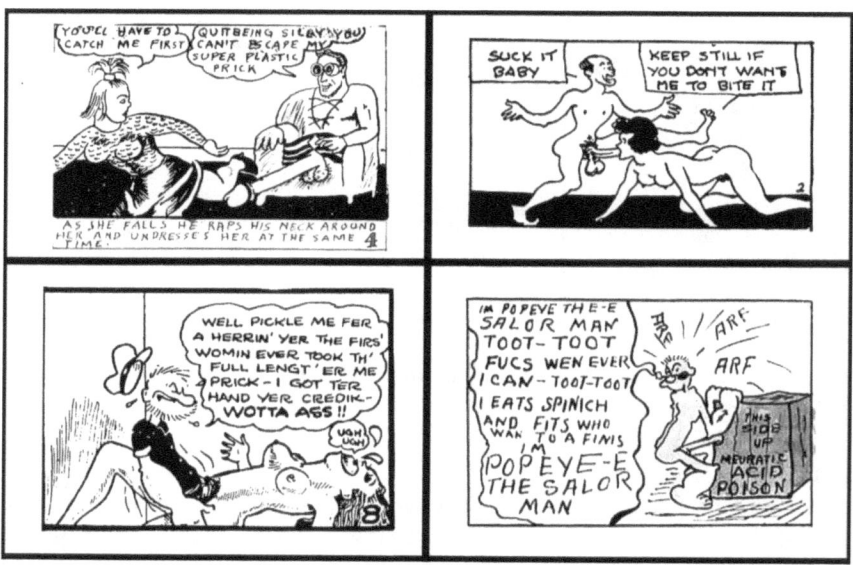

Figure 2: These are representative images from Tijuana Bibles. Because they were published anonymously, it's difficult to know when they were drawn and by whom. These images are taken from Bob Adelman's *Tijuana Bibles: Art and Wit in America's Forbidden Funnies, 1930s–1950s* (courtesy Bob Adelman).

Superhero comics were also well established by the time the underground comix movement began—indeed, some superheroes were even depicted in Tijuana Bibles (see Plastic Man in Figure 2). The superhero certainly had exaggerated muscles and perfect form, but, for the most part, things were in proper proportion, faces were drawn to look realistic, and it was clear the artists were attempting to make superheroes look as if they could exist in the "normal" world. The art of superhero comics was much more akin to the representations of the human form, particularly male, in classic art. This is not to suggest that the superhero artists were classically trained, or drew upon Greek statues when creating their art, but rather that, on the spectrum of idealized human forms, superhero artists and classic artists were closer in artistic style than the underground comix artists, in general. This is easily explained in part because the comix artists took inspiration primarily from two sources: *Mad Magazine* (specifically the work of Harvey Kurtzman) and Tijuana Bibles. These inspirations provided a foundation from which comix artists could work against conventions in comics, primarily: house styles, simplistic and childish story lines, characters with clean moral compasses, and the like.

The inspiration from *Mad* and Kurtzman on the underground movement is pretty obvious—and has been well-documented—but the influence of the Tijuana Bible on the movement was generally overlooked until 1997.[9] Bob Adelman's collection *Tijuana Bibles* (1997), and more specifically Art Spiegelman's introduction, "Those Dirty Little Comics," help to rectify that problem. Here, Spiegelman speaks about the influence of the Tijuana Bible on the underground movement:

> The Tijuana Bibles weren't a direct inspiration for most of us; they were a precondition. That is, the comics that galvanized my generation—the early Mad, the horror and science-fiction comics of the fifties—were mostly done by guys who had been in their turn warped by those little books... [and] without the Tijuana Bibles there would never have been a Mad magazine... and without Mad there would never have been any iconoclastic underground comix in the sixties [5].

If, as Denis Kitchen suggests, Kurtzman is the "'father-in-law' of underground comix," then the granddaddy of the underground comix movement is the Tijuana Bible.[10] It is this anti-authoritarian nature of Tijuana Bibles, and the underground comix movement, that evoke a sense of the "spirit" of the punk movement. But distribution and "shock value" aside, the Tijuana Bibles and the majority of the early underground comix movement shared more in common with the psychedelics and the hippie movement than the punks. In part, this is because Crumb is thought of as the father of the underground movement, and his work is so closely associated with the psychedelics and the notion of "free love."[11] However, as I will argue in the next section, *Binky Brown* is clearly a punk text inside and out.

Binky Brown's Penis

While Justin Green certainly is an underground comix artist, and he shares some common influences, he is not precisely in the same camp as

Crumb, Spiegelman, and the others who are more indebted to the ethos of the 1960s—though he is frequently lumped in with them. Green admits to having read *Mad* and even aping Crumb's style for a time, but he said (in a 1982 interview with Mark Burbey) that he "learned how to read and write from Fox & Crow Comics when he was four or five years old, and then went through the standard Scrooge, Donald Duck routine. Then became kind of fixated on Superboy, as a budding neurotic. Then totally disavowed comics." However, the biggest influence on Green's development was, "Treasure Chest comics ... a Catholic comic that was distributed free" by the Church. In addition to these graphic influences, Green also cites print influences as well: Joyce's *Portrait of the Artist as a Young Man*, Philip Roth's *Portnoy's Complaint*, James T. Farrell's *Studs Lonigan Trilogy*, and J.D. Salinger's *Catcher in the Rye*.[12] Another trait that sets Green apart from the other comix artists is that Green was actually a classically trained artist and has a degree in fine arts. Though Green certainly was a child of the 60s and shared the same cultural experience as his other contemporary underground artists, he came at his work with a unique set of skills, ideas, and inspiration.

Much of the attention paid to Green's *Binky Brown Meets the Holy Virgin Mary* focuses on the autobiographical content. Nearly every article that discusses the work and every review of the book states that *Binky Brown* is the first autobiographical comic. This autobiographical content certainly sets it apart from the other underground comix of the time: "Before Justin Green, cartoonists were actually expected to keep a lid on their psyches and personal histories, or at least disguise and sublimate them into diverting entertainments" (Spiegelman 4). Indeed, it was Green who advised a young Spiegelman to write from his own life rather than using animals to tell a story about racial divisions in the U.S.—the resulting comic was the start of *Maus*. In drawing from life, Green exposed himself in a way that later came to embarrass him; in 1982 (in the same interview with Burbey mentioned earlier) Green reflected: "It's kind of shocking for me to look at. I'm not especially proud that I put so much of my internal life on the line." However, beyond the autobiographical elements of *Binky Brown*, the look and style of the book feel distinctly different from Crumb and his comix disciples. As discussed earlier, with regard to Raymond Pettibon's work, Green's art is less cartoonish and more "real." It relies on less exaggeration and distortion, and instead is more grounded in reality. This more realistic look mirrors the very real story that unfolds throughout the comic.

In short, *Binky Brown* tells the tale of a young boy struggling to understand sexual urges, maturation, Obsessive Compulsive Disorder, and how to resolve his Catholic guilt—which is also Justin Green's life story. Each of these neuroses might have been manageable on its own, but the combination proved nearly fatal. It isn't until 1989, when Green heard an interview on

NPR with the author of *The Boy Who Couldn't Stop Washing*, that Green finally had a name for the neurosis that he's struggled with his entire life: Obsessive Compulsive Disorder.[13] Before that moment, Green was left to believe that his urges and obsessions were as a result of sin. When he rejected the church—which at least allowed for confession to atone for sin—it left him with no explanation or resolution. Even something relatively simple, such as maturation proves difficult for Binky to navigate.

During Green's time in school, sex education was limited at best, and there were no "self-help" books for individual study. As Spiegelman states in the introduction to *Tijuana Bibles*, "the Tijuana Bibles were the sex-education manuals of their time" (Spiegelman 10). Given the distortion of reality that these texts suggest, it's no wonder the anxiety youths felt with regard to sex. The few popular "sex books" that did exist were taboo and limited in their usefulness. The earliest of these is *An ABZ of Love*, which was published in Demark in 1961 and then translated into English in 1963. Unlike the clinical descriptions offered in textbooks, the *ABZs* was written with a casual tone and included drawings—though, these drawings were (with few exceptions) very cartoonish in nature (see Figure 3).

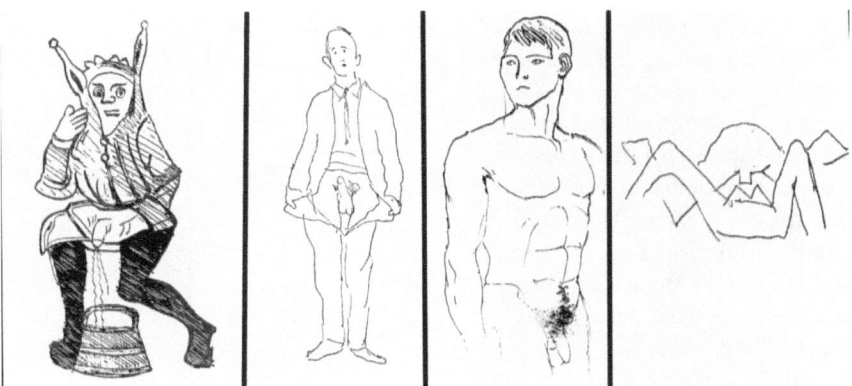

Figure 3: Images from *An ABZ of Love* (1961, first edition) by Inge Hegeler, Sten Hegeler, and Eiler Krag.

The book offered a "Note" on the flip side of the title page, stating that this book was for "couples in their thirties or forties" and acknowledges that, "there will always be those who claim it was written for pornographic reasons," before warning, "we feel it only fair to warn those who are looking for pornography that they will be disappointed." What's more, several images were censored in the English edition. In lieu of a drawing, English readers were treated to a black box with the following message: "Here was an illustration, though legal in all Scandinavian countries, our legal department advised us to delete it for the reason that it would, most likely, prove too shocking in the USA. We apologize to the reader for our cultural timidity." Other censored images simply had the black box with the words, "See page 62" where this warning first appeared. The image that was censored? A man with an erection (see Figure 4).

Despite the shortcomings of this book, it was the one that Kurt Vonnegut, Jr., turned to and suggested to his wife, writing: "If you are as interested in sex as you say you are, there is a really lovely book about it in my study—on a top shelf. It's red, and it's called *The ABZ of Love*."[14] ABZs aside, the next most popular "sex books" were *Everything You Always Wanted to Know About Sex (But Were Afraid to Ask)* (1969)—which offered no drawings or photos and was based purely on the experience of the author, and the experience of his clients, and is written from a clearly biased and judgmental voice—and *The Joy of Sex* (1972)—which then set the standard for a "sex book." And while sex education did exist in public schools by the 50s, it lacked a national standard. Indeed, it was not until 1970 when the White House Conference on Children recommended publicly funded programs for "sex and population education" that something approximating the modern sense of "sex education" came into existence. The early 1980s finally found frank

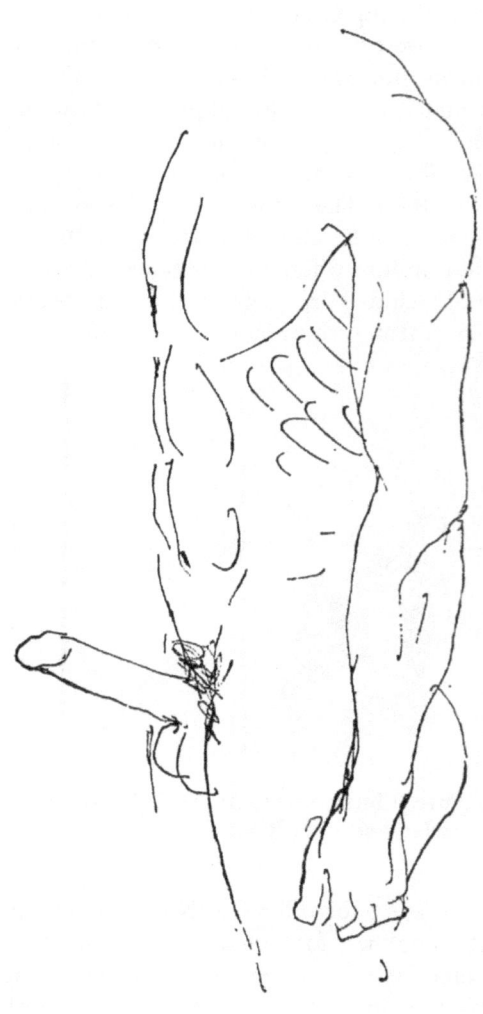

Figure 4: Image from *An ABZ of Love* (1961, first edition) by Inge Hegeler, Sten Hegeler, and Eiler Krag.

discussions of sexuality, sex in general, and sex education come into existence. For youths of the 1940s and 1950s, specifically the comix artists that this essay concerns itself with, "sex education" was limited to Tijuana Bibles, clinical textbooks, and pornography. It should come as no surprise that this repression of a natural desire became an essential element of the comix artists' art.

And yet when it comes to discussing *Binky Brown*, the discussions tend not to focus on the prolific and obsessive depictions of the penises; they are instead about Green's struggles with the church, about Green's use of autobiographical details, about Binky's obsessive compulsions, and about the rays that extend from Binky's penis (and penile appendages later). While critics have gone to great lengths to discuss the "rays" that appear later in the text, it is the penis that should be the focus of the discussion. The penis is the initial cause of Binky's distress. Phallic imagery (a baseball bat held at waist level) appears on page one, and actual penises (Binky's and his father's friend's) appear on page four, while the rays don't appear until page twenty-four (more than halfway through the book). The rays are important, but they are only an extension of his confusion with regard to his very real, very natural, penis. The rays are a fabrication of Binky's imagination, and they are created only as a result of the suppression of natural urges and a lack of discussion about maturation. Though Binky blames himself for the rays and his impure thoughts, in effect the Church and his parents, the two most omnipresent "systems" in his young life, created the rays, not Binky. Not coincidentally, these are the same authoritative systems that "aspiring revolutionaries" railed against. Add the government to the mix, and you have the punk trifecta (or its holy trinity). *Binky Brown* is about maturation and rebelling against the Church, but it's also, on a much grander scale, about questioning the validity of systems that attempted to control Binky Brown.

For Justin Green, having lived through the world depicted in Binky Brown, his rebuke to these systems was to bare his penis—the source of his anxiety and the one thing that the church and his parents refused to acknowledge. Whereas punk bands, Tijuana Bibles, and comix (in general) tend to exaggerate the male member, Justin Green draws earnest, unflattering penises to depict his reality, his suffering, and to talk about that which must be not spoken of, that which is unclean, that which is "private." *Binky Brown* is not about exploitation or shock value; this is about desire and the expression of a young man's frustration and, even more importantly, about his desire to question authority. At the same time punk bands were naming themselves after euphemisms for male genitalia, or using phalluses on their album art and t-shirts, Justin Green's Binky Brown was less cock-sure. The penis-in-your-face approach of the punk bands of the 70s, was the very thing that sent Binky into hiding and despair.

Punk musicians hoped to shock their audiences and catch their attention; Binky wanted nothing more than to blend in and disappear. His own phallus and sexual desire produced great anxiety for him; for the bands, it's the audience that feels anxious and uncomfortable by the assertion of the male member. For Justin Green, baring his phallus was therapeutic. In a day and age that didn't readily acknowledge OCD and anxiety disorders, this was the way he coped with his neuroses. Drawing them was painful, but through the expression, he allowed others to confront their fears and "heal" with him. Intentionally, or otherwise, the punk bands of the period also forced people to confront these feelings as well. Their songs about masturbation and "real sex" (as opposed to the sanitized version expressed on TV and in film) was startling and shocking only because it was so rare in the time. Punk bands played the penis angle for affect, whereas Justin Green wrote about it because he had no other option. Some saw the art as a cheap gimmick, like the punk bands, but his was the most real expression. It was him baring his soul, and penis.

Depending on how you count them, there are 124 penises in *Binky Brown Meets the Holy Virgin Mary*.[15] There are some, but fewer, phallic objects sprinkled throughout the text as well. As noted earlier, these phallic items have received more critical attention than the actual penises; perhaps this is because a focus on the phallic objects allows the discussion to move one step away from actually discussing the phallus itself. Spiegelman, again from the "Introduction" to the McSweeney's edition, suggests that the very reason *Binky Brown* is not "recognized in the worlds of Art, Literature, Clinical Psychology and Religious Studies" is because of all "those drawn penises casting their rays all over the pages" (n.p.). So, let's focus on the penises, why they are there, and what they mean.

There are four types of penises throughout the text: (1) the realistic; (2) the romanticized; (3) the Tijuana-inspired (generally these are of the appendage penis variety); and, (4) the imaginary—aka, rays without a phallus or with the phallus covered or obscured by clothing. Just as with Pettibon's flaccid male members, the "realistic" penises present in *Binky Brown* are just a matter of course; Binky is a teenager, going through puberty, and male nudity is simply a matter of his reality. Whether it is the locker room scene (depicted in Figure 5, from page 19), his father's friend offering to "have a sword fight" (in the lower right panel of Figure 5, from page 4), or Binky's struggles with "impure thoughts" (all of page 29), these depictions are in keeping with the male nude tradition, and reflect Binky's anxiety with regard to "normal" adolescent concerns about size, hairiness, and self control.

Young Binky had no outlet for this shame, and these anxieties led to his imagined self and the "romanticized" penises. In these depictions, Binky imagines himself to be muscular, well-endowed, and a confident artist, rather than the scrawny, average, tortured artist that he really is. Ironically, it is only

Figure 5: Images from Justin Green's *Binky Brown Meets the Holy Virgin Mary* (courtesy Justin Green).

through the complete immersion in his anxiety and shame that Binky becomes, if only for a fleeting moment, the Romanticized version of himself (depicted in the top left panel of Figure 5, from page 40). Then, the muscular, hairy-chested, well-endowed, Binky stands holding a hammer amid the shattered remains of Madonna statues, before returning to "normal" Binky who has to clean up the mess and move on with his life.

The "Tijuana-inspired" penises are, in some ways, an extension of the "romanticized" penises. These are certainly exaggerations, but they go beyond the simple distorted perception of size. These depictions are when Binky imagines his fingers, feet, and limbs are becoming penises. With these penises, Binky has supplanted the actual phallus with anything resembling a phallus. No longer does he need to be nude to be reminded of his anxiety, but instead shame and anxiety surfaces when he sees his fingers or a phallic-like object (firehose, baseball bat, 7-Up bottle, tube of toothpaste, a rubber bumper guard from a '58 Cadillac, etc.).

The "imaginary" penises, or rays, take this anxiety to the next level by extending the range of even the Tijuana-inspired penises to infinity. Now the penis has been abstracted to the point of not even needing to be seen and yet still cause Binky undue hardship. To understand how these imaginary penises work, Green includes a couple of panels of boxy-Binky who attempts to use math and geometry to navigate the rays. But, even geometry and right angles fail when Green points out that these objects have a "common vanishing point at which their projection rays converge, so in Binky's world every object has its dominant ray, based on length rather than width.... The object in Binky's game was never to let a ray connect with an illicit vanishing point; but to try to make them veer harmlessly into outer space or Iowa" (32–33). The culmination of the four penises occurs on page 32, and it is here that Binky realizes, "the more vehemently he denied the existence of the rays, the more real they became" (see Figure 6).

So much of *Binky Brown* is about attempting to be "normal," attempting to blend in, and conforming in general; the penises, the reluctance to talk about puberty, and the anxiety these changes and differences cause Binky are just one aspect of the book. Whether it is penis size, or whether or not Binky has a "hairy dick" like the other guys in the locker room (19), or how one reconciles faith with "impure thoughts," Justin Green is continually wrestling with what it means to be "normal." When Binky Brown hears a patch of grass ask him to keep it from getting wet, he immediately retorts, "You don't hear all the other grass complaining! What makes you so special!" (2). Later, Green informs the reader, "Like most God and Father fearing male warbabies, Binky Brown yearned to serve his country and mother as flamboyantly as possible" (4). And, of course the nuns, "had an obsessive way of imposing order, uniformity, rigidity, and obedience" (8). Furthermore, Green sprinkles tongue-in-cheek authority throughout the text with footnotes, references, and definitions (pages 7, 17, 18, 20, 22, and 34). But, for Green as a sufferer of obsessive compulsive disorder, the bigger issue is just what is "normal," and (perhaps more importantly) who gets to decide? In "The Binky Brown Matter," he poses the question this way: "Are the effects of OCD preoccupation any less real because their bogus origin is known with certainty by the suffering individual? No. There's even a guessing game which explores the theme: 'WHAT WOULD I NORMALLY DO?'—as if there were a parallel universe where the unimpaired self is functioning in complete mental health" (83). Just as Binky

Figure 6: Image from Justin Green's *Binky Brown Meets the Holy Virgin Mary* (courtesy Justin Green).

was made to believe he was not "normal," because of his OCD, shame and anxiety with his penis, and his guilt over sin, Green too was made to feel like he was slowly going crazy because there was nothing to validate his experience.

In *Binky Brown*, it is the Church and society that are imposing their normalizing glare at the youthful Binky, and it is only after he comes to terms with his difference that his shame and anxiety fade. The authority of these systems is littered throughout the work: ventriloquism dummies and marionettes (9); blindly repeating Church doctrine, "the Church is infallible" (11); a news report on the television about the Comics Code (12); Binky's father admonishing him for defending himself against his brother (14); the picket signs loaded with Church slogans and campaigns (18); the schoolmasters and nuns (throughout the text); the mentions of music and books that were burned by the Church (20); the campaign advertisements (25); the various images of Jesus; and of course the many, many depictions of the Virgin Mary who haunt Binky and are the primary source of his guilt and shame. It is only when Binky finally abandons all attempts to juggle these various authoritative controls that he frees himself: "At least I don't have to worry about committing anymore sins—I know I'm damned for eternity" (34). Binky then attempts to fill the void left with beer, gambling, speed, crime, masochism, Hesse novels, obsessive love, protest, yoga, Zen, pot, mysticism, psychiatry, painting, the blues, and acid (35). Finally, in an orgasmic moment of destruction, Binky smashes all of his idols (literally and figuratively) and realizes, "my prick is just a prick.... I'm alive!" (39). Then, and only then, can Binky at least be free from, "the primeval morass of superstition and guilt fostered by well-meaning institutions like the Catholic Church" (40).

The penises in Binky Brown are all about Binky's struggle into manhood, and they're all about the awkwardness he feels about his body because no one provides him with straight talk about sex and sexuality. And, yes, the penises most certainly are a "fuck you" to the church and all those who would repress these normal thoughts. Ultimately Binky Brown is a punk text, reacting to and rejecting authority and their systems—the Catholic Church, Freud's approach to psychology, parents, etc. By the end of the book, Binky Brown doesn't care about living in harmony with others; he wants to find himself, understand who he is, and find others who feel the same way. He bares his penis and waves it around as a way of saying, "Hey! I reject you, and I reject a society that says I'm broken." This, too, is the rallying cry of the punk movement.

Conclusion

As with any movement, the punk movement faded. It was replaced by hardcore, then new wave, then goth, and eventually industrial. Justin Green also found a new calling: billboard painting. Just as punk musicians found they could only play hard and fast for so long before the emptiness of angst overtook their lives, so too did Justin Green find he had cleansed his palate of rallying against the system. While so much of the punk movement was about posing and posturing, feigning strength and brashness, Green bares his penis not because he wants to shock and awe, but because he needs to talk about it. This makes *Binky Brown* even more punk because it's sincere. As Patrick Rosenkranz, in *The ABCs of Autobio Comix* (2011), writes:

> Most people prefer to deny their deep dark secrets, even from themselves, but Green gave us everything he'd stored up—angst, nausea, sexual humiliation, and morbid obsessions. He didn't waste any time building up his ego or making himself look heroic [1].

I would take Rosenkranz's comments a step further and say, it is the earnestness of the depictions of the penises that really make the work unsettling to readers. In the era of the Tijuana-inspired exaggerated penises (see Crumb et al), the frankness of Green's art stands in stark contrast.

Even though the art in *Binky Brown* is not ultra-realistic, it seems more authentic. It is the realism and personal nature of this text that makes it unique and uncomfortable. Readers seem more at ease talking about the exaggerated art in comix than about what they are confronted with in *Binky Brown*. Similarly, the world was "shocked" by the Sex Pistols and their overt, exaggerated, sexual innuendo, but they were willing to talk about it and discuss it. However, when someone wants to have a frank discussion about sexuality, maturation, and masturbation, the world turns a deaf ear to him. *Binky Brown* has been saved from the sidelines of history thanks to the autobiographical elements present in the book, and then again due to its unique and early depiction of OCD, but if not for those claims to fame, one could easily imagine a world without *Binky Brown*, where the book has been glossed over and forgotten in favor of a safer, more palatable text. In such a world, Pettibon's nude male posters would be forgotten in favor of his album art covers and controversial critiques against the LAPD.

Underground comix and punk came out of a mixture of desire to shock audiences into conversations about taboos and uncomfortable topics, to challenge authority, and to cope with a volatile period of American history. Whether by music, or by art, or by performance, punk bands and comix artists push the boundaries and challenge audiences. However, by not engaging the work in its entirety, we are somehow missing the point. By ignoring the 124 penises, and 38 phallic items in the 42-page comic book, our discussion of *Binky Brown* is incomplete. Yes, it's an Underground Comic. It's independently made. It deals with topics that are less than dinner-conversation material. More importantly, it's an earnest look inside a young man's world and his attempt to understand it. Despite the Church's desire to suggest it, and Binky Brown's own attempt to ignore it, pretending the penis isn't there, doesn't make it so.

Notes

1. Certainly there were artists before the MC5 that used "fuck" and its various forms in their songs; look no further than the Blues artist known as Lucille Bogan/Bessie Jackson for an example from 1934. Jefferson Airplane hold the distinction for singing "motherfucker" live on television during a performance of their song "We Can Be Together" for the first time (August 19, 1969)—their album *Volunteers*, which featured the song, was released in November 1969. But, the MC5 released "Kick Out the Jams" as a single in 1968, and their album was released the following year. They launched into a dispute with their record label, Hudson's (the largest distributor of music in Detroit at the time), and fought for their right to have true artistic freedom. Many artists followed suit, citing the MC5 as an example.

2. The trend of offensive band naming is not limited to penis references, as the following list of band names demonstrates: Anal Cunt, Anne Frank and Beans, Cunts, Crucifucks, Dayglo Abortions, Dying Fetus, Hitler's Other Nut, and the Revolting Cocks. Alternatively, a controversial name can work against a band, as the surviving members of Death recall in the documentary *A Band Called Death* (2012). The Hackney brothers actually say they were rejected time and time again because of the name Death, and were even offered a contract contingent on them changing the name. Of course, that was 1971 and most of the more offensive names, listed above, are from the 1980s and later.

3. As a result, his work can be found on album sleeves for the Minutemen, Saccharine Trust, and then later Foo Fighters, Unknown Instructors, Cerebral Ballzy, 1208, Mike Watt, and Sonic Youth, among others.

4. This is by no means meant to be an exhaustive search, but this claim is supported by examples of: the *Apollo Belvedere/Pythian Apollo*; the *Artemision Bronze*; the *Kroisos Kouros*; the *Riace Bronzes*; Agesander, Athenodoros, and Polydorus' *Laocoon and His Sons*; Alexendre Alexandrovitch Deineka's *Shower After the Battle*; Anton Raphael Mengs' *Seated Nude Male*; Antonio Canova's *Apollo Crowning Himself*, *Damoxenos*, *Hercules and Lychas*, *Napoleon as Mars the Peacemaker*, and *Perseus with the Head of Medusa*; Antonio del Pollaiuolo's *Battle of Ten Naked Men*; Apollonios' *Belvedere Torso*; Auguste Rodin's *The Age of Bronze*, *The Kiss*, and *The Thinker*; Baccio Bandinelli's *Hercules and Cacus*; Balthasar Permoser's *Apollo*; Barberini's *Faun/Drunken Satyr*; Benvenuto Cellini's *Persesus with the Head of Medusa*; Bernini's *David* and *The Rape of Prosperpina*; Caravaggio's *Amor Vincit Omnia*, *John the Baptist (John in the Wilderness)*, *John the Baptist (Youth with a Ram)*, and *Sleeping Cupid*; Donatello's *David*; Edvard Munch's *Les baigneurs (Bathers)*; Epigonus' the *Dying Gaul*; Eric Fischl's *Emptying of the Estuary*; Fernando Botero's *Adam*, *Protestant Family*, and *Tribute to Bonnard*; Francois Girardon's *Pluto Abducting Proserpine*; George Minne's *Adolescent* and *Kneeling Youth at the Fountain*; Germaine Richier's *The Storm*; Giambologna's *Rape of the Sabine Women*; Glykon's the *Farnese Hercules*; Hieronymus Bosch's *Garden of Earthly Delights*; Jacopo Pontormo's *Venus and Cupid*; Jan van Scorel's *Venus and Two Cupids*; Jean-Baptiste Pigalle's *Voltaire*; Jean-Francois Millet's *Nude Study*; John De Andrea's *Couple*; John Flaxman's the *Fury of Athamas*; John Singer Sargent's *Reclining Male Nude*; Koloman Moser's *Le Printemps (Spring)*; Leonardo da Vinci's *Anatomy of a Male Nude*, *Coition Figure*, and *Vitruvian Man*; Luca Signorelli's *The Resurrection of the Flesh*; Lucian Freud's *Naked Man with a Rat*, *Naked Man, Back View*, and *Reclining Male*; Marius-Jean-Antonin Mercie's *David*; Masaccio's the *Expulsion of Adam and Eve from Eden*; Michelangelo's *Bacchus*, *Christ*, *David*, *Dying Slave*, *Ignudo*, and *The Creation*; Myron's *Discobolus*; Pablo Picasso's *Les adolescents (Teenagers)*; Paul Cezanne's *Seated Male Nude*; Peter Paul Rubens' *Drunken Hercules*; Philip Pearlstein's *Male and Female Models*; Pierre et Gilles' *Vive La France*; Pierre Puget's *Milon of Croton*; Pierre-Charles Simart's *Orestes Sheltered in the Pallas Altar*; Pietro Faccini's *Man Seated Nude*; Pietro Perugino's *Apollo and Marsyas*; Polykleitos' *Doryphoras*; Praxiteles' *Apollo Saurok tonos*; Rembrandt van Rijn's *Adam and Eva*, *Seated Male Nude*, and *Standing Male*

Nude; Richmond Barthe's *Feral Benga*; Robert Mapplethorpe's *Charles Bownman, NYC*; Sylvia Sleigh's *The Turkish Bath*; Theodore Gericault's *Study of a Male Nude*; and Wolfgang Tillmans' *Kneeling Nude*.

    5. I think few would argue with this claim, but between 1982 and 1985 the following comics are "born": *Love and Rockets, V for Vendetta, AKIRA, Lobo, Peter Pank, Fashion Beast*, etc. Arguments could be made for the underground comix (which I address in the next section) or the earlier examples of *OMAC* (Buddy Blank) (1974), *Judge Dredd* (1977), or issues of, or particular characters from, the *Uncanny X-Men*. But, in terms of the general consensus about "definitive" punk comics, my initial claim stands.

    6. See Bob Adelman's *Tijuana Bibles* and the introductory essay by Art Spiegelman for an excellent discussion of the history of these books, the names, and their far-reaching influence.

    7. Some suggest Tijuana Bibles were first created by bored World War I soldiers longing for female companionship, and others point to soldiers being exposed to overseas pornography as the inspiration.

    8. I use "the 60s" as a rather general starting point, but more specifically I see the start of the underground movement beginning with Frank Stack's *The Adventures of Jesus* (1962) and Jack Jackson's *God Nose* (1964). Crumb's *Fritz the Cat* begins in 1965, *Zap* in 1968, *Jiz, Snatch*, and *Cunt* comics in 1969, and in 1973 the Berkeley Comix Convention is held.

    9. Mark James Estren's *A History of Underground Comics* (1974) does acknowledge a possible link between Tijuana Bibles and the Comix movement, but it's not really until Spiegelman's essay in Adelman's collection that the connection is solidified. Since then, Dez Skinn (2004), Duncan & Smith (2009), and Mazur & Danner (2014), have continued to build on that link and explore the connections in greater detail.

    10. In his foreword to Dez Skinn's *Comix: The Underground Revolution*, p. 6.

    11. One look no further than the popularity and prevalence of Crumb's "Keep On Truckin'" image, or the *Fritz the Cat* films.

    12. See the "Afterword" in the McSweeney edition of *Binky Brown Meets the Holy Virgin Mary*, specifically p. 62.

    13. See "Afterword" in the McSweeney's edition, p. 61.

    14. See *Kurt Vonnegut Letters*.

    15. In my count, I included each individual finger and foot.

WORKS CITED

Alaniz, Jose. "'I Want': Women in post–Soviet Russian Comics." *Ulbandus Review*, vol. 11, 2008, pp. 142–79. *JSTOR*, www.jstor.org/stable/25748187. Accessed 18 Apr. 2014.

Burbey, Mark. "On Comics and Catholics." *Comics Journal*, no. 104, 1986, pp. 37–49.

Chaney, Michael A. "Animal Subjects of the Graphic Novel." *College Literature*, vol. 38, no. 3, 2011, pp. 129–49. *EBSCOhost*, search.ebscohost.com/login.aspx?direct=true&db=eue&AN=508443205&site=ehost-live. Accessed 18 Apr. 2014.

Chute, Hillary. "Our Cancer Year, and: Janet and Me: An Illustrated Story of Love and Loss, and: Cancer Vixen: A True Story, and: Mom's Cancer, and: Blue Pills: A Positive Love Story, and: Epileptic, and: Black Hole (review)." *Literature and Medicine*, vol. 26, no. 2, 2007, pp. 413–29. *Project Muse*. Accessed 7 May 2013.

———. "Temporality and Seriality in Spiegelman's In the Shadow of No Towers." *American Periodicals: A Journal of History, Criticism, and Bibliography*, vol. 17, no. 2, 2007, pp. 228–44. *Project Muse*. Accessed 7 May 2013.

Duncan, Randy, and Matthew J. Smith. *The Power of Comics: History, Form, & Culture*. Continuum, 2009.

El Refaie, Elisabeth. "Life Writing from the Colorful Margins." *Autobiographical Comics: Life Writing in Pictures*, Mississippi UP, 2012, pp. 11–48.

Estren, Mark James. *A History of Underground Comics*. Roni Publishing, 1993.

Foltz, Mary Catherine. "The Excremental Ethics of Samuel R. Delany. *SubStance*, vol. 37, no. 2, 2008, pp. 41–55. *Project Muse*. Accessed 18 Apr. 2014.

Friedman, David M. *A Mind of Its Own: A Cultural History of the Penis*. The Free Press, 2001.

Gardner, Jared. "Autobiography, 1972–2007." *Biography*, vol. 31, no. 1, 2008, pp. 1–26. *Project Muse*. Accessed 7 May 2013.
Green, Justin. "Apocrypha." *Justin Green's Binky Brown Sampler*. Last Gasp, 1995, pp. 78–90.
_____. *Binky Brown Meets the Holy Virgin Mary*. McSweeney's Books, 2009.
_____. "Harvey Kurtzman Tributes." *The Comics Journal*, no. 153, 1992, pp. 70.
_____. "Justin Green's Sketchbook." *The Comics Journal*, no. 152, 1992, pp. 121–25.
Hamilton, Terri. *Skin Flutes & Velvet Gloves*. St. Martin's Press, 2002.
Haslanger, Andrea. "What Happens when Pornography Ends in Marriage: The Uniformity of Pleasure in *Fanny Hill*." *ELH*, vol. 78, no. 1, 2011, pp. 163–88. *Project Muse*. Accessed 18 Apr. 2014.
Hatfield, Charles. *Alternative Comics: An Emerging Literature*. Mississippi UP, 2005.
Levin, Bob. "Rice, Beans, and Justin Green." *Comics Journal*, no. 203, 1998, pp. 101–7.
Levitz, Paul. *The Power of Comics: History, Form, & Culture*. Continuum, 2009.
Manning, Shaun. "Justin Green on 'Binky Brown.'" *Comic Book Resources*, 22 Jan. 2010, http://www.comicbookresources.com/?page=article&id=24518. Accessed 2 Aug. 2012.
Mazur, Dan and Alexander Danner. *Comics: A Global History, 1968 to the Present*. Thames & Hudson Ltd, 2014.
Micciche, Laura R. "Seeing and Reading Incest: A Study of Debbie Drechsler's *Daddy's Girl*." *Rhetoric Review*, vol. 23, no. 1, 2004, pp. 5–20. *EBSCOhost*, search.ebscohost.com/login.aspx?direct=true&db=eue&AN=11960928&site=ehost-live. Accessed 18 Apr. 2014.
Miller, Toby. "A Short History of the Penis." *Social Text*, no. 43, 1995, pp. 1–26. *JSTOR*. Accessed 18 Apr. 2014.
Mitchell, Carol A. "The Sexual Perspective in the Appreciation and Interpretation of Jokes." *Western Folklore*, vol. 36, no. 4, 1977, pp. 303–29. *JSTOR*. Accessed 18 Apr. 2014.
Perper, Timothy, and Martha Cornog. "The Education of Desire: Futari etchi and the Globalization of Sexual Tolerance." *Mechademia*, no. 2, 2007, pp. 201–14. *Project Muse*. Accessed 18 Apr. 2014.
Randall, Jon. "The Goblin Meets Binky Brown Who Met the Holy Virgin Mary." *Goblin*, 2 Aug. 2012, http://www.sonic.net/~goblin/Just.html. Accessed 18 Apr. 2014.
@RaymondPettibon. "Iyt's been fairly consistent; tho pnkrckrs knowledge o my art stops at 15 whtever their age is:50–60 years." 30 Jul. 2014, 9:09 p.m. https://twitter.com/RaymondPettibon/status/494666237561954304.
_____. "They chose them frm 100's.Not my proclivity.I by no means called the shots.The dck is like the letter "I"to me." 30 Jul. 2014, 3:17 p.m. https://twitter.com/RaymondPettibon/status/494577431303311360.
_____. "Yes Fugs;have some o their records somewhere.AndJustin Green is my favrite of socalld Underground comic.Will do collabo." 31 Jul. 2014, 7:06 a.m., https://twitter.com/RaymondPettibon/status/494816462130122752.
Renne, Elisha P. "Condom use and the popular press in Nigeria." *Health Transition Review*, vol. 3, no.1, 1993, pp. 41–56. *JSTOR*. Accessed 18 Apr. 2014.
Rollins, Henry. "The Art of Punk—Black Flag." *YouTube*, uploaded by The Museum of Contemporary Art, Los Angeles, 11 Jun. 2013, http://youtu.be/N0u04EqNVjo?t=18m17s.
Rosenkranz, Patrick. "The ABCs of Autobio Comix." *The Comics Journal*, 6 Mar. 2011, http://www.tcj.com/the-abcs-of-auto-bio-comix-2/. Accessed 2 Aug. 2012.
Ruffel, Ian. "Humiliation?: Voyeurism, Violence, and Humor in Old Comedy." *Helios*, vol. 40, no.1–2, 2013, pp. 247–77. *Project Muse*. Accessed 18 Apr. 2014.
Seizer, Susan. "On the Uses of Obscenity in Live Stand-up Comedy." *Anthropological Quarterly*, vol. 84, no.1, 2011, pp. 209–34. *Project Muse*. Accessed 18 Apr. 2014.
Shannon, Edward. "Shameful, Impure Art: Robert Crumb's Autobiographical Comics and the Confessional Poets." *Biography*, vol. 35, no. 4, 2012, pp. 627–49. *Project Muse*. Accessed 7 May 2013.
Shulman, Robert. "The Serious Functions of Melville's Phallic Jokes." *American Literature*, vol. 33, no. 2, 1961, pp. 179–94. *JSTOR*. 18 Apr. 2014.
Skinn, Dez. *Comix: The Underground Revolution*. Thunder's Mouth Press, 2004.
Spiegelman, Art. "Symptoms of Disorder/Signs of Genius." *Justin Green's Binky Brown Sampler*. Last Gasp, 1995, pp. 4–6.

Stehle, Eva. "The Body and its Representations in Aristophanes' Thesmophoriazousai: Where Does the Costume End?" *American Journal of Philology*, vol. 123, no. 3, 2002, pp. 369–406. *Project Muse*. 18 Apr. 2014.

Van Driel, Mels. *Manhood: The Rise and Fall of the Penis*. Translated by Paul Vincent, Reaktion Books Ltd., 2009.

Von Bisack, Richard. "Memoirs of a Catholic Boyhood: The Birth of the Comic Book Autobiography." *Metroactive Arts*, 12 Oct. 1995, http://www.metroactive.com/papers/metro/10.12.95/comics-9541.html. Accessed 2 Aug. 2012.

Whitlock, Gillian, and Anna Poletti. "Self-Regarding Art." *Biography*, vol. 31, no. 1, 2008, pp. v-xxiii. *Project Muse*. Accessed 7 May 2013.

Witek, Joseph. "Justin Green: Autobiography Meets the Comics." *Graphic Subjects*, edited by Michael A. Chaney, Wisconsin UP, 2011, pp. 227–230.

Reinventing a Carnivalesque Public Sphere

(Re)imagining and (Re)drawing Madrid in the Long 1970s

LOUIE DEAN VALENCIA-GARCÍA

In 1975 the catchphrase "Generalissimo Franco is still dead" entered the American lexicon after being featured in a satirical newscast on the television show *Saturday Night Live*. The skit mocked the American news media for its obsession with the dictator; in the mid–1970s, all eyes were on Spain. After 40 years of rule, both Spaniards and the outside world watched as Madrid, a grey city under Franco, became the center of both a young democracy and a vibrant punk scene. This youth culture, which finds its roots in the 1960s, a period in which young Spaniards first started challenging the authoritarian regime, reflected a mixture of sexual liberalization, a rejection of the perceived "backwardness" of the Francoist dictatorship, a reinvention of native Iberian pluralistic traditions, and a burgeoning global youth culture that connected the New York Underground, British punks, Californian hippies, and Spanish *frikis* and *punkis* (freaks and punks). In the years just before the dictator's death in 1975, young Spaniards began to create an underground scene that challenged Spanish normativity vis-à-vis creative expression, clandestine gatherings, explicit comic books, street drinking, sex, drugs, and punk rock—resurrecting a "carnivalesque" tradition in what became known as the *Movida Madrileña*, or the Madrid Scene. In this essay, I will first explore punk culture as carnivalesque, then I will analyze the creation of a punk culture and describe the role carnivalesque comic books played in allowing young Spaniards to imagine alternatives to the dictatorship, teaching them how to subvert the Francoist regime through producing, distributing, and reading punk comics.

Setting the Stage

In the aftermath of the Spanish Civil War in 1939, Francisco Franco's newly installed fascist dictatorship banned the centuries-old tradition of carnival, the often-debaucherous period leading up to the Catholic tradition of Lent, a six-week period of fasting and reflection in preparation for the Easter celebration. During the carnival festival, Spaniards from the largest cities to the smallest *pueblos* would drink, dance, and subvert social norms in preparation for the solemn Easter holiday. Carnival allowed people to "let out steam" before having to undergo the restrictions of the Lenten season. However, as a result of the nearly three decades of suppression, by 1965, as noted anthropologist Julio Caro Baroja declared, the carnival celebration was essentially dead in Spain; Caro Baroja saw no hope for its revival (25).

While punk culture has often been associated with anti-authoritarian tendencies in other parts of the world, the Spanish case provides a unique example in which an *actual* authoritarian regime was pitted against a subversive punk culture. Aesthetically resembling the child of British punk and Warholian pop, this underground Spanish youth culture drew influences from Patti Smith, Pablo Picasso, Joan Miró, Woody Allen, Arthur Rimbaud, Joy Division, and Robert Crumb, to name a few. By the mid–70s, Madrid had begun its transformation into a Dionysian party scene.

The *Movida*, also called "la nueva ola española" (Spanish New Wave), was a hybrid Spanish youth culture of the mid–1970s that drew from the New York Underground, British punk, Barcelonese hippie culture, and native Spanish traditions—reminiscent of the bricolage punk style described by Dick Hebdige in his *Subculture: The Meaning of Style*. Elsewhere, Hebdige has described youth culture, and the teenager (what the Spanish would call *adolescente*), as a "permanent wedge between childhood and adulthood" (*Hiding* 29). Hebdige writes:

> The wedge means money. The invention of the teenager is intimately bound up with the creation of the youth market. Eventually a new range of commodities and commercial leisure facilities are provided to absorb the surplus cash which for the first time working-class youth is calculated to have at its disposal to spend on itself and to provide a space within which youth can construct its own immaculate identities untouched by the soiled and compromised imaginaries of the parent culture [*Hiding* 29–30].

The *Movida*, and the youth culture surrounding it, functioned to both separate young people from the previous generation and create a new space for what would become a youth-based consumer culture. The *Movida*'s association and intersections with marginal and working class culture even created a generation of young people that saw a way of self-identification that existed outside of class and gender norms, and, at times, even ethnic divisions. Even though many of the participants of the *Movida* often came from middle class or élite backgrounds, most of them had experienced some sort of repression by the conservative, authoritarian regime. In response to this repression, Spanish punk subculture exhumed a suppressed carnivalesque tradition, functioning to transgress rigid societal norms in Franco's Spain. In effect, young Spaniards created a post-modern variation to the traditional carnival, borrowing their aesthetic from punk culture to express their rejection of Francoism. Unlike the annual carnivals of old, which lasted just a week, the *Movida* acted as a discharge for decades of pent-up suppression.

The Appeal of Punk as Carnivalesque: The Place of Popular Culture and the Grotesque

Taking from Mikhail Bakhtin's analysis of the place, nature, and importance of the carnivalesque, Peter Stallybrass and Allon White's *The Politics and Poetics of Transgression* translates Bakhtin's theories into a framework and praxis that is not only useful for historical analysis, but brings into focus the central role of that which is "grotesque," or of "low culture," as a necessary component for understanding systems of power, urban life, and economic spheres. The study does not merely translate Bahktin's theories, but rather, removes those theories from an ageless model separated from historical analysis to further demonstrate the struggles involved in the production of culture in contentious or ambiguous places within a society. The authors argue, "The bourgeois subject continuously defined and re-defined itself throughout the exclusion of what is marked out as 'low'—as dirty, repulsive, noisy, contaminating. Yet that very act of exclusion was constitutive of its identity. The low was internalized under the sign of negation and disgust" (191). Stallybrass and White go on to explain that bourgeois culture is, in fact, historically rooted in carnivalesque (and working class) culture, despite the bourgeoisie's desire to reject working class culture. For the authors, the bourgeois coffee shop, a place of democratic dialogue, is rooted in working class (and peasant) carnivalesque culture.

Stallybrass and White convincingly argue that cafés, too, find their origins in the tradition of the bars, taverns, and other seedy places where people with different experiences interact. Indeed, the bourgeois carnival celebrations of Venice, Italy evidence how the rising bourgeoisie transformed a folk carnivalesque tradition into a decadent celebration that became more associated with the middle (and even aristocratic) class than the working class. Whether seen in the middle class cafés of Madrid or the haute fêtes of the

Venetian carnival, the bourgeoisie can both define itself against a "filthy" culture, or appropriate and "gentrify" the carnivalesque culture of the lower classes to suit its needs. In the case of the *Movida*, that "filth" came to represent a rejection of traditional Catholicism and the Franco regime.

This understanding of how the bourgeoisie can both appropriate and define itself against carnivalesque "filth" is important to consider in order to understand how "punk rock" in Spain developed as an intersection between bourgeois and working class youth cultures. Spanish punk culture's connection to filth was evident in the early translations of "punk" as "rock *macarra*"— *macarra* being an insult used to describe vulgar, low culture often associated with marginal(ized) people. In fact, Diego Manrique's punk how-to-guide from 1977, *De Qué Va el Rock Macarra*, explicitly emphasizes the use of "macarra" as a translation for "punk" while simultaneously using a "punk rock" sticker on the cover (see Figure 1). Spanish punks, of all classes, were attracted to the idea of their culture as low culture, as filthy, vulgar, and disruptive to Francoist constructions of gender, sexuality, class, and nationalism—in other words, carnivalesque.

The Revival of the Spanish Carnivalesque: Identity, Counterpublics and Imagining a Community

In order to understand the underground scene depicted in Spanish punk comics, as well as the role of comic books in the *Movida*, first it is helpful to look at the types of spaces in which those comics circulated. The emergence of the *Movida* engendered a period of tension between the old guard of the regime and a new generation of young people who had no memory of the Spanish Civil War—a generation that looked toward both Spanish pluralistic traditions of old and to a budding global youth culture, embodied by punk. The *Movida* represented a shift in what was accepted as normative expressions of gender and sexuality—particularly dangerous to the patriarchal regime. The *Movida* sustained nearly a decade of sexually transgressive behavior as young Spaniards revived the moribund tradition of subverting authority through carnivalesque performance—all once common in Spanish carnivals. Like in carnival, cross-dressing, public nudity, partying, and drug-induced celebration fueled the *Movida Madrileña*.

The *Movida* was not an organized movement, but was an intersection of antiauthoritarian tendencies operating from what I call "carnivalesque counterpublics." In *Publics and Counterpublics* Michael Warner defines "counterpublics" as "…by definition, formed by their conflict with the norms and

138   Part III: Underground Punk Comics

Figure 1: Image from *De Qué Va el Rock Macarra* by Diego A. Manrique, La Piqueta, 1977 (courtesy Diego A. Manrique).

contexts of their cultural environment, and this context of domination inevitably entails distortion. Mass publics and counterpublics, in other words, are both damaged forms of publicness, just as gender and sexuality are, in this culture, damaged forms of privacy" (63). Moreover, Warner describes counterpublics as forming through "an address to indefinite strangers," different from a community or group (120). Warner further argues that "...counterpublic discourse also addresses those strangers as being not just anybody. They are socially marked by their participation in this kind of discourse; ordinary people are presumed not to want to be mistaken for the kind of person who would participate in this kind of talk or be present in this kind of scene" (120). For Warner, a counterpublic exists as an alternative to a dominant public sphere; however, is it not exclusively limited to subaltern spaces. It is located in the public sphere. Counterpublics require active participation. A counterpublic is not necessarily a group of anarchists cohabiting together, a Roma street market, or young socialists organizing a protest—but they *could* all be part of an underground scene. Counterpublics are composed of participants who are active in producing, reading, and distributing cultural practices that act against dominant culture *in* the public sphere. Counterpublics require a "scene."

While "*movida*" is often translated as "movement," I use the alternate translation of "scene," as *movida* implies a (re)appropriation of physical places to create interconnected spaces for "happenings," i.e., drugs, concerts, parties, art exhibits, or even street drinking. As such, any of these "happenings" might become "carnivalesque counterpublics" where a carnivalesque inversion of the hegemonic public sphere can take place. The carnivalesque scene (made up of these counterpublics) intersects with, operates parallel to, and acts against the hegemonic public sphere. A "scene" further implies mobility, ephemerality, interconnectedness, and commonality in the spaces and places that make up the scene. For example, a young Spaniard of the period would ask, "Where is the *Movida* tonight?" Similar to other punk cultures, the *Movida* was not a cohesive social or political movement—although it certainly had many social and political implications. In many ways, the *Movida* represented an aesthetic of dissent, always moving and changing.

The extension of this transgressive and post-modern youth culture throughout Spain not only subverted Franco's controlling regime, but also exemplified the ways young people adopted new technologies to spread their pluralistic message through new and adapted media. By the time Franco died, not only were young subversives already creating their own newspapers, fanzines, films, and comic books that implicitly, if not outright, criticized the regime, but their underground culture also had a following that would grow exponentially by the time the Spanish Constitution of 1978 was ratified. By creating and consuming material such as transgressive comic books, young

Spaniards were able to imagine what the world might look like without the oppressive chains of an authoritarian régime. By the end of the 1970s, young people were partying in the streets—making real a carnivalesque culture that subverted the ideals of the conservative regime through a culture of drugs, sex, drinking, and art performed in the streets of Madrid. These young Spaniards had begun to act out the scenes previously only imagined in the pages of zines and comics from imported American comics and those self-produced in Spain.

Before punks could create their scene they had to first imagine it. The images in punk comics not only allowed young people to imagine what an antiauthoritarian culture might look like, but those counternormative images gave young people a language and aesthetic with which to identify. In the long twentieth century, young European urbanites have attempted to carve out spaces for themselves in their society while simultaneously trying to gain recognition of their own subjectivity by those same authorities that they might even reject. Unlike adults, young people generally do not own property, and are thus restricted to spaces they are "given" by their caretakers, "public" spaces that are allotted to them, or spaces that they have (re)appropriated for themselves. As a result, young people tend to inhabit marginal, and arguably queer, spaces within society. Moreover, in modernity, young people have a propensity to "imagine" spaces (and what Benedict Anderson would call "imagined communities") where they can demonstrate agency—creating counterpublics. From these counterpublics, they dictate both rules and norms, most obviously seen in European mod, hippie, and punk youth culture of the post-war years. From these marginal spaces young people can, in effect, imagine "virtual" spaces from which they can forge counterpublics—creating the possibility of subversion of hegemonic power,[1] authority and normativity.[2] A carnivalesque scene allows for ephemeral spaces where normative social roles can be subverted. These punk comic books allowed young Spaniards to adopt an aesthetic of transgression against the dictatorship—appropriating dress, attitude, and scene from the New York Underground and British punks. While often the lyrics to the punk songs might have escaped young Spaniards, the style and the affect of punk culture certainly came through. The subversive, confrontational message was clear.

Making a Scene: From Carnivalesque Space to Public Sphere

As a colonizing force, fascism necessitates an active destruction, or assimilation, of competing systems of power to impose its own hierarchical structure. During both the Spanish Civil War and its aftermath, Franco's regime recognized a need to disrupt the populist networks (Republican, Anarcho-syndicalist, Socialist, and Communist) that would have challenged the dictatorship, effectively preventing contestation to Franco's power by disassembling the Spanish public sphere. To accomplish this, through surveillance by secret police, the regime created a state in which people policed themselves in places that traditionally incubated dissent, such as cafés, bars, and universities. Spaces that were especially transgressive toward authority, that allowed carnivalesque celebrations, were made illegal. In the 1940s, the dictatorship instituted requirements that mandated that all film, music, and publications go through a process of censorship—effectively disrupting normal sociality and information flow under the emergent dictatorship.

However, by the 1970s, since young people had over a decade of experience trading and distributing banned superhero comic books under the dictatorship, many young people grew up hiding comics from authorities. Moreover, increasingly fewer and fewer young people even bothered to submit their publications for censorship.[3] The *Movida* represents what I describe as a "subversive horizontal network" composed of counterpublics, nodes that created an underground network that undermined Francoist values, developing into the Madrid Scene. This network facilitated the production and distribution of the underground comic books of the *Movida* in three ways. Firstly, comics of higher quality were often published by independent, small presses that would send those comics to various local printers for publication—these works were often more experimental and transgressive. While many initially were produced in small numbers, many "pirated" photocopied editions often appeared. Secondly, comic anthology magazines were also common, usually composed of both imported, translated comic books (often without accreditation) in conjunction with comics produced by Spaniards. Many of the Spanish writers and artists of these anthology magazines, such as *Star*, *El Vibora*, and *Madriz*, were later featured in youth oriented magazines such as *La Luna de Madrid* (*The Moon of Madrid*), arguably the most prominent publication of the *Movida*. Last, comics were also often found in the dozens of cheaply produced, photocopied fanzines. Distribution of all these comics ranged from formal to informal spaces. Some comics/fanzines were sold at locally owned record stores and bookstores; others were sold by hand at bars and clubs. Many were traded amongst friends or cheaply copied using Xerox machines.

Much like the early printing press, as described by Benedict Anderson in his *Imagined Communities: Reflections on the Origin and Spread of Nationalism*, these zines and DIY comics allowed members of the punk community to imagine a broader community of subversives to which they belonged. Comics were particularly important because of their inherent visual nature; they allowed young people to imagine (and create) spaces and an aesthetic that stood counter to Francoism. Drawing from these images from punk cultures abroad, young Spaniards turned everyday spaces into places from which they could act out agency. They were able to create an expanding scene (or network) of interconnected people and ideas (seen in the cultural production of comics, music, poetry, etc.) from which a counternormative public sphere was able to emerge, culminating in rejection of Francoism through a valorization of carnivalesque, punk norms that intentionally subverted the regime.

Whereas this transgressive behavior previously might have played out in the cafés and universities, under the dictatorship, it showed up first in comic books and cheap photocopies that allowed Spaniards to *visually* imagine alternatives to Franco's Spain. The copy machine, like the printing press before it, allowed for a rapid construction of the punk identity in the imagination of its participants, what Benedict Anderson calls "simultaneity" (22–26). More importantly, as Anderson might argue, these comics provided a language and "imagined community" with which antiauthoritarian youth could identify; it even gave them a word to describe themselves, "punk." Not only was punk media produced and distributed by young people, but it also took advantage of new technologies that allowed for them to produce media that was both affordable and easily distributed—such as the Xerox machine. Moreover, photocopied comics and zines allowed for young people to self-publish material that was not easily censored by the fascist state. While in a limited sense these comics were affected by a capitalist system (Xerox was, after all, a large international company), photocopied comics such as *La Piraña Divina* (1975) were often printed at the lowest cost possible, using cheap paper and printing, and without the intention of profit. An edition of *La Piraña Divina* was even published and circulated (photocopied without authorization) in the Netherlands in 1977. By reading, photocopying, and passing along these comics European punk comics were able to develop a language and culture for themselves that stood in opposition to the Francoist system.

Unlike hierarchies, or vertical systems of power, subversive horizontal networks function like nodes in a graph, bouncing through a hierarchical structure that is slow to move and adapt to new ways of subverting said structure. That is to say, the rigid structures of the dictatorship were ill prepared to deal with the new ways young people created subversive spaces. While not all these nodes (or counterpublics) connect, they are still traceable and operate from spaces where power is absent. When left alone, hidden from hegemonic power, these nodes can act as counterpublics from which hegemonic structures can be subverted—using what Michel De Certeau calls "tactics" of subversion (39). When a significant number of these counterpublics are connected, hegemonic power structures can be subverted, forcing power structures to change. In a post-structural world, even the hegemonic structures we imagine are composed of networks that are constantly "re-assembling"[4] and competing with each other—constructing what we imagine to be unmoving structures. These carnivalesque scenes subvert social norms and authority, presenting a stage (or scene) for what amounts to an inversion of acceptable behavior. While Bakhtin argues that the carnivalesque ultimately reinforces hegemonic power, the question must also be asked what happens when the carnivalesque is suppressed into hiding, where authority is absent over decades? Can the carnivalesque, in fact, produce social change? Can these seemingly disparate carnivalesque tactics against dominant culture affect change if continually, publicly, and consistently acted out over time?

The comics and zines of the *Movida* produced an alternate model and created a style and aesthetic that allowed for those participants to identify each other—appropriating the antiauthoritarian, punk aesthetic for themselves. Within the pages of Spanish punk comics an alternative way of living life was imagined, one that left out the Catholic Church and the Francoist state. Nancy Frazier describes "subaltern counterpublics" as "parallel discursive arenas where members of subordinated social groups invent and circulate counter-discourses, which in turn permit them to formulate oppositional interpretations of their identities, interests, and needs" (67). In what amounts to privileging political narrative, most historical treatments of the Spanish transition from authoritarian rule to democracy have tended to rely primarily on the Francoist state's perspective of the role of young people, continuing to marginalize counter narratives, rather than considering the subjectivity of young people themselves. This top-down approach situates youth movements within a more general political milieu, but doesn't consider political change as being the product of youth culture.

Clashing with Fascism: Disrupting Patriarchal Authority

The formation of an underground culture that emerged under the Franco regime sheds light on a palpable shift from the conservative culture to the popularization of a transgressive and carnivalesque culture where constructions of Spanishness, patriarchy, and heteronormativity were not only subverted, but also ultimately transformed. While the carnivalesque nature of the *Movida* certainly became more visible during the years after Franco's death, by looking at the cultural production of young people during the first half of the 1970s, scholars can see a burgeoning movement that was actively attempting to (de)construct gender roles, Spanish identity, and power relationships through the depiction of counter-normative ideologies transmitted through punk comics, zines, music, and film.

Madrid's punk *Movida* owed a debt to the post-hippie/pre-punk culture of Barcelona's own underground subculture, "*el Rrollo*," which cultivated an underground comic book culture that eventually spread across Spain. As early as 1973, 1,000 copies of the comic *El Rrollo Enmascarado*, or "*The Masked Rrollo*," were printed in Barcelona—arguably, the first comic of the Spanish Underground. *El Rrollo Enmascarado* was both named after the movement and solidified the appellation popularly. "Rrollo" can be translated as both an atmosphere, a general subject matter, and a way of being. As per infamously strict censorship regulations, the artists behind *El Rrollo*, the two brothers "Farry" and "Pepichek" (Miquel and Josep Farriol), along with Javier Mariscal and Nazario Luque Vera, had to submit the publication to Francoist authorities for approval. While the strict Francoist censorship laws had loosened by the 1970s, to play it safe the collective claimed that only 300 copies were printed, keeping the number low to avoid suspicion—although thousands of copies would eventually be printed.[5] Without delay, authorities confiscated the 300 issues, and charged the writers and artists with "public scandal" and "immorality" for the "depraved" images and scatological content found in the comic. Despite the charges, the authors still clandestinely sold the work.

At trial, the young men were, surprisingly, found innocent of the crimes on the claim that they had no malicious intent. As previously mentioned, even seemingly puerile superhero comics, such as *Superman*, had been banned until the 1970s.[6] Here, even though the comics were drawn and produced by the collective, the judge found that their "immoral" and "depraved" images were not made with malicious intent. This loosening of state controlled censorship had, in fact, started in the late 1960s with the passing of new laws that gave more autonomy to publishers, such as the *Ley de la Prensa* of 1966. While there was a provision that stated children's books had to undergo censorship, *El Rrollo Enmascarado* included on its cover three key phrases, "Only for select minorities," "Only for progressive adults," and "Total or partial reproduction of this "rrollo" is permitted." In effect, the trial concluded that these "adult" comics were being produced by adolescents who didn't know better. This effectively gave the green light for what would be the first wave of Spanish underground culture. Indeed, at least 45 different comics/zines were identified as originating in Madrid in the second half of the 1970s alone.[7] Young people who produced these comics and zines existed in an ambiguous space—not quite responsible for breaking the rules.

Inspired in style and content by the work of Robert Crumb and the New York Underground, *El Rrollo Enmascarado* presents *historietas groseras*—tales of sex, drugs, and partying. One transgressive comic even offers a critique of the homophobia ubiquitous in Spanish society. The untitled two-page comic featured in *El Rrollo Enmascarado*, dated 1973, features a man being followed by strangers through the streets of an unnamed city. The protagonist's internal dialogue reads: "I have to be careful. They say the city is full of them./Oh, no! Here's one!/Maybe he won't see me./He's looking at me with a fixed stare. He is coming closer!" (n.p.). The unnamed protagonist finds himself face to face with a man that looks to be holding *something* in his hands, between his legs; the naïve protagonist takes off running. The man reaches a dead end, and finds himself surrounded by three men ... trying to sell him lottery tickets so they can pay for an end-of-semester holiday. The comic, while playing on a fear of homosexuality, suggests to the reader that one should be more afraid of salesmen's (read: capitalists') shenanigans than queer men. *El Rrollo Enmascarado* glorifies sex-capades, and successfully pushes the envelope of normative taste. While many of these stories would hardly be considered feminist, any expression of a libertine sexuality *was* considered transgressive. Once that sexuality was freely exhibited, a conversation about the role of women, and feminism could begin.

In 1976 Producciones Editoriales, a Barcelona-based publisher famous for printing the monthly underground comic magazine, *Star*, published *El Comix Marginal Español*, which collected the work of marginal comics artists and writers across Spain. *El Comix Marginal Español* worked to both define what an underground in Spain might look like, but also to draw specific connections to a global underground youth culture. The introduction of this comic not only gives a heavy nod to the American underground comics that influenced the genre, but simultaneously acknowledges those artists' attempts to use comic books to critique American imperialism from within. Referring to the United States as "Yanquilandia" ("yankee-land"), a not-so-uncommon jibe at the U.S., *El Comix Marginal Español* simultaneously lauds the likes of New York artist Robert Crumb. At the same time, the introduction also critiques the French underground for its elitist tendencies. The comic praises the hippie movement, and decries a consumerist society that is obsessed with consumption. The 176-page tome not only gives space to introduce artists and writers in Spain, but also acts to create a Who's Who of young Spanish comic writers. It is an introduction to a Spanish Underground and a map of the scene.

Historia de la Censura, published in 1977 by Manuel Quinto and the artist Esparbe, even uses the comic form to re-open a dialogue about censorship by outlining a graphic history of censorship, starting with ancient Egypt and Greece, moving through the Renaissance and Modernism, and bringing that history to the Franco dictatorship. Heavy in both text and comic depictions, the comic demonstrates that by 1977 not only could a dialogue be started about censorship, but that the dialogue was already happening in a genre that primarily targeted young people. Esparbe's rough lines not only reflect a punk aesthetic, but they also appeal to both audiences that would be interested in a sequential art narrative and a more traditional textual analysis.

Vicios Modernos, or "Modern Vices," a black and white comic produced by Spanish artists Ceesepe (Carlos Sánchez Pérez) and Alberto García-Alix between the months of March and May of 1978, nearly half a year before the Spanish Constitution of 1978 was finalized or ratified, featured exactly what its title promised: a graphic guide to modern vices: sex, drugs and partying. While the cover features a young punk rocker smoking a joint, a stylized depiction of García-Alix himself, the more explicit scenes within the work show sex, heroin use, and even drug overdose. Other scenes include: the protagonist dreaming of having sex with a nun, an all nude female punk group taking a concert stage, explicit drug use, masturbation, street drinking, and dance. In one celebratory confessional scene, a man claims to have more alcohol than blood in his veins, a woman claims to have more than 30 venereal diseases, and a man claims to have sex with "momma's boys," such as himself. An anonymous crowd of attractive people claim to be a lost generation of "pimps, whores and faggots." The story then disappears back into a dreamlike chaos composed of sex and drugs, in an aesthetic style that distinctly resembles a sort of convergence of 1950s Americana mixed with British punk style, with its rockabilly hair, spiked hair, and heavy leather. While some of the depictions of women in *Vicios Modernos* might seemingly overly sexualize women, unlike many works of the period, the message in this comic is explicitly queer and feminist—challenging normative constructions of sexuality. Images of male nudity and masturbation also appear. This nudity acts more so to transgress the boundaries of the public/private spheres. Depicting carnivalesque party scenes, many of underground comics of the period, like *Vicios Modernos*, brought those taboos that had been long suppressed under the regime into the public sphere. Notably, the drawings in *Vicios Modernos* are based on García-Alix's own photography, but were rendered graphically as a psychedelic comic by Ceesepe. Together, the two formed the arts collective "Cascorro Factory," inspired by Andy Warhol's "Factory," and named after the Madrid plaza of the same name in which they lived. Stylistically, *Vicios Modernos* is reminiscent of the punk comic "The Legend of Nick Detroit," a comic narrative depicted with photographs by John Holmstrom, featuring the likes of punk rockers Richard Hell, David Byrne, and Debbie Harry.

While the aforementioned comics were produced by young people living in Spain, most of the punk comics of the era were not exclusively dedicated to the work of Spaniards. More often than not most underground comics would inevitably have at least one imported British or American comic featured. In fact, *Nick Detroit* was reprinted and translated in the second issue of the Spanish punk comic series *Rock Comix*—a semi-regular title that often reprinted American and British punk comics, but also released original content. The translation of Holstrom's comic appeared in Spain the same year as its original publication, 1976—although the Spanish comic did not credit its original source, *Punk Magazine* issue #6. Despite the dictatorship, Spain was far from isolated from British and American punk culture. *Punk Magazine* issue #6 had arrived particularly early to Spain, being transported, translated and published that same year. Each edition of the Spanish *Rock Comix* was dedicated to a particular artist or genre, from Frank Zappa, to Lou Reed to Pink Floyd and "Californian rock" to the Rolling Stones. One issue, a Lou Reed tribute by Spanish artist and writer Nazario Luque, was used as the cover art in Lou Reed's live album, *Take No Prisoners*. Spanish punk comics both borrowed from other punk sources, but also influenced the broader punk movement by connecting the antiauthoritarian punk message to international audiences.

The mid–1970s represented a noticeable shift toward an explicit appropriation of the punk aesthetic. *Vicios Modernos* and *Rock Comix* were not the only places where intersections between different types of visual culture such as photography and comic books could be found. Young Spaniards of the mid–1970s also were seeing photographs of the British punk scenes from which they could draw (in both senses of the word). One example of this, the photographic collection *Punk*, by Salvador Costa, was published in 1977 by Producciones Editoriales (the publisher of *El Comix Marginal Español*) after Costa had visited London the year before. The work visually brings its reader into the British punk scene with its patchwork, pinned together aesthetic—underlined by a love of filth (even featuring a filthy looking WC on its cover.

Moreover, *Vicios Modernos* was published in conjunction with another collective known as *La Banda de Moebius*, edited by Javier Rodríguez de Fonseca and Juan Luís Recio. *La Banda de Moebius* produced dozens of short texts visually drawn from the punk aesthetic, even featuring the work of comic artists such as Ceesepe. The publications of *La Banda de Moebius* were mostly small, portable editions that contained themes that were sometimes political, sometimes literary, often both, and always graphically appealing. They wrote about everything from poetic tributes to John Lennon at the time of his death to the communist manifestos and treatises on contemporary Middle Eastern politics.

In fact, Ceesepe, Alix, and Rodríguez de Fonseca and Recio all met and collaborated in such a place where such "modern vices" were well practiced, a bar called *La Vaquería*, poetically located on a street named "Libertad," or "Liberty," in what is now Madrid's gay neighborhood, Chueca. In places such as the *Vaquería* bar, which opened in 1974, groups of young people experimented with art, music, poetry, literature, sex and debauchery. The locale was even featured in the underground comic *Carajillo*, a 1975 comic published in Madrid, which depicted it as a place to find libertine thinkers (see Figures 2 and 3).[8] In effect, such counterpublics helped create a stage to experiment with the freedom that participants did not yet have outside those places. In an interview I conducted with Emilio Sola, one of the bar's founders, he described the bar as a place where sex, drugs, poetry, and music could find a home—even offering room for writers and artists to live and work. The artist Ceesepe even painted a mural on the doors that led into the bar. According to an interview I held with the editors of the *Vicios Modernos*, Javier Rodríguez de Fonseca and Juan Luís Recio, who themselves were in their twenties at the time of its publication, the texts were distributed in cafés, bars, universities and in the famous Madrid street market, *El Rastro*—known for second-hand goods being sold by Spanish Roma, as well as an extensive underground comic and fanzine publication scene that ran largely under-regulated on Sunday mornings in the working class neighborhood *La Latina*. In that same street market, a group of kids created a collective, *Liviandad del Imperdible*, and dedicated themselves to comic books, music, poetry, and challenging social norms. The members created their own comics and translated foreign comics. After a time, many of those members of *Liviandad* left and reformed as *Kaka De Luxe*, or "Crap De Luxe," a collaboration by Fernando Márquez, Manolo Campoamor, Carlos Berlanga, Enrique Sierra, Olvido "Alaska" Gara Jova, and Nacho Canut. What started as a fanzine dedicated to comic books, theory, and music later metamorphosed into the mythic Spanish New Wave punk band of the same name. Initially known for a raw, unpracticed punk-pop style, *Kaka* dissolved, transforming into the Spanish pop group sensations *Paraíso* and *Alaska y los Pegamoides*,[9] protagonists of the music of the *Movida*. Alaska, the daughter of a Cuban mother and a Spanish Civil War exile, grew up in México and arrived in Spain in her teenage years to become the queen of the *Movida*—demonstrating the important role of women in taking back the public sphere.[10] The transformation of *Liviandad* to *Kaka* to *Paraíso* and *Alaska y los Pegamoides* mirrors the different phases of Spanish punk, from *El Rrollo* to Spanish New Wave to the *Movida*. Transforming from fans of the punk aesthetic to musicians and representatives of the *Movida*, the members of Kaka de Luxe reflected an actualization of the punk aesthetic into the real world—no longer just imagined.

The representation of women and queer characters in these comics worked to displace heteronormativity. One fanzine published in 1980, *96 Lágrimas*, even featured short comics that depicted the punk scene as feminist, or at least recognized the need for feminism to combat a traditionally sexist patriarchy. Like *Vicios Modernos*, *Lágrimas*' scenes showed young

Figures 2 and 3: Images from the underground comic *Carajillo*, a 1975 comic published in Madrid by Juan Rodriguez Ortega, which depicted "the *Vaquería* bar, which opened in 1974, [where] groups of young people experimented with art, music, poetry, literature, sex and debauchery," as a place "to find libertine thinkers. In effect, such counterpublics helped create a stage to experiment with the freedom that participants did not yet have outside those places" (11–12) (courtesy Juan Rodriguez Ortega).

women walking the streets, dressed in punk clothing, and surrounded by music. In the story, a young woman is raped. Upon returning home, the survivor joins with other woman as they search out the rapist to teach him a lesson. *Lágrimas*, and zines like it, reinforced the image of the vibrant punk scene that was inclusive and feminist. While it might be a chicken-egg sort of question, which came first, the representation or the carnivalesque places, it becomes obvious that the two did indeed help propagate and reify the myth of such a libertine scene—further inspiring the creation of more carnivalesque places.

(Re)imagining a Public Sphere

Henri Lefebvre, when discussing the childlike nature of Symbolist French poet Arthur Rimbaud, writes that a childlike perspective allows young people, and those with childlike perspectives, to see animals, angels and incredible cities where most people only see the ordinary. Lefebvre explains that for children, and/or those with young *mentalities* such as Rimbaud, "the word 'image' takes on a new meaning, working on two levels, that of the senses and that of the mind or the dream. In this heightened confusion of the abstract and the concrete, symbol and sensation are no longer distinguishable" (109). Punk comics, and the aesthetic depicted in those comics, provided young Spaniards a model with which to imagine a new Spain.

In the aftermath of the dictatorship, real life began to slowly reflect the images found in the comic books, as seen in one famous mid–1970s photo by Félix Lorrio, from a celebration in Madrid's Plaza de Dos de Mayo, in which nudity is prominently celebrated as young people climbed a triumphal arch located in the plaza in an explosion of Dionysian revelry. The scene, published in May of 1977 in the leftist magazine *Triunfo*, as described by *Movida* scribe Eduardo Haro Ibars, remarkably resembled the cover of *Rock Comix*'s reprinted collection, S*an Reprimonio y las Pirañas*, a 1976 special edition of Nazario Luque's earlier works. The cover features nude people, young and old, dancing around a statue, as framed by a triumphal arch. While the naked young people might not have been specifically thinking of Nazario's work when climbing the statue, in a plaza famous for initiating a Spanish revolt against Napoleon in the nineteenth century, the aesthetic surely resonated.

Spanish punk comics, in effect, allowed young Spaniards to imagine sexuality and sociality in a way that had been effectively banned under the regime—rooted in the hedonistic and carnivalesque. This gave young Spaniards the ability to imagine a scene where they could play pluralistic and diverse ideas—and later even act it out. Imagining a space where authority does not exist is necessary to believe that alternative possibilities can happen—and to create a community. The *Movida* more broadly encouraged Spaniards to "act out" their transgression against the regime through a carnivalesque display that could otherwise be written off as "making a scene." These carnivalesque transgressions that spread from the heart of the capital prepared a generation of Spaniards to both participate democratically and think pluralistically through the practice of (re)appropriating public spaces, hegemonic discourses and culture that culminated with the creation of an underground "scene," the *Movida Madrileña*. Having taken the winding Madrid streets, punk culture allowed for alternatives to the conservative dictatorship.

NOTES

1. See: Gramsci, Antonio. *Prison Notebooks*, edited by Joseph A. Buttigieg. Columbia UP, 1992.

2. See: Lefebvre, Henri. *Critique of Everyday Life*. Verso, 2008.

3. See my chapter "Truth, Justice and the American Way in Franco's Spain" in *The Ages of Superman: Essays on the Man of Steel in Changing Times*, edited by Joseph J. Darowski, McFarland, 2012, pp. 45–61.
4. See: Latour, Bruno. *Reassembling the Social: An Introduction to Actor-network-theory*. Oxford UP, 2005.
5. See censor report: Archivo General de la Administration, Expediente 3200/75.
6. See my chapter "Truth, Justice and the American Way in Franco's Spain" in *The Ages of Superman: Essays on the Man of Steel in Changing Times*, edited by Joseph J. Darowski, McFarland, 2012, pp. 45–61.
7. See: Babas, Kike and Kike Turrón. *De Espaldas al Kiosco: Guía Histórica de Fanzines y Otros Papelujos de Alcantarillas*. Los Libros del Cuervo, 1996. Babas and Turrón's guide is an excellent reference of most, if not all, the significant fanzines and comics during the period. The work includes the address when available, as well as a brief description of the work.
8. The author and the editors would like to thank Juan Rodriguez Ortega for his permission to reprint his work in this essay.
9. Pegamoide: Substance composed of cellulose dissolved and applied to a fabric or paper to obtain resistant imitation leather.
10. For those interested, Alaska also starred in Pedro Almodóvar's first feature film, *Pepi, Luci, Bom y las Otras Chicas del Montón*.

Works Cited

Abellán, Manuel L. *Censura y Creación Literaria En España (1939–1976)*. Península, 1980.
Anderson, Benedict. *Imagined Communities: Reflections on the Origin and Spread of Nationalism*. Verso, 2006.
Babas, Kike and Kike Turrón. *De Espaldas al Kiosco: Guía Histórica de Fanzines y Otros Papelujos de Alcantarillas*. Los Libros del Cuervo, 1996.
Bakhtin, Mikhail M., and Michael Holquist. *The Dialogic Imagination Four Essays*. University of Texas Press, 1996.
Bernecker, Walther L. "El Cambio de Mentalidad en el Segundo Franquismo." *España En Cambio: El Segundo Franquismo, 1959–1975*, edited by Nigel Townson, Siglo XXI, 2009, pp. 49–70.
Carajillo Vacilón, Iniciativas Editoriales, 1976.
Caro Baroja, Julio. *El Carnaval: Analysis Historico-Cultural*. Taurus Ediciones, 1983.
Cascorro Factory, editors. *El Rrollo Enmascarado*, no. 1, 1973.
Castillo, David. *Barcelona, Fragments de la Contra Cultura*. Ajuntament de Barcelona, 2010.
Cazorla, Sánchez Antonio. *Fear and Progress: Ordinary Lives in Franco's Spain, 1939–1975*. Wiley-Blackwell, 2010.
Ceesepe. *Vicios Modernos*. La Banda de Moebius, 1979.
Costa, Salvador. *Punk*. Producciones Editoriales, 1977.
de Certeau, Michel. *The Practice of Everyday Life*. University of California Press, 2006.
Dopico, Pablo. *El Cómic Underground Español, 1970–1980*. Cátedra, 2005.
Fraser, Nancy. "Rethinking the Public Sphere: A Contribution to the Critique of Actually Existing Democracy." *Social Text*, no. 25/26, 1990, pp. 56–80.
Gallero, José Luis. *Sólo Se Vive Una Vez: Esplendor y Ruina de la Movida Madrileña*. Ediciones Ardora, 1991.
García-Alix, Alberto. *Alberto García-Alix, 1978–1983*. Ardora, 1999.
Haro Ibars, Eduardo. *De Qué Van las Drogas*. La Piqueta, 1978.
_____. *Gay Rock*. Ediciones Júcar, 1975.
_____. "Un Dos De Mayo Goyesco." *Trunfo*, vol. 1, no. 746, 1977, pp. 38–39.
Hebdige, Dick. *Hiding in the Light: On Images and Things*. Routledge, 1988.
_____. *Subculture: The Meaning of Style*. Routledge, 2008.
Kaka de Luxe (fanzine). Kaka de Luxe, 1977.
La Liviandad del Imperdible. La Liviandad del Imperdible, 1976–1977.

Latour, Bruno. *Reassembling the Social: An Introduction to Actor-network-theory.* Oxford UP, 2005.
Lefebvre, Henri. *Critique of Everyday Life: Volume 1.* Verso, 2008.
Manrique, Diego A. *De Qué Va el Rock Macarra.* La Piqueta, 1977.
Nazario. *Los Años 70 Vistos por Nazario y Sus Amigos.* Ellago Ediciones, 2004.
Nichols, William J., and H. Rosi Song, editors. *Toward a Cultural Archive of La Movida: Back to the Future.* Fairleigh Dickinson UP, 2013.
96 Lágrimas, no. 1–4 (1980–1982).
Ordovás, Jesús. *De Qué Va el Rrollo.* La Piqueta, 1977.
Ortega, Juan Rodriguez. *Carajillo.* Editorial Madrágora, 1975.
Quinto, Manuel, and Esparbe. *Historia de la Censura.* Ediciones Sedmay, 1977.
Radcliff, Pamela Beth. *Making Democratic Citizens in Spain: Civil Society and the Popular Origins of the Transition, 1960–78.* Palgrave Macmillan, 2011.
Rodríguez de Fonseca, Javier and Juan Luís Recio. Personal interview. 26 June 2013.
Sola, Emilio. Personal interview. 10 June 2013.
Stallybrass, Peter, and Allon White. *The Politics and Poetics of Transgression.* Cornell UP, 1986.
Stapell, Hamilton M. *Remaking Madrid: Culture, Politics, and Identity after Franco.* Palgrave Macmillan, 2010.
Valencia-García, Louie Dean. "Truth, Justice and the American Way in Franco's Spain." *The Ages of Superman: Essays on the Man of Steel in Changing Times*, edited by Joseph J. Darowski, McFarland, 2012, pp. 45–61.
Warner, Michael. *Publics and Counterpublics.* Zone Books, 2002.

Drawing Istanbul's Asshole
Turkish Punk Comics

CAN YALÇINKAYA

In the last few years of the 1970s, the heyday of the punk movement in the Anglo-American world, Turkey was in a time of upheaval for other reasons. There were armed conflicts between different camps of politicized youth on the streets (Aydın and Taşkın 295–296).[1] Those who fought for a cause didn't seem to have time for a western youth subculture. Regardless, in 1984, Turkish President Kenan Evren visited a high school in Ankara, and declared, "I don't want a punk youth" ("Evren" 7). Evren was a former military officer who led the most heavy-handed *coup d'etat* in the history of Turkey, during which many left wing activists—as young as 16–were arrested, tortured, hanged or disappeared with no trace. How, then, did punk become a threat for President Evren, who suppressed radical youth with tanks on the street a mere four years before that statement? How did the punk movement manifest itself in Turkey, and what did it mean to be a punk in an Islamic country with a secular state?

This essay sets out to provide answers to these questions, but its primary focus is to trace the influence of the punk subculture in Turkish comics and cartoons, particularly in two magazines, *L-Manyak* ("L-Maniac") and *Lombak* ("Pop Eyed"). It outlines the history of the punk subculture in Turkey, discussing how punk has been appropriated by the Turkish youth. The role of cartoonists, who often act as disseminators of underground culture within the mainstream humor magazines, is vital to this process. Since the 1980s, during which the global youth subcultures of metal and punk entered Turkey, cartoonists have been their ambassadors.

"I Want to Piss on Your Face": Turkish Punk Rock

During the 1920s and 1930s, the ruling ideology in Turkey aimed to establish a modern, western nation-state through political, economic and cultural reforms. The government felt modern Turkish music should aim to create a synthesis between Turkish folk music and western music (Tekelioğlu 204).[2] This idea became a defining discourse for much of Turkish popular music from the 1960s onwards. Turkish rock musicians invented a style they called "Anatolian Pop," combining Turkish instruments and tunes with western guitars, keyboards and percussion (Stokes 133).

Tünay Akdeniz was one of these musicians, influenced by western beats and rock music, and bands like Led Zeppelin. He claims that his record *Salak* ("Stupid," Kent Plak, 1975) was the first Turkish rock record with Turkish lyrics. His contribution to punk in Turkey was his single *Mesela Mesele* ("For Instance, the Problem," Pardon, 1978), which had the caption "Punk Rock" on the cover along with the artist's name (Tünay Akdeniz & Çığrışım). In musical terms, it was hard to say *Mesela Mesele* is strictly a punk record, but Akdeniz boasted a punk image with dark, messy hair, tight jeans, leather jacket, safety pins, chains and lockpads. Akdeniz admits that while he could relate to punk's defiant attitude, he considered its musical style too simplistic. His image was influenced by a media interest in punk fashion (Boynik and Güldallı 15–25). Indeed, though it was nearly impossible to find punk records in Turkey at the time due to a general lack of foreign imports and a lack of public interest, images of British punks were in circulation in the mainstream media, which often framed punk in sensationalist terms, defining it as an "ugly, abject, vile, tasteless" fashion ("Çirkinlik" 20). Punk's initiation in Turkey, then, was based more on its visual aspects than its sounds, and in this sense, Tünay Akdeniz's case constitutes a peculiar example of how punk was initially appropriated by the Turkish youth. Turkey was to wait for another decade before bands with a punk sound as well as image started to emerge and actively create a scene.

The 1980s were a period of immense change in Turkey. After the 1980 military coup, it took three years before Turkey resumed parliamentary democracy. With the election victory of the Motherland Party (ANAP) in 1983, Turgut Özal became the Prime Minister. Özal adopted neoliberalist new right policies, similar to Thatcherism in the UK and Reaganism in the USA, with an emphasis on liberal economics and traditional conservatism (Keyder 297). The trade liberalization policies introduced by the Özal administration in the late 1980s enabled an acceleration in the free flow of foreign products into Turkey, which not only included goods but also cultural commodities, like American films and music.

During the early 1980s, it was still relatively difficult to find original recordings of western rock, metal, and punk bands, although pirated tapes of such records were available (Boynik and Güldallı 36). Due to the limited scope of these scenes, there weren't clearcut distinctions between rockers, punks and metalheads. Often, these youth groups gathered together in the same places and played gigs together (39). The first real Turkish punk band is considered to be Headbangers, who started playing together in 1987. Having not released any official records, some of their rehearsal tapes survive, with song titles like "Suratına işemek istiyorum" (I Want to Piss on Your Face") and "Beni ilgilendirmez" ("I Don't Care"), representing the grotesque and nihilist facets of punk.³ This politically disengaged but morally offensive attitude also informed the cartoonists of the time.

"I don't know if there is such a thing as punk comics..."

During an interview I conducted with Cengiz Üstün, a cartoonist who worked for humor magazines such as *Pişmiş Kelle* ("Grinning Skull"), *H.B.R. Maymun* ("Weekly Independent Disturbed Monkey"), *L-Manyak* and *Lombak* since the early 1990s, he gave an ambiguous response to my question regarding the punk influence on his work: "[My brother] Bülent and I liked Exploited and Sex Pistols. [Punk] was so simple, we loved it. I don't know if there is such a thing as punk comics, but we felt close to punk. There was an affinity between the music and our life styles. The spirit of punk resonated with us" (C. Üstün n.p.).

This interview was part of my research that started with a master's thesis on subversive Turkish comics, and I wanted to extend it into a documentary about two periodical publications, *L-Manyak* and *Lombak*. These two monthly magazines boasted an underground style with themes of sex, drugs and violence. I was aware of Cengiz Üstün's (and his brother Bülent's) interest in punk subculture from their earlier work in the 1990s in magazines like *Pişmiş Kelle* and *H.B.R. Maymun*. I had hoped that Cengiz would mention some punk comics influences but in retrospect, his doubts about the existence of a punk style of comics was not surprising.

It is not easy to pinpoint what a "punk comic" is. In one of the few scholarly works on the influence of punk in comics, Guy Lawley identifies "punk sensibilities" in the works of mainstream American comics writers and artists, including Neil Gaiman and Grant Morrison (117). Lawley even mentions Gary Panter, who though often "thought of as a punk artist ... wouldn't use the word punk himself" (107). The question, then, is how to define "punk comics"–with the exception of those with punk characters. In addressing this question, Lawley identifies "a drawing style," "subject matter," "thematic concerns," and "punk attitude" as criteria to consider (100). Thus, one could look for the "ratty line," or perhaps the situationist practice of détournement, "punk characters," themes of anarchy, nihilism, anti-authoritarianism, and offensive, subversive attitudes among others (100). In the context of this essay, we would also need to ask how national and cultural context affects comics influenced by punk, particularly in the example of *L-Manyak* and its successor *Lombak*. The cartooning styles of the two magazines in question should be seen within the wider of context of similar, preceding magazines, as they are influenced by and are often a reaction to earlier styles.

Humor magazines have been popular publications in Turkey since the late 19th century. *Gırgır* ("Fun," 1972—ongoing with several changes in editorship since 1989) a weekly publication that was similar to the American *Mad Magazine* in its humor style, was the most popular among its peers and very influential for contemporary cartoonists. Under the editorial leadership of Oğuz Aral, *Gırgır* trained dozens of young artists and published their works. Many current Turkish humor magazines are published and staffed by Aral's "students." It was in the pages of *Gırgır* that the first rock-influenced cartoons appeared. Abdülkadir Elçioğlu (a.k.a. Aptullica), a cartoonist who identified as a rocker, created the strip series *Grup Perişan* ("Band of Miserables"), telling the adventures of three university students who shared a flat in Istanbul: Mazhar, a metalhead, Sadi, a left-wing intellectual, and Danyal, a provincial young man with get-rich-quick schemes. The style of the series is somewhere in between the British sitcom series *The Young Ones* and Gilbert Shelton's *The Fabulous Furry Freak Brothers*.

In 1989, Aptullica moved *Grup Perişan* to the newly established magazine *Hıbır*, and introduced the first punk character in Turkish cartooning history, Çivi Kafa ("Spike Head"). The character occasionally appeared in *Grup Perişan* strips. Having been raised in Germany, his punk outlook and lifestyle often clashed with his family's and society's more conservative views (Elçioğlu n.p.).

Elçioglu was only one of the many cartoonists who left *Girgir* in the second half of the 1980s to join newly emerging humor magazines. One of the reasons for the separations from *Gırgır* was the lack of creative freedom on the part of many of its cartoonists. Some of Aral's former employees mentioned the authoritarian attitudes of their editor (Şen 55). It is said that Oğuz Aral made "corrections" on the works of the young artists and tried to create a uniform visual character in the magazine. There were also some forbidden subjects in *Gırgır*, such as depictions of genitals or using obscene language (Cantek 214). This atmosphere was one of the elements that resulted in the separations from the magazine.

Limon (later *Leman*) became the first enduring humor magazine published by the former young cartoonists of *Girgir*.⁴ *Limon* ("Lemon") was a significant magazine, as it didn't shy away from producing humor based on ugliness, filth, violence, and sex. Many of the punk cartoonists of the 1990s were influenced by the cheerful, anti-social attitude of the magazine. Creators like Gökhan Dabak, Can Barslan and particularly Kemal Aratan drew new road maps for future cartoonists with manic, hyper-energetic, absurd, nonsensical comics and cartoons. It is noteworthy that Dabak and Aratan were also musicians and part of the rock and punk scenes of the mid-1980s.

The 1990s were the decade when humor magazines started to become independent. *Limon*'s cartoonists quit from the *Güneş* Media Group which financed the magazine, and began to publish *Leman* (1991). *Leman* became the only humor magazine to be able to criticize anyone and everyone as radically as it pleased, and it was the most popular magazine of political opposition. *Leman* increased the number of political pages and included such columns as "Lemanti-Medya" (a combination of the words "Leman" and "Anti-Media"), where they adopted a critical and satirical approach towards the media, and "Haftanın (Göt) Laleleri" ("[Ass] Tulips of the Week"), where they declared people and institutions related to politics, the business world, and the media as "ass tulips," slang for hemorrhoids. The D.I.Y. attitude of *Leman*, along with its anarcho-communist politics, its anti-authoritarianism and subversive cartoons established it as a punky magazine, even if it didn't overtly identify as punk.

As *Leman* became the best-selling humor magazine, its creators opened a café/bar chain under the name of Leman Kültür ("Leman Culture"), sold merchandise of Leman characters, printed the books of its cartoonists and published more magazines starting from the mid-1990s. Their monthly comics anthology, *L-Manyak* (1996) became one of the significant humor magazines of the period, and was able to create its own distinct humor style rather than being a monthly extension of *Leman*. The two other significant humor magazines of the 1990s, which were *Pişmiş Kelle* and *H.B.R. Maymun*, both of which were instrumental in cultivating *L-Manyak*'s style.

Pişmiş Kelle was founded under the editorship of Engin Ergönültaş. The dominant drawing style of *Pişmiş Kelle* was not as bright and clean as *Gırgır*'s. It was shabby, dark, and more open to alternative, distinct styles than *Gırgır*, thanks to Ergönültaş's vision. The dominant themes in *Pişmiş Kelle* were poverty, shantytowns and street life, and the dominant characters were sex workers, pimps, drug addicts, the poor, and other marginalized people. Ergönültaş's affinity with American underground comix and the punk movement is clearly articulated in *Pişmiş Kelle*. In the March 20, 1992, issue, Ergönültaş writes about punk and comics, saying that cartoonists like Cengiz Üstün and Memo, who started their career in *Pişmiş Kelle*, are punks themselves (15). Ergönültaş published the rest of the article the following week.

He described underground comix as the ancestor of punk style in comics due to their "dark, violent, confronting" content and style. He defined the main characteristics of punk comics as an amateur drawing style with themes of "hopelessness, corruption, impurity, uncanniness, violence, darkness" (2, 12, 15). The article was accompanied by a one-page comic, written and drawn by the 19-year old Mehmet Coşkun (a.k.a. Memcoş) featuring a punk character.[5] Cengiz Üstün, Memo (Tembelçizer) and Memcoş would later become part of the "gang" that shaped *L-Manyak*'s style.

What was missing in the discussion of punk comics by Ergönültaş in *Pişmiş Kelle* is the fact that it excludes the more cheerful aspects of punk, and associates the punk influence with mere bitterness. Ergönültaş's works are generally grim stories set in slums, with poverty-stricken characters who have nothing to lose. Arguably, this might have had an impact on his perception of punk. However, humor has been a significant aspect of the punk movement. Tricia Henry describes punk humor in fanzines as:

> Characterized by outrageousness in graphics and content, it was designed not only to entertain the readership, but to alienate the general public. *Punk* #1 features sexist humor ("Cars and Girls"), and scatological humor ("Joe"). In *Punk* #3 we find examples of black humor ("Father No's Best"), antireligious humor ("10 Warning Signs of Blessedness") and a bizarre piece by Legs McNeil entitled "A Story to Fill Space," in which he describes throwing up on a subway [111].

Many of these elements are seen in *L-Manyak* and its successor *Lombak*. What was portrayed in *L-Manyak* and *Lombak* had, in effect, a punk flavor, in that they shared the same desire to revolt and shock. The characteristics Tricia Henry identifies in punk fanzines, "chaotic appearance, subversive graphics, offensive subject matter, aggressive antisocial tone, and liberal use of profanities and off-color humor" (112), were used as primary sources of humor in these magazines. In addition to these, the influence of punk on these magazines may be divided into three: scatological humor, the DIY aspect, visual aesthetics and subject matter.

L-Manyak began as a side project of *Leman* cartoonists. Bahadır Baruter, a popular cartoonist for *Leman*, was assigned as the editor of this new publication. In 1995, when Baruter started reviewing submissions, there weren't many comics published outside of humor magazines. Due to their limited spaces, weekly deadlines, and stylistic requirements, humor magazines weren't ideal places for longer form comics to flourish. A 64-page, A4 size monthly magazine was met with excitement among cartoonists (C. Üstün n.p.).

Baruter says he had a vision for *L-Manyak* from the beginning. His own weekly page of cartoons in *Leman* (created with writer Fatih Solmaz), "Lombak," featured single panel cartoons, which aimed to "break taboos" in the words of Baruter (n.p.). "Lombak"'s symbol was two naked lower bodies attached to each other from the waist, and their cartoons involve extreme hardcore sex, masturbation, bodily fluids, disabled people, homosexuality, religion, and violence. Solmaz and Baruter did not concern themselves with politics and political correctness.[6] His vision for the new magazine was to follow similar themes and styles in longer comic forms.

Baruter gathered several like-minded cartoonists from *Leman*, *H.B.R. Maymun* and *Pişmiş Kelle*, who shared the same aesthetic vision with "Lombak," in the creative team of the magazine. During the first year, the influence of *Leman* gradually decreased. The magazine's future stars, such as Bülent Üstün, Cengiz Üstün, Memo Tembelçizer (Memo the Lazycartoonist), Oky, Kenan Yarar, Emrah Ablak, and Ersin Karabulut were from *H.B.R. Maymun* and *Pişmiş Kelle*. According to Cengiz Üstün, while *Limon* had a great influence on his generation, *Leman* didn't have a similar impact. *Leman*'s popular cartoon pages, such as Ahmet Yılmaz's "Cümbür Cemaat" focused more on observational details about the everyman. Their humor became more situational and was based on words rather than action. *L-Manyak* wanted a return to a manic, action-based humor style (C. Üstün n.p.).

Along with Baruter, Bülent Üstün (a.k.a. Büstün) played a significant role in envisioning *L-Manyak*'s aesthetics and narrative structure. He created the most popular character of the magazine, "Kötü Kedi Şerafettin" ("Şerafettin the Evil Cat"), and wrote many of the scripts drawn by other cartoonists throughout the magazine's lifespan. In an interview I conducted with Baruter, he stated that he would happily share credits with Bülent Üstün in conceptualizing the magazine (n.p.). Bülent Üstün had a weekly page in *H.B.R. Maymun*, called "Kabız Kuğu" ("Constipated Swan")—its logo showing a swan trying to defecate in pain. This image conveyed the idea that behind anything that was supposedly beautiful leered something ugly or grotesque. His cartoons presented a world of filth and absurdity, visual aesthetics drawing from underground comix and punk. His style is cartoony and exaggerated. He draws energetic, action-filled panels with a violent slapstick tone, and almost all of his characters, men and women alike, are ugly, hairy, and sweaty. His cartoons are an attack on middle class bourgeois morals and values, such as good manners and cleanliness.

Bülent Üstün was also the most "punk" of all the creators in question. Memo Tembelçizer talks about how Büstün introduced him to punk music when he shared a flat with him and his brother Cengiz. They started a band together called Testis ("Testes"), and sang obscene and humorous lyrics to basic, three chord punk tunes (Tembelçizer n.p.). Bülent Üstün's punk attitude surfaced through declarations he made in "Kabız Kuğu" in 1995. In issue #79, he published a call for contributions:

> Announcement: Psychopaths, mad people, the manic depressive, paranoids, those of the threshold, the stupid, geniuses and idiots, perverts, the waste of the society, those who can leave the door open to anarchism and to the bearded and long haired people who have perceived the drawbacks of committing to the nation, ideologies and any other masks and deceptions without any room for debate, the disconnectus erectus.... Write! Draw! Shit [punctuation missing in original] But send them! They will be used in Kabız Kuğu [Üstün, "Duyuru" 5].

This announcement links to punk philosophy in three ways. Firstly, it calls to all the marginalized sections of the society to send their work, and expects them to resist the social formation in some form. Secondly, it employs anarchism in the same way punk does, by framing it as a distrust against politicians, nations, states, ideologies, and organized religion. Thirdly, the way Üstün asks for people to produce, to send their own work is reminiscent of the DIY philosophy of punk.

In *H.B.R. Maymun* issue #80, Üstün writes:

> The satirist or the master of irony is basically a hopeful person, on the side of change and evolution. If s/he swears, mocks, or speaks sarcastically it is because s/he invests in the existence of a better world. There is no such hope for the BLACK humorIST. Like a prophet of apocalypse, s/he sheds light on the hypocrisy hidden beneath the hope, the desire for change and the belief in evolution. For him/her, nothing has changed since the beginning and his/her mission in this bloody farce, i.e., "Life," is to unveil (Üstün, "Not Not Not Not Not" 5).

This piece has clear connections to punk negationism, in the vein of the slogan "No Future." It is a manifesto for overthrowing meaning formed by the signifying practices of the dominant culture.

"Drawing the City's Asshole"

Bahadır Baruter describes *L-Manyak* and *Lombak*'s stance as antipolitical and disengaged from current affairs, but claims that the magazines were informed by the spirit of their times (n.p.). It is possible to claim that, starting from the eighties and through the oppressive politics of the military regime and Özal's application of the new right policies in Turkey, a new common sense was constructed and naturalized. Engaging in radical (especially left-wing) politics became "outdated." The education system and parental authorities contributed to the ideological programming of the younger generations in a conservative strain. Economic breakthrough, consumption and depoliticization became the keywords to describe the social tendencies of the young people raised in this period.

As Sezgin Boynik maintains, rock and punk youth subcultures were often seen as a product of the free market economy introduced by Turgut

Özal and the Motherland Party. The left-wing critics of Özal framed consumption of western-style subcultures and music genres as conforming to western cultural imperialism. Boynik opposes this, suggesting Turkish punks were open to these new sounds and ideas coming from the west, but did not care about the "open society" ideal Özal's policies promised (350–352). Based on Boynik and Güldallı's interviews with punks of the time, the Turkish scene in the 1980s did not seem to be as politically engaged as their western counterparts, but instead adopted nihilistic and hedonistic aspects of the subculture.

Here, it might be worthwhile to think about some of the artistic and cultural precedents of punk. One link that always comes up in early scholarship on punk is the influence of Dadaism on punk. Dick Hebdige quotes George Grosz's reflection on Dada in order to shed light on its connection with punk: "Nothing was holy to us. Our movement was neither mystical, communistic nor anarchistic. All of these movements had some sort of programme, but ours was completely nihilistic. We spat on everything, including ourselves. Our symbol was nothingness, a vacuum, a void" (Grosz qtd. in Hebdige 106). According to Greil Marcus, though, punks, unlike Dadaists, were not nihilists; they were negationists. Their symbol was not nothingness or meaninglessness. They aimed to destroy the meanings produced by the dominant culture, through their signifying practices. Greil Marcus says "you can find punk between every other line of [Adorno's] *Minima Moralia*: its miasmic loathing for what western civilization had made of itself by the end of the Second World War was, by 1977, the stuff of a hundred songs and slogans" (72). He adds "what Adorno's negation lacked was glee—a spirit the punk version of his world never failed to deliver" (73).

This spirit of gleeful negation is the most significant commonality *L-Manyak* and *Lombak* share with punk. The apolitical attitude of these magazines is also a result of distrust against politicians and the social formation in which they are produced. They also have a pessimistic outlook on life and believe that there is "no future." Yet, they also embraced the more hedonistic aspects of punk, portraying lives spinning around sex, drugs and humorous situations. They seek to negate the norms and values of the dominant culture, as well as their "parent's" (*Leman*'s) culture in a way a youth subculture does. *Leman*'s political standpoint didn't mean anything to the "gang" of cartoonists in *L-Manyak*, who aimed to subvert social moral norms through the scatological humor of comics series such as Kaan Ertem's "Zıçan Adam" ("Shitting Man") and later Memo Tembelçizer's "Zort" ("Fart") and grotesque themes in many of their comics, including "Kötü Kedi Şerafettin" by Bülent Üstün, "Aşık Memo" ("Memo the Minstrel") by Memo Tembelçizer, and "Kunteper Canavarı" ("Buttbanger Monster") by Cengiz Üstün (see Figure 1).[7]

Ayşe Öncü labels humor magazines as "transgressive cultural spaces for

162   Part III: Underground Punk Comics

Figure 1: "Kötü Kedi Şerafettin" by Bülent Üstün in *L-Manyak* issue #28, April 1998, page 8 (courtesy Bülent Üstün).

Istanbul's youth" (176). Their independence, being devoid of advertisements and use of cheap paper grants them the position of being alternative to such magazines as "*Cosmopolitan, Marie Claire, Burda, Playboy* etc.," all of which are presented in glossy papers and are under the umbrella of big media groups (Öncü 176). Öncü deems the world represented in humor magazines as the antithesis of the "shiny, clean, orderly world inhabited by good-looking people" as represented in television commercials and magazines which focus on upper-middle class lifestyles. The sexuality in humor magazines of the 1990s, unlike the aforementioned glossy magazines, is also far from being clean, erotic, or pornographic, but is obscene and humorous (Öncü 181).

Sex, obscenity, and the grotesque—in varying proportions—have always been among the ingredients of humor magazines in Turkey. *L-Manyak* and

Lombak are no exceptions. However, what makes them exceptional is the particular attitude they adopt, which could be defined as "grotesque realism" as outlined by Bakhtin. Cantek emphasizes the grotesque and carnivalesque attributes of such *L-Manyak* and *Lombak* cartoons as Cengiz Üstün's "Mokar Hastası Nihan" ("Nihan the Cock Addict")—a strip series featuring a woman who shoves anything she finds in her vagina—Memo Tembelçizer's "Aşık Memo"—a series portraying Memo as a bard with a giant penis, who refrains from sex and only masturbates—and Cengiz Üstün's "Kunteper Canavarı"— a comic series about a monster with yet another giant penis, punishing his adversaries by raping them anally (310–314).

While characters with extraordinary genitals were abundant in *L-Manyak* and *Lombak*, the fascination with excrement sometimes outweighed the phallic obsession. According to Bakhtin, defecation, in grotesque imagery, means death for the person who is subject to it, yet it also signifies birth and regeneration, and thus becomes ambivalent (151). Defecation brings death for the old and birth for the new. In *L-Manyak*, defecation as a method of debasement was the main theme of Kaan Ertem's "Zıçan Adam" ("Shitting Man"). The character, Zıçan Adam, defecates on people from all backgrounds who offend him, such as hooligans, disturbers of peace, hunters, those who pollute the environment, and rich people. The exaggeration of the amount of "Zıçan Adam's" excretion and the manner in which he excretes associate the series to grotesque realism, particularly to what Bakhtin refers to as "Malbrough Theme," which can be summarized as "degrading death" related to defecation (151). People who are drenched in "Zıçan Adam's" feces are not only degraded but also die a symbolic death.

Another significant artist who portrays images of defecation in a grotesque way is Memo Tembelçizer. His two works from *Lombak*, issues #53 and #54, particularly reflect the ambivalent nature of defecation Bakhtin talks about. These two narratives, both titled "Dünyanın En İğrenç İnsanı Memo Tembel Çizer" ("Memo Tembelçizer, the Most Disgusting Person on Earth"), contain both poles of becoming, namely destruction and regeneration. Memo depicts himself as a supernatural "shit-being" that is the accumulation of modern people's excreta. This creature invites humanity to the righteous way, which is to "Eat shit!," and be on good terms with their feces. He calls them to "shit on civilization!" In the end, all is drenched in defecation, and the universe is reborn out of shit (Tembelçizer, *Zort* 44–47) (see Figure 2).[8]

"Kötü Kedi Şerafettin" also hosts a number of grotesque themes, the most particular of which lies in Şerafettin's origin story. Şerafettin is a half cat-half human creature. As Bakhtin points out, "(...) the combination of human and animal traits is, as we know, one of the most ancient grotesque forms" (316). In *L-Manyak* issue #7, Şerafettin recites the succession of events concerning his birth. His mother was accidentally impregnated after she sat

Figure 2: "Dünyanın En İğrenç İnsanı Memo Tembelçizer" by Memo Tembelçizer in *Zort*, published by Murekkep, 2009, p. 44 (courtesy Memo Tembelçizer).

on the ejaculate of a man (Üstün 12–15). Through the course of his adventures, Şerafettin becomes involved in both human and cat affairs, often resulting in violence, and has both human and cat lovers. This state of liminality is what defines the character's body in a constant state of becoming between the human and the animal.

Another aspect of *L-Manyak* and *Lombak* that links them to a punk attitude is the DIY spirit of these magazines. This is apparent in *L-Manyak* and *Lombak* in two ways. Firstly, they come from a tradition of self-publishing. *L-Manyak* was published under the independent humor magazine *Leman*, but Bahadır Baruter and his "gang" left *Leman* to publish their independent magazine *Lombak* in 2001. *Lombak* took over the flag of self-publishing, and parted ways with *Leman*, which became a "corporation." Secondly, the crude, primitive, naïve and "anyone-can-do-it" (anti-) aesthetics of DIY became one of the dominant drawing styles in these magazines. Especially, the "ratty line" is favored among a number of artists such as Emrah Ablak, Memo Tembelçizer in "Ben Bir Eşşeğim" ("I Am an Ass"), Yetkin Gülmen, Alpay Erdem, Göxel, Bahadır Baruter in "Kahraman Barut" ("Barut the Hero"), and Bülent Üstün in "Lombak Kerizleri" ("Idiots of Lombak") and "Prensiplerim Vardır" ("I Have Principles").

In terms of subject matter, i.e., "punk characters, gigs, and bands," *L-Manyak* and *Lombak* had limited space. Cengiz Üstün, Memo Tembelçizer and Mehmet Coşkun, the cartoonists whom Ergönültaş identified as punks in *Pişmiş Kelle*, as well as others like Oky occasionally place punk characters in their strips and cartoons. However, it is mostly due to Bülent Üstün that punk characters are used in *L-Manyak* and *Lombak*. He turned himself into a character in "Kötü Kedi Şerafettin," and draws himself as a punk, with spiked hair, ripped clothes, t-shirts with anarchy symbols or the logos of punk bands, and a leather jacket. The only comic strip with an overt punk subject matter was "Mongollar" ("The Mongols"). This short-lived series was written by Bülent Üstün and illustrated by Hakan Karataş and was about an untalented punk band, who try endlessly to record a demo and give concerts but fail each time.

One of the main influences of punk on *L-Manyak* and *Lombak* was related to the street credibility, or the "streetwise" facet of punk. The artists in *L-Manyak* and *Lombak* imply in their works that they have an intimate knowledge of the language and practices of the street. The use of drugs and alcohol, street violence, and slang are indispensable elements of these magazines. The setting in a lot of their comics was Beyoğlu, Tarlabaşı and Cihangir, places that were associated with night life, drug use, and prostitution in the 1980s and 1990s, but which gradually became gentrified. According to Baruter:

Places like Cihangir and Tarlabaşı, the margins, are areas that lack much validity or officiality. The language and the slang of the ghetto are connected to the out-of- the-ordinary. The things which are covered, suppressed and hidden make us laugh most, right! Because life is not in Bağdat Caddesi. The asshole and the shit of the city is there [in Cihangir and Tarlabaşı]. Those people are the closest characters to the shit and filth which we are interested in. I mean, we are naturally on the same side with them. We have a chemistry with the man who carries a knife, with the *tinerci* ("glue sniffer"), the junky, the unjustly treated, the *jiletçi* ("self-mutilator"), the loser. But do we raise our children as junkies, heroin addicts or homosexuals? Or do we expect such characteristics from our brothers/sisters or friends? I cannot say that. We can never give such a moral message. There is no such thing in humor, either. We laugh and have fun, but the warmest relationship I have is with my family [qtd. in Cantek 315].

This quote is an indication of the magazines' solidarity with the down and out, but also raises questions about their authenticity. While *L-Manyak* and *Lombak* cartoonists boast their ability to navigate these "dangerous" streets, and co-exist with marginalized figures of society, they also draw a distinct line between themselves and those figures, in what could be considered a bourgeois sensibility. It would also be worthwhile to investigate how humor magazines contributed to the gentrification of the neighborhoods of Cihangir and Tarlabaşı through their depiction of them as "cool" places, but that is beyond the scope of the current study.

Conclusion

Boynik and Güldallı, in their oral history of punk in Turkey, describe the 1990s in which the punk subculture flourished, with many bands recording demos and distributing them nationally and internationally, and the emergence of numerous punk fanzines. They end their discussion of punk in Turkey with the release of the first legally released punk album by the band Rashit in 1999. This symbolic end could be seen as a statement regarding punk's supposed incompatibility with the mainstream and corporate music industry.

In addition to the questions of authenticity, *L-Manyak* and *Lombak* could also be implicated with "selling out" to the corporate, free market ideals of the new, global Turkey. After the launch of *Lombak* as an independent magazine by the former *L-Manyak* cartoonists, Baruter followed a similar route to that of *Leman* and went on to establish a corporate media company. In 2002, he came together with three of his former colleagues from *Leman* to publish a new weekly humor magazine, *Penguen* ("Penguin"), which was followed by a magazine of culture and arts, *Hayvan* ("Beast"). However, when the producers of *L-Manyak* became independent from *Lombak*, they had to confront trials against what was defined as their immoral comics. Before, the editors of *Leman* had dealt with such trials. As a result, characters such as "Kunteper Canavarı" and "Aşık Memo" disappeared.

In 2002, *Penguen* founded a company called Cominic, which described their aims on their website cominic.com as working in five basic areas: "Mobile Entertainment, Publishing, License Sales, Consumption Products, and Production (Animation & Broadcast)" (n.p.). In 2003, it was announced that Cominic established a partnership with Sony Ericsson "to bring popular humor, which is followed by everyone through different channels, into Sony Ericsson mobile phones via mobile internet technologies (Oymacı n.p.). In this context, wallpapers, screen-savers, EMS'es, and games (such as those featuring Şerafettin the Evil Cat) were designed for mobile phones. Another deal was established by giant publishing corporation Doğan Publications, who started publishing books of collected works by the cartoonists of *Lombak* and *Penguen*.

Today, it would not be wrong to say that *L-Manyak*'s and *Lombak*'s humor has been appropriated by the mainstream culture and media. As Kumru Berfin Emre and Göze Orhon point out, the functioning of the culture industry is directed towards containing and melting the elements of resistance and difference (Emre and Orhon 134). The oppositional aspects of popular texts start to get included in the range of standardized products. The mainstream culture is no longer repulsed by the humor of *L-Manyak* and *Lombak*, as it appropriated their humor and reproduced it as profitable products (i.e., books by Doğan Publications and Mobile Phone Entertainment in cooperation with Sony Ericsson). Bahadır Baruter was introduced in a website as the manager of a magazine (*Lombak*) with an annual turnover of 500,000 US Dollars and a monthly circulation of 70,000 (Oymacı n.p.).

In our interview, Baruter suggested his involvement with running the business, and "being the boss" brought the end of the "gang" spirit in *Lombak*. In 2006, Bülent Üstün left the magazine to publish *Fermuar* ("Zip"), another weekly humor magazine. Many of his friends from *Lombak* followed him, including his brother Cengiz, Memo Tembelçizer and Oky. The magazine wasn't long-lived. *Uykusuz* ("Insomniac"), first published by cartoonists who left *Penguen* (including Memo Tembelçizer, Oky, Ersin Karabulut, Yiğit Özgür, Umut Sarıkaya and Bülent Üstün) in 2007, has been more successful and continues to be published at the time of writing.

After the departure of its most popular cartoonists, *Lombak* didn't survive very long and was shut down in 2007. *L-Manyak* continues to be published with a different crew but it is hard to say it still captures the vision of the magazine with its original staff. The violent, oversexed, action-based, offensive style of humor was replaced by a calmer, more naive, nostalgic and situational humor approach. As the Justice and Development Party (AKP) has gained more power since 2002 and Recep Tayyip Erdoğan was elected Prime Minister for three consecutive terms, previously apolitical cartoonists have become more politically engaged, and critical of government policies. However, the increasing conservatism in the public and mainstream media has made it impossible to publish the likes of *L-Manyak* and *Lombak* today. Perhaps, in Turkey at least, it is time to declare punk dead.

Notes

1. See also Zürcher, Erik Jan. *Turkey: A Modern History.* New Edition. I.B. Tauris, 2004.
2. See also, Karahasanoglu, Songül, and Gabriel Skoog. "Synthesising Identity: Gestures of Filiation and Affiliation in Turkish Popular Music." *Asian Music*, vol. 40, no. 2, 2009, pp. 52–71.
3. There were a handful of punk bands in Istanbul and Ankara during the late 1980s, including Noisy Mob, Spinners (an all-female anarcho-punk band) and Hong Kong Virus. There were also many rock and metal bands, some of whom wrote English lyrics to their songs.
4. The first separation from *Gırgır* actually took place in 1978, when cartoonist Engin Ergönültaş led a group of cartoonists in a new magazine called *Mikrop* ("Microbe"). *Mikrop* was more involved in radical left-wing politics than *Gırgır*. Its handling of sexuality and obscenity was also more liberal compared to Oğuz Aral's editorial direction. *Mikrop* wasn't long lived, and was shut down in 1979. Ergönültaş continued working for *Gırgır* until 1989, and soon after that he became the editor of a new humor magazine titled *Pişmiş Kelle* ("Grinning Skull").
5. Mehmet Coskun's short comic "Duvar" ("The Wall") portrays a punk character attempting to climb a symbolic wall, a metaphor for an existential struggle to free oneself from social norms.
Translation:
Panel 1 Caption: "To transcend," to go beyond what exists.
Panel 2 Caption: To steal your thoughts from your skull. Just think.
Panel 3 Caption: "The wall" is the obstacle you must surpass.
Panel 4 Caption: There is some courage right in front of you.
Panel 5 Caption: Just climb, and don't look down.
Panel 6 Caption: If I didn't have to hold on to the wall, I would applaud your courage, dear skeleton.
6. In 2011, Baruter came under conservative media scrutiny and received death threats for drawing a cartoon that proclaimed "There is no God, Religion is a lie" in the popular weekly magazine, *Penguen*. The magazine felt obliged to apologize to its readers for offending religious sensibilities.
7. This panel from Bülent Üstün's "Kötü Kedi Şerafettin" ("Şerafettin the Evil Cat") depicts a particularly gory scene, in which Şerafettin violently kills his adversary. It is a good representation of the overall violent nature of comics in *L-Manyak*.
Translation:
Şerafettin: "Fuck you!.."
Caption under the panel: Wow, Sero [Şerafettin], what have you done dude? Phew [whistling effect].
Side caption: Information about a Bülent Üstün signing.
8. This panel from "Dunyanin En Igrenc Insani Memo Tembelcizer" ("Memo Tembelcizer, the Most Disgusting Person on Earth") portrays the artist himself as a "shit-being" in which he asks people to embrace their feces, and criticizes them for being too sterile.
Translation:
Caption: We all know that humanity will never reconcile with its shit. They will always live with the sterilization lie!
Caption: But there is still a way for salvation!

Caption: The way for salvation is in you!
Caption: YOU! And everyone like you who believe in the cause of shit!

WORKS CITED

Aydın, Suavi and Yüksel Taşkın. *1960'tan Günümüze Türkiye Tarihi*. İletişim, 2014.
Bakhtin, Mikhail. *Rabelais and His World*. Translated by Héléne Iswolsky, Indiana UP, 1984.
Baruter, Bahadır. Personal interview. February 2009.
Boynik, Sezgin, and Tolga Güldallı, editors. *Türkiye'de Punk ve Yeraltı Kaynaklarının Kesintili Tarihi 1978-1999/An Interrupted History of Punk and Underground Resources in Turkey 1978-1999*. BAS, 1999.
Cantek, Levent. *Türkiye'de Çizgi Roman*. İletişim, 2002.
"Çirkinlik, iğrençlik, kötülük, zevksizlik de moda oldu: Punk." *Milliyet*, 20 November 1977, pp. 20.
"Evren: 'Punk Gencligi istemiyorum.'" *Milliyet*, 21 December 1984, pp. 7.
Elçioğlu, Abdülkadir. *Grup Perişan 1989'dan 1995'e Seçmeler*. 4M Yayıncılık, 1996.
Emre, Kumru Berfin, and Göze Orhon. "1990'lı Yıllarda Türkiye'de Kültür Endüstrisi." *Pasaj*, no. 2, 2005, pp. 125-142.
Ergönültaş, Engin. "Kelle'den Mektup Var." *Pişmiş Kelle*, 20 March 1992, pp. 15.
———. "Kelle'den Mektup Var." *Pişmiş Kelle*, 27 March 1992, pp. 2, 12, 15.
Hebdige, Dick. *Subculture: The Meaning of Style*. Routledge, 1991.
Henry, Tricia. *Break All Rules!: Punk Rock and the Making of a Style*. UMI Research Press, 1989.
Karahasanoglu, Songül, and Gabriel Skoog. "Synthesising Identity: Gestures of Filiation and Affiliation in Turkish Popular Music." *Asian Music*, vol. 40, no. 2, 2009, pp. 52-71.
Keyder, Çağlar. *Türkiye'de Devlet ve Sınıflar*. İletişim, 1993.
Lawley, Guy. "I Like Hate and I Hate Everything Else: The Influence of Punk on Comics." *Punk Rock: So What?*, edited by Roger Sabin, Routledge, 1999, pp. 100-119.
Marcus, Greil. *Lipstick Traces: A Secret History of the Twentieth Century*. Harvard UP, 1990.
Öncü, Ayşe. "Global Consumerism, Sexuality as Public Spectacle, and the Cultural Remapping of Istanbul in the1990s." *Fragments of Culture: The Everyday of Modern Turkey*, edited by Deniz Kandiyoti and Ayşe Saktanber, I.B. Tauris, 2002, pp. 171-190.
Oymacı, Sinan. "Sony Ericsson—Cominic İşbirliğiyle Türkiye Cep'ten Gülmeye Hazırlanıyor." *Net Yorum*. 6 March 2003, www.netyorum.com /sayi/124/20030306-02.htm. Accessed 21 Mar. 2018.
Şen, Necdet. "Gırgır bir Okul muydu?" *Serüven*, no. 1, 2004, pp. 52-58.
Tekelioğlu, Orhan. "The Rise of a Spontaneous Synthesis: The Historical Background of Turkish Popular Music." *Middle Eastern Studies*, vol. 32, no. 1, 1996, pp. 194-215.
Stokes, Martin. "Sounding Out: The Culture Industries and the Globalisation of Istanbul." *Istanbul: Between the Global and the Local*, edited by Çağlar Keyder, Rowman and Littlefield, 1999, pp. 121-140.
Tembelçizer, Memo. *Zort*. Mürekkep, 2009, pp. 44-47.
———. Personal interview. February 2009.
Üstün, Bülent. "Duyuru." *H.B.R. Maymun*, 7 December 1995, pp. 5.
———. "Kötü Kedi Şerafettin." *L-Manyak*, July 1996, pp. 12-15.
———. "Not Not Not Not Not." *H. B. R. Maymun*, 14 December 1995, pp. 5.
Üstün, Cengiz. Personal interview. February 2009.
Zürcher, Erik Jan. *Turkey: A Modern History*. New Edition. I.B. Tauris, 2004.

PART IV : PUNK MANGA

Bōsōzoku Motorcycle Gangs, the Bubble Economy and Psychic Children
Reaffirming Giri *Through Ōtomo Katsuhiro's* Akira *(1988)*

CHRISTOPHER C. DOUGLAS

The appearance of punk's influence outside of punk's birthplace in English and American cultures creates an interesting space wherein some of the most iconic punk attitudes are developed separately from what many Westerners might consider the defining aesthetic principles of the movement. Whereas many of the ideas of punk explored in other essays in this collection are developed in the context of Ōtomo Katsuhiro's *Akira* manga (1984–1993), one feature that is noticeably missing in the film version of *Akira* (1988) is the "do it yourself" attitude prevalent in Western punk movements.[1] While the conclusion of the manga reaffirms a do-it-yourself aesthetic, the movie insists instead upon utilizing the aesthetics of punk to reaffirm social duty and obligations. This unexpected twist is notable for its importance to the plot of the film; for its status as an authoritative alternate ending, as the film was written and directed by Ōtomo himself; and, perhaps most importantly, for its specific relevance to the cultural moment of the movie's production.

1988 was a watershed year for Japanese animation. Three iconic Japanese animated movies were released in that year: two by Studio Ghibli—*My Neighbor Totoro* (となりのトトロ) and *Grave of the Fireflies* (火垂るの墓)—and the third, *Akira*, written and directed by Ōtomo Katsuhiro. Little would seem to tie these three films together other than the year of their appearance, although both *My Neighbor Totoro* and *Grave of the Fireflies* appeared together as a mismatched double-feature. However, all three films address, each in its own way, the concept of *giri* (義理) or societal obligation: a concept which in effect extends the bond between parents and children to the more generalized sense of connection between an individual and society. *Giri* might be easiest to see in *My Neighbor Totoro*. Set in the 1950s, this film portrays the efforts of a transplanted city family to thrive in a rural society, with the help of neighboring farmers and a number of kindly forest spirits, all of whom help the family integrate into rural life. *Grave of the Fireflies* concerns itself with the subject of *giri* as well, although from the negative standpoint. Here a young boy, Seita, decides to cut off himself and his sister from his remaining family members during the last days of World War II because of his desire to be free from an uncaring aunt. Seita's abandonment of his societal obligations, his refusal to remain with his family and with adults who can provide for himself and his sister while supporting the war effort, and his turn to petty thievery, clearly lead to his sister's death—and swiftly thereafter, his own. The film's judgment is clear: it is not starvation, per se, but rather Seita's defiant alienation, that causes the siblings' deaths. *Akira*, as the manga was re-envisioned in its 1988 theatrical release, also promotes the idea of social obligation. This essay seeks to discuss the context that these three films appeared in, to explain why the most iconic anime films from 1988 are concerned with the idea of traditional values, and to explore exactly how *Akira*, a film about a *bōsōzoku* (暴走族)[2] motorcycle gang, military oppression, and a post–World War III Tokyo simmering with homegrown terrorism can be seen as expressing that concern. Much of its success in doing so, I'll argue here, lies in its usage of liminal figures who straddle both youth and old age: preternaturally aged psychic children known in the film as the espers.[3] It is through these key characters, with their privileged sense of history, that the ongoing importance of *giri* is urged.

Curiously, although, nearly every commentator on *Akira* notes its status as a record-breaking, number one film in the Japanese market the year of its release, with Susan Napier vaunting it "as the film that started the anime boom in the West" (41), the context of its production has gone almost unnoticed, as critics focus tightly on the film's content. The figure of the loner is briefly discussed as a contextual part of Japanese culture in Napier's "*Akira* and *Ranma ½*: The Monstrous Adolescent," but her finding of catharsis in "the image of a youth going up against and destructively triumphing against a repressive [Japanese] society" totally ignores the film's key figures of resolution, the espers (48). The idea of identity, conveyed through a focus on body transformation, that may be analyzed along psychoanalytic lines, recurs in the criticism on this film, including Napir and Gerald Miller's "'To Shift to a Higher Structure': Desire, Disembodiment, and Evolution in the Anime of Ōtomo, Ishii and Anno." These psychoanalytic readings tend to ignore the specific cultural context of the film's production. Thomas Lamarre's "Born of Trauma: *Akira* and Capitalist Modes of Destruction" does attempt to place the film in the historical context of Japan post–World War II as a "repetition of historical trauma" (141), but in doing so, ignores the mid–1980s anxieties about Japan's youth culture that gave rise to the film's emblems of violence and anomie.

Correcting this oversight is crucial because of the influence which both this manga and film have had in Japanese comics and animation. The mid- to late-1980s saw a sudden interest in cyberpunk visions of the future in Japanese manga, something not popularly present before Ōtomo's series. While the 1970s saw a number of punk or dystopic manga—*Devilman* (デビルマン; 1972–73) by Nagai Gō and *The Drifting Classroom* (漂流教室; 1972–74) by Umezu Kazuo, for example—the cyberpunk manga did not really take form as a popular genre until *after* the publication of *Akira* from 1982–1990. In manga, Shirō Masamune's *Appleseed* (アップルシード; 1985–1989) and *Ghost in the Shell* (攻殻機動隊; 1989–1997), and Kishiro Yukito's *Battle Angel Alita* (銃夢; 1990–1995) followed soon after *Akira*'s publication, and a number of cyberpunk anime—*Bubblegum Crisis* (バブルガムクライシス; 1987–1991)[4] and *Neo-Tokyo* (迷宮物語; 1987), which featured a story written and directed by Ōtomo, and *Genesis Survivor Gaiarth* (創世機士ガイアース; 1992)—premiered either during or soon after *Akira*'s publication. Therefore, understanding the context in which the film and movie versions of *Akira* were produced is crucial to understanding not only the works themselves, but also the increasing interest in cyberpunk in Japanese manga and animation.

Three introductory sociocultural phenomena must be understood if we are fully to grasp the context for the film version of *Akira*. The first is the Bubble Economy. The Bubble Economy, according to Eric Johnston was "[t]he period between roughly 1985 and 1990[, which] was a time of unparalleled prosperity in Japan. But it was also a gilded age defined by opulence, corruption, extravagance and waste" (n.p.). Thanks largely in part to land speculation, the Japanese economy grew rapidly in the mid–1980s. The Bubble Economy era was one where many Japanese people were concerned for the very idea of what it meant to be Japanese, as the concept of *giri* was, for many, being carelessly tossed aside.

Giri, too, needs further elucidation here. The term has no direct cognate in Western culture, but it is foundational to the Japanese understanding of society, where it is "the most valued standard in human relationships: master-subordinate, parent-child, husband-wife, brothers and sisters, friends, and sometimes even enemies and business connections. If pressed to define it, *giri* involves caring for others from whom one has received a debt of gratitude and a determination to realize their happiness, sometimes even by self-sacrificing" (Gillespie and Sugiura, qtd. in Davies and Ikeno 95). Most scholars trace the concept to the rise of rice-farming, which created strong community bonds, as a thousand years ago, raising rice was an activity upon which the entire community depended, and at times involved a great deal of communal assistance, which in turn was expected to be paid back (Davies and Ikeno 96). During the Bubble Economy, the practice of *giri* was threatened: "The frugality and austerity that defined the country during the postwar era gave way to extravagance and conspicuous consumption. Stories of housewives in Nara sipping $500 cups of coffee sprinkled with gold dust or businessmen spending tens of thousands of dollars in Tokyo's flashy restaurants and nightclubs were legion" (Johnston n.p.). Today, Johnston finds that the Bubble Economy is looked upon with mixed reactions, but that many view it "as the moment in Japan's history when the country abandoned it's [*sic*] traditional moral, social, [and] cultural values and became greedy in an allegedly Western or American sense" (n.p.). Mary Brinton notes the prevalence of "fanciful stories" told about reckless young people in the late 1980s who would work for a few months, while sponging off of their parents, then take months-long vacations (6). Japanese society was under the belief that the economy was ruining its youth.

A third background element, validating that belief for many in the Bubble era and its aftermath was the popularity of *bōsōzoku* motorcycle gangs. Comprised of rebellious young men, these gangs were in themselves considered a major threat to the stability of Japanese society, and in the 1980s a common target of older adults' ire. Indeed, Sato Iyuka in *Kamikaze Biker* states that they caused a "moral hysteria" in the nation (2). The gangs peaked in the early 1980s, though they remained a viable presence throughout the 1990s; over 96,000 arrests were made of *bōsōzoku* members for reckless driving in 2000 ("Fall in Traffic Offense…"), although there were only 9,064 known *bōsōzoku* members in 2011, down from a peak of 42,510 in 1982 ("Biker gang ranks…"). The beginning of *Akira*'s publication in 1982 coincides with the peak of biker gangs in Japan. Yet despite the gangs' diminished presence, the image of the *bōsōzoku* gang member continues to be a popular one in Japanese culture, as figures evoking both fascinated terror and sympathy (Sato 197–200). The *bōsōzoku* gang member is a particular manifestation of a common figure in modern Japanese culture, that of the reckless young man, unbound by the constraints of society, who is often prone to violence and self-aggrandizement. Thus, even as *Akira* as manga was first published in 1982, at the very height of the *bōsōzoku* phenomenon, it also draws from a broader iconography.

The figure of the young man unable to fit into the normal confines of Japanese society is a trope in Japanese culture that stretches, in its modern form, back into the Meiji Era (1868–1912). Marie Morimoto notes the common analogy in *jidaigeki*, or period-piece dramas which are typically set in the Edo period (1603–1868), of "the lone warrior struggling against all odds" working "as a metaphor for Japan as a nation" (21–22). Although earlier examples exist, perhaps the most influential appearance of this figure appears in Natsume Sōseki's[5] novel *Botchan* (坊っちゃん),[6] published in 1906. The novel's title translates approximately to "Young Master" in English, in a familiar, but old-fashioned sense; this is the name given to the novel's main character by an aged female servant. Known only as Botchan in the text, the central figure is a graduate from a western-style university in Tokyo who becomes a mathematics teacher for a school full of delinquent boys, as he has nothing better to do with his degree. Interestingly, Botchan himself acts as a liminal figure between these juvenile delinquents and society at large. Due to his own personal code of ethics, Botchan is unable to act as a member of modern Japanese society in good standing; the novel's first line hints at this outcome: "Ever since I was a child, my inherent recklessness has brought me nothing but trouble" (Sōseki 5). Although the kanji characters used to describe Botchan's recklessness (無鉄砲) are different from those used to describe reckless driving (暴走), the idea of a lack of restraint is shared in both the figure of Botchan and in that of the motorcycle gang member. Botchan eventually gives up his teaching position after he and another instructor attempt to stop a fight between their students and a rival school, and get caught up in the fight themselves; this fight is later used as a pretense to fire Botchan's only friend at the school, a man named Hotta. Botchan's affirmation as to his fighting prowess as he is pummeled with a stone, and dives into fight himself, presages the attitudes of *bōsōzoku* gang members yet to come: "'Who do you think I am?' I shouted again. 'I may be small, but Tokyo's the home of fighting, and I can still show you a thing or two'" (196). Botchan himself is not fired, although unlike Hotta, he actively fought back against the boys. What follows is a shocking sequence of voluntary exile and retaliatory violence that seems to almost predict the *bōsōzoku* phenomenon. Before leaving the town and the school where he had worked, Botchan and Hotta ambush their two rivals, who had convinced the school's principal to fire Hotta because of his involvement in trying to stop the fight; Botchan and Hotta beat their rivals until they are unable to resist their blows anymore (218–21). Botchan goes back to Tokyo to take a job as an assistant mechanic (223). This outcome further forecasts the cultural understanding of the manual laborer, especially the mechanic, as allied with the *bōsōzoku* gang member, whose connection to his motorcycle is seen as paramount. The influence of Sōseki on modern Japanese culture is difficult to overstate; the translators of another of Sōseki's novels, *I Am a Cat*, claim that "Sōseki rapidly achieved, and has since maintained, wide-spread recognition as the best of modern Japanese novelists" ("Introduction" viii). A joke referencing this novel's nameless cat narrator found its way into the videogame *Mother 2/EarthBound*

(1994, 1995) in the form of the nameless mouse who accompanied a strange inventor named Apple Kid. Andrew Lee states that "*Botchan* is required reading at school in Japan" (n.p.). The perennial interest in Sōseki's novels, and the place that *Botchan* has in the Japanese school curriculum positions the figure of the reckless young man clashing with society directly into the heart of Japanese popular culture. While some of Botchan's actions may be reprehensible, then, the intense sympathy Sōseki encourages toward him lays the groundwork for the *bōsōzoku* mythos some 80 years later.

Just as the reckless young man and the school full of delinquent boys are common motifs in Japanese literature and art (often they coincide, naturally, as the troubled young man will belong to a school full of other delinquents), so too are they linked in Japanese manga and videogames. The *bōsōzoku* archetype has remained popular, despite the actual number of *bōsōzoku* gangs dropping severely in the past two decades. This sympathetic rebel, the high school aged *bōsōzoku* gang member, finds its hold in many different series: Ōtomo's *Akira* (1982–1990), in which all of the main characters belong to a motorcycle gang; Fujisawa Tōru's comedy series *Shōnan Jun'ai Gumi* (湘南純愛組 ; 1990–1996) and *Great Teacher Onizuka* (グレート・ティーチャー・オニヅカ, officially abbreviated as *GTO*; 1997–2002), the former of which features two hapless *bōsōzoku* gang member high school students looking for love, and the latter featuring one of those two gang members as a teacher in a school full of delinquents; Miyashita Akira's comic *Sakigake!! Otokojuku* (魁!!男塾; 1985–1991), which features a motorcyclist among its many male delinquent school characters; and Kase Atsushi's *Kamereon* (カメレオン; 1990–1999), a comedy series about a young high school boy who dreams of one day running his own *bōsōzoku* gang.[7] More recently, the videogame/visual novel *Danganronpa* (localized in America as *Danganronpa: Trigger Happy Havoc*; 2010) also has as one of its main characters a *bōsōzoku* gang leader. While the majority of the appearances of this figure make him a figure of either irony or comedic buffoonery, when handled seriously, as in the case of *Akira,* the rash juvenile delinquent takes on new dimensions, and in the film adaptation of this manga, provides a means of understanding the common neuroses in Japan plaguing a society being redefined by new money.

Nosaka Akiyuki, the author of the short story that was later turned into the film *Grave of the Fireflies*, shortly before the release of the film in Japan in 1986, gave an interview with that film's director, Takahata Isao, that speaks to this neurosis and crystallizes the fears about Japanese youth culture that both this film and *Akira* reflect.[8] Both interviewees were children during World War II, and felt that the children of the mid–80s in Japan were losing their connection to a sense of duty:

TAKAHATA: ... Seita is different. When he's insulted by his aunt, he isn't stoic but withdraws and goes away to do other things. He doesn't *endure* it. I think Seita's feelings, those kind of feelings, are better understood by today's children. It's my generation that thinks he has to endure it. Today's children... base their decisions on whether something is pleasant or not. [...] It's not only the children.... I think the times are becoming that way, as well.

NOSAKA: That main character is rather spoiled for a wartime child. In that sense, I think today's children would become just like him if they were put into the same situation [Takahata "Two Grave Voices" 7].

Both the director and author of the short story this film is based on find that the difference between Seita and his cohorts is his inability to live a life not centered around pleasure; the same fate exists for the children of the 1980s. Nosaka later clarifies the context in which he wrote his story, which ironically forecasts the Bubble Economy era in which this film was produced: "I wrote this book in 1967, right in the middle of Japan's high economic growth years. From my perspective it looked like an abnormal time. I thought the real spirit of humanity was different..." (9). The idea of the dissolution of what held society together was present, for Nosaka, in the 1960s, and for Takahata, this was similarly reflected during the Bubble Economy. The reckless young man in *Grave of the Fireflies* is shown as a cautionary tale for Japanese youth. As Dani Cavallaro so aptly and succinctly states, it is "Seita's determination to take his and his sister's fate solely into his hands—thereby refusing to help his compatriots with the war effort" that dooms the two children (29). This film and its message, appearing in the same year that *Akira* debuted, crystallizes the contemporary Japanese concern over the erosion of *giri*. Nosaka calls his story "a double-suicide" narrative, which Takahata compares directly to "Chikamatsu's double-suicide plays" (7). An editor's note to this translation of the interview states that Chikamatsu was the eighteenth-century "playwright and author of 'The Love Suicides at Amijima,' a play which dramatically contrasted the *ninjo* of 'individual emotion' of a pair of doomed lovers against the *giri* or 'social obligation' of society" (7). The failure of Seita is seen as one boy's failure to enact *giri*.

This is the underlying framework that enables us to understand the aims of *Akira*. What we are presented with in Ōtomo's film is a world where *giri* is no longer valued by society at large. Instead, each sector of society has become disassociated from all others, and most of the characters in the film seek out selfish interests. The resolution of the film, the fantastical vanquishing of this selfishness, is ultimately a reaffirmation of *giri*, achieved paradoxically by members of an anarchic motorcycle gang. The film opens with this gang's brutal attack on a rival *bōsōzoku* group: hardly an auspicious start, but one intended to confirm its audience's sense of living within an urban dystopia.

A brief synopsis of the film version of *Akira* is required to understand the regeneracy of the characters and their various motivations, for it is important to clarify here that the majority of my argument is based upon the film, which was written and directed by the manga's creator, Ōtomo, and which thus forms an alternate-yet-authoritative retelling of his still-ongoing print narrative. I do occasionally refer to the divergencies between the film and the manga, especially concerning the film's development of events in volume 2 and beyond, but space does not allow here for a full discussion of all six volumes. Ōtomo sets his story thirty years after WWIII, and whereas the manga briefly discusses the nuclear conflict as having destroyed many cities around the world, the film takes us straight to a dystopic Neo-Tokyo. Neo-Tokyo is a gritty, dangerous city full of neon lights and mobs barely controlled by brutal police violence, one where groups of teenagers engage in violent, drug-fueled assaults. One such gang, led by high school student Kaneda Shōtarō crosses paths with a strange, withered child, whose immense psychic powers seem to awaken similar abilities in Kaneda's best friend, Shima Tetsuo. Tetsuo is promptly abducted by the military, and enlisted in a top-secret program along with the mysterious child, one of the espers. These figures are ancient, withered children, all with psychic abilities and physical ailments; Kiyoko, the only female, is a bedridden clairvoyant, while Takashi, who can walk with some difficulty, and Masaru, who is restricted to a hovering wheelchair, can both use psychokinetics, or the ability to move objects with their minds. These three espers are key figures, and their back histories are revealed in the film's climax. As characters who embody connections both to the past— they have been children for decades, yet are preternaturally old—and the future—they embody the future of human evolution—they eventually become the ideal representative force for *giri* in this film. Though the relation of Tetsuo to the espers is unclear at first, viewers are aware that Tetsuo's mental powers are surgically enhanced, and that the Colonel and Doctor—figures referred to in most cases only by their titles—behind the program see the captive boy as a military asset. Meanwhile, a scheming politician named Nezu secretly influences a group of radical dissidents, led by a man named Ryu, to foment discord and terrorism in Neo-Tokyo. Kei, a teenaged girl in this terrorist movement, meets Kaneda, the motorcycle gang leader, and—as underdogs in the whole sordid system—they embark on a rocky courtship. Eventually, after much death and destruction wreaked by the militarily-enhanced psychic powers of Tetsuo, the three espers summon Akira, the most powerful psychic in existence, whose power began WWIII three decades prior, when he accidentally destroyed much of Tokyo. Akira takes Tetsuo and the espers with him to a safe-haven in another existential realm, leaving behind a partially destroyed Neo-Tokyo, but with Kaneda, Kei, and the Colonel left alive at the end.

The motives of most characters for most of the film are baldly selfish. Tetsuo, on discovering his psychic abilities, steals Kaneda's motorcycle and his crimes later escalate to the wholesale slaughter of hundreds or thousands of people. Tetsuo makes it clear that his ambition is to be better than Kaneda, to whom he has felt subordinate for most of his life. After Kaneda shows up to attempt to rescue him, Tetsuo informs his would-be rescuer: "That's okay, Kaneda. I won't be needing you to save me anymore. From now on, I'll be saving you. All you have to do is ask, Kanny," before becoming upset and violently knocking Kaneda around the room via telekinesis.[9] Kaneda, for his part, acts as a constant reminder in this film of the danger of abandoning past relationships and prior obligations for the thrill of new experiences. In this way, Kaneda acts as a stand-in for the commonly held fears about what might happen to Japan's youth during the Bubble Economy, even as Tetsuo represents a figure from the then-present moment, a rebellious young man whose social duty lies only with his closest friends. As Tetsuo releases himself from previous bonds by specifically harming those who make up the fabric of his daily life—stealing Kaneda's motorcycle, killing the owner of a bar that he and his friends frequented, and murdering one of the members of his own motorcycle gang—he becomes increasingly destructive to society at large. His uncontrollable rise is the greatest threat to Japan since the beginning of World War III. Thus, Tetsuo even more than Kaneda, who reforms, represents a doomsday scenario about youth culture separated from the concept of *giri*.

This is, however, but one facet of the problem. While Ōtomo's film contains these fears about a disconnected youth culture, it also contains a harsh critique of the adults whose greed corrupts the economy. Here, a single character, Councilman Nezu, leads a double life as rightwing plutocrat and leftwing insurrectionist, and in both forms flouts *giri* for the sake of personal enrichment. He does so from the position of a greedy, rich, older generation, more concerned with titles and stocks than the welfare of the nation. Fittingly, although the kanji for his name are comprised of characters for root/source (根) and harbor (津), his name sounds very similar to *nezumi* (鼠) the word for mouse or rat. Considering his appearance, abnormally short, with a pinched face and buck teeth, it is clear that Ōtomo intends for viewers to associate him with a rodent. The film establishes, first, his failure as a councilman to protect the public welfare, through his hypocritical funding of an insurrectionist movement ostensibly intended to redress social injustice, and secondly, his betrayal of those who join the movement in good faith. Near the end of the film he is seen, during the middle of a military coup of the government, burning documents and shoving money and legal papers into a suitcase. His right-hand man, Ryu, is shot by Nezu during the attempted escape; Ryu lives to see Nezu die, but it seems clear from the film that, though we never see Ryu himself die, the gun-wound to the stomach will make his fate certain. Ōtomo shows both of these characters, one as a greedy, morally bankrupt city councilman, and the other as a political dissident, one whose goal is to totally upend society, as having no concern for their obligations to the rest of their city or nation. Ryu's goals may be more noble, but his means of achieving them, involving the bombing of public spaces, show a further disregard for *giri*.

Both of these characters' roles in Ōtomo's film are noticeably different from their appearance in his manga, and show marked attention by Ōtomo to simplify their characters, and thusly the lesson they teach. Ryu, over the course of the manga, moves from being a terrorist into part of the force instrumental in taking out both Tetsuo and Akira. Although he dies in the sixth volume of the manga after shooting Akira (6.266–269), by this point he has had some chance to reform; such a chance is denied to him in the film.[10] Nezu, too, is somewhat different from his appearance in the manga. In the original source material, Nezu is secretly working for a character almost entirely cut from the film, Lady Miyako, the psychically gifted leader of a religious cult. Ōtomo limits Lady Miyako's presence in the film to two or three brief scenes, and he renders her gratuitous to the resolution of the plot, whereas in the manga, is she is instrumental in opposing slowly the deterioration of society in Tokyo. Her sacrificial death at the end of the sixth volume (6.317–322) provides the catalyst for Tetsuo's downfall. She, in many aspects, embodies the concept of *giri*, and Ōtomo's choice to remove her from the film simplifies and focuses his message about *giri* by restricting its full expression to one group of characters. Nezu's death in the manga comes as, in his attempts to betray Lady Miyako, he is shot by Ryu in the stomach (3.204–206) and, shortly thereafter, shot again by the military after attempting to assassinate Akira (3.231–233). One perceives in the manga, too, that Nezu's attempt on Akira's life is the inverse of Lady Miyako's sacrificial death, as his efforts result in a terrible psychic explosion that levels much of Neo-Tokyo (3.244–271). The death sequence in the manga, then, including Nezu's last moments, reflects more on Nezu's isolation through his private ambitions than on his public sins. But in the film, worthless stacks of money and bonds blow away in the wind as he slumps over and dies, making the message about the futility of his greed for money and property especially clear. His money cannot save him from the rottenness of his heart in the same way that the sudden influx of real-estate cash will not be salvific for Japan. The film makes a subject whose layers of treachery are complex in the manga a figure with more obvious economic motives. The third volume of the Japanese manga, which had developed the character of Lady Miyako and seen the death of Nezu, had been published in full as a collection in August of 1986 ("AKIRA (3)"). The film was released almost two years later, in July of 1988. The choices to minimize Lady Miyako and to simplify Nezu's character for the film were clearly conscious on Ōtomo's part, and should be read jointly as an indictment of the world of "extravagance and conspicuous consumption" that Japan had rapidly overtaken Japanese culture in that brief interval (Johnston n.p.).

Of the other characters in the film, only two sets of people can be said to retain, or to rediscover, a sense of social obligation: the maturing Kaneda and the remaining members of his *bōsōzoku* gang, and the three espers. Kaneda acts out of a sense of personal duty, seeing it as his task to kill his friend for the betterment of the world. In this way, Kaneda acts out of a sense of *giri*. There is a strong emotional bond between both Kaneda and Tetsuo, and Kaneda's initial attempts to rescue him from the military show his deep concern for his friend. Both may be juvenile delinquents, but Kaneda understands both his obligations to his friend, and to society as a whole, when he moves from attempting to rescue Tetsuo to attempting to kill him. At the end of the film, when Tetsuo is devoured by Akira's power, he begs for Kaneda's help, and Kaneda tries to go to him, even though he is warned by one of the espers, Takashi, that he should not. The dreamscape that Kaneda enters after entering into Akira's psychic bubble shows his long-lasting relationship with Tetsuo, along with the long-lasting relationship the espers have with each other, and their connection with Akira. Although the film and manga versions of *Akira* differ greatly in their conclusions, this dreamscape sequence appears in both, and is key to understanding the sense of *giri* that holds these key characters together (6.344–361).

In the film version of the sequence, Kaneda and Tetsuo are shown riding their motorcycles together, with Kaneda instructing Tetsuo how to ride, and then shows how Tetsuo was, before this, a lonely orphan. The scene then shifts, to show the espers and Akira as young, regular-looking children, at a strangely scenic institute where they undergo harmful experiments. Even as their bodies deteriorate, they still find happiness in their friendship with each other. The action shifts back to Tetsuo as a bullied child, being befriended by Kaneda, who restores to him a stolen toy and instructs him on how to handle the bullying. The parallels between Tetsuo, Kaneda, and the espers are made clear here, especially in reference to their established social connections. While these moments are brief in the film, lasting less than four minutes, they serve as a reminder during the film's climax as to the only force which can bring resolution to Neo-Tokyo's chaos—the duty of social bonds. Indeed, this force is vulnerable if just one person tries to enact it. In the film, Kaneda attempts to act out according to his *giri* but since his only idea is framed in *bōsōzoku*-style vigilantism, he cannot neutralize Tetsuo without outside intervention.

As we have seen, Ōtomo's critique of Japanese society in the late 1980s exposes both the problems inherent in youth culture, and the problems inherent in business culture. Still, an interesting reevaluation of these punk teenagers in the context of the Bubble Economy is demanded by this film. Of all of the film's many characters, the only mortals to show a sense of social duty outside of the espers, are the violent, delinquent teenagers. The adult figures in this film are almost universally irredeemable. The Colonel does make the attempt to restore order in Neo-Tokyo (and survives at the end of the film), but his disrespect for any authority other than himself shows his methods to be simply a means to an end, the maintenance of his pet project, the espers. At one point in the film, the Colonel literally shoots the messenger when the Executive Council informs him of his being removed from military control. By contrast, there is great value shown in this film in the attitudes of the marginalized delinquents; their alternative lifestyle has fostered positive understandings of interpersonal relationships. While their methods are reprehensible, their social bonds are foundational. By implication, it will take another group of eternal children to fully develop the essence of *giri*.

Pointedly then, the only characters who can presently resolve the conflict and are aware of their social obligations are the extra-human espers themselves. They initially take some actions which prove fruitless to combat Tetsuo—attacking him with golems made out of toys, and abducting Kei to fight Tetsuo at Akira's storage facility—but ultimately they resolve the conflict through what amounts to a formal consecration of both their own past relationships and their joint relationship, as a group, to society as a whole. As figures that are at the same time both youthful and ancient, small children yet with white hair, wrinkles and pallid skin, they are the perfect connection to the past, attesting to the power of old obligations in the present.

Two-thirds of the way through the film, the esper Kiyoko most clearly announces the espers' intentions in terms of relationship to Tetsuo, and in a way that acknowledges their own faults for mishandling him earlier: "When [psychic] power is awakened inside, it is important to wisely choose how to use it. When the time comes, you might not know it, yet alone be prepared for it. Your friend has already made this choice. Tetsuo is our newest companion. He's our friend, also. His actions are out of control, and for that we're partly to blame, too." There is a clear message in this exchange about the importance of personal responsibility, and failing that, the responsibility that others have to guide and take care of their friends and fellow members of society. Kaneda shouts "Tetsuo's our friend, not yours!" in complaint, as his personal sense of *giri*, at this moment in the film, does not extend beyond his own long-established social bonds. Kaneda and the other members of the *bōsōzoku* gang are the only ones in this film who have a long-lasting friendship with Testuo, but the espers here see him as a member of their own society as well. They are aware of the social impact that Tetsuo can have, having seen the destruction of Tokyo first-hand due to an uncontrollable psychic blast three decades prior. Kaneda sees Tetsuo only as his own problem, but the espers are aware of him as their own responsibility as well, as he belongs to their broader society of psychics.

The film's climax invokes a sense of self-sacrificial duty and reverence for past social obligations as a solution to social conflict. As Tetsuo and Kaneda fight in the Olympic stadium, the espers appear and, before the remains of Akira—set up as if they were relics or objects of veneration—they place themselves in what appears to be the action of prayer. They are here to honor their lost friend and their past relationships. The veneration of the dead as spiritual intercessors is common in *Shinto*, the native religion of Japan; the souls of especially important people were frequently enshrined and officially installed as a deity, or *kami* (神) throughout Japanese history.[11] This act of recognizing their past relationships to try to influence their present is the essence of *giri*. Through their prayers before the relics of their lost friend, they manage to resurrect Akira, who envelops Tetsuo in his own psychic power, a growing bubble of whiteness which proves the film's *deus ex machina*.[12]

The esper Takashi's attempt to stop Kaneda from going to Tetsuo as Akira's psychic power enveloped him shows the espers's willingness to sacrifice their own lives for others; their responsibilities to others supersedes their own personal desires. As Takashi goes into the growing psychic bubble after Kaneda to attempt to rescue him, the remaining two espers, Masaru and Kiyoko, at first try to prevent Takashi from entering the psychic bubble, and then debate on what they should do:

> Kiyoko: "No don't, wait Takashi!"
> Masaru: "If you went in now, you'd be trapped along with him."
> Takashi: "But he... none of this is his fault at all!" [Takashi enters into the psychic bubble after Kaneda.]
> Masaru: "Takashi!"
> Kiyoko: "Takashi!"
> Masaru: "If we went in there, we wouldn't be strong enough to come back out again."
> Kiyoko: "But if the three of us tried, maybe we could save that boy."
> Masaru: "You're right. Us three together..."

Ultimately, all three espers join together to save Kaneda's life, recognizing the justness of Kaneda's attempts to rescue his friend, and acknowledging his blamelessness in his attempt to right his friend's uncontrolled wrongs. Once these characters have entered into the psychic bubble, the audience is reminded of each of these characters' own past relations. The importance of traditional ideas of *giri* is stressed through the memories and actions of Kaneda, and especially of the espers.

This focus does not appear in the ending of the manga. The film implies that while the espers, Akira, and Tetsuo have left the world, they are not dead but merely beyond or above it in some way. The voices of Kiyoko and Masaru, some of the final lines of the film, imply that they will someday return, completing their initial hesitation about not being able to return from Akira's psychic power:

> KIYOKO: "But some day we ought to be able to…"
> MASARU: "Because it has already begun."

The manga does not include such a positive note to end on. In the last major action which takes place in the manga, Kaneda appears with a new *bōsōzoku* gang to attack a United Nations peacekeeping military force and tell a group of foreign aid workers to leave the rubble of Tokyo: "This is a sovereign nation! If you come again without an invitation, we're gonna treat you as invaders, got it ?! … Akira still lives among us!" (6.421–422). The idea of Akira still being present exists in this version as a threat, instead of a promise of return and progress as it is in the film. The idea of *giri* on a societal level is not held up here, although on an individual level it is maintained.[13] By the time the manga had ended on June 25th of 1990, the bubble economy had burst—the week of December 25, 1989, the Nikkei 225 had peaked at 38,916, but by the week of April 9th, 1990 it was down to 29,214, a drop of 9,702 points (nearly 25 percent of the stock market's peak value) which completely erased *all* of the stock gains for the year of 1989 (Yahoo!Finance)—and the widespread concern that spendthrift young people were going to ruin the country as they abandoned their morals died with the housing market. The Bubble Economy's bursting proved a moment of deep introspection in Japan (Laura Hein 459–61). Japanese beliefs about the economy fell, but what briefly replaced them was a moment where Japanese youth "began exploring new directions, knowing that they were as likely to succeed by striking out on their own as with the now uncertain standard lifetime-employment path," before there was a cultural backlash (Hein 461). There seemed to be a moment where the hopes of the Japanese youth to find a new, better structure, outside of the established economy, could provide a new way forward. What is fascinating about this film's assertion of *giri* is its focus on young people being the bastions of social obligation. Whereas the expected seat of *giri* might be seen in an older generation, in this film, the ones to change society are youth, and briefly, in the early 1990s, this appeared to be happening, before social beliefs in the power of the Japanese economy reasserted themselves.

The film ends on a much more hopeful and reconciliatory note than the manga does, as to the efficacy of *giri* for future change. While this film may be ostensibly about psychic powers and motorcycle gangs, one message Ōtomo sent to his intended audience was that only self-sacrifice for the good of others can ultimately resolve the problems faced by society. Ōtomo's film has a pointed focus, relevant to the moment in which it was produced during the Japanese Bubble Economy; the fears hiding in the background of this film, of a youth culture out of control while a world of greedy businessmen existed only to generate more personal wealth as the ruination of Japan, are addressed in such a way that there is a clear hope for the future for those who are willing to remember the obligations that persist despite social change.

NOTES

1. This essay uses the Modified Hepburn method of Romanization for all Japanese words and names, following the ALA-LC guidelines for Romanization, located at http://www.loc.gov/catdir/cpso/roman.html. Except for in the works cited entries, Japanese names retain traditional Japanese naming conventions, wherein the family name precedes the given name. Japanese words which have attained common English spellings, most notably Tokyo, will retain the common English spelling. Occasional Japanese words in common use in the field of Japanese comics and television are also used, most notably *manga*, the Japanese word for comics, and *anime*, the Japanese word for animation; when referring to Japanese examples, neither of these words appear in italics throughout the text. As *Akira* (アキラ) is spelled using *katakana*, the writing system usually reserved either for emphasis or foreign loan words, it would normally be Romanized in Japan as *AKIRA*; however, Western naming conventions for titles have been preserved throughout, except for specific references to Japanese-language resources.

2. The kanji characters for *bōsōzoku* translate literally to "runaway" or "reckless driving" (暴走) paired with "tribe" or "band" (族). Thus, it is a motorcycle gang that is characterized specifically by the uncontrollable nature of its driving.

3. Esper is derived from combining ESP (Extra Sensory Perception) with the -er suffix, to arrive at an in-world term for psychic. Both esper and psychic, when referring to a person, are used interchangeably in this essay.

4. *Bubblegum Crisis* includes many references to the film *Blade Runner*, and so is not only influenced by *Akira*, but can be seen to be part of a growing interest in cyberpunk in Japanese popular culture which occurred after *Akira*'s publication. *Bubblegum Crisis* also saw a large number of spinoffs of its own, including *AD Police Files* (ADポリス; 1990), *Bubblegum Crash* (バブルガムクラッシュ!; 1991), and *Bubblegum Crisis Tokyo 2040* (バブルガムクライシス TOKYO 2040; 1998–99), just to name a few, showing the continuing popularity of cyberpunk during this era.

5. Although typically an author would be known by a family name in a formal essay, as Sōseki is this author's penname (his given name is Kin'nosuke), he is most commonly referred to in scholarly literature as Sōseki.

6. Two editions of this work are cited in this essay: the Japanese-language version posted on Natsumesosekiwww and an English-language version translated by Alan Turney. References to specific kanji characters used refer to the former source, and quotes in English from the latter.

7. While the prior examples have been translated into English, *Sakigake!! Otokojuku* and *Kamereon* remain Japanese-language only texts.

8. The only English-language translation of this short story is Nosaka, Akiyuki. "A Grave of Fireflies." Translated by James R. Abrams. *Japan Quarterly*, vol. 25, issue 4, 1978, pp. 445–463.

9. Direct quotes in English come from the 2001 Pioneer dub of *AKIRA*, the most recent translation of the film available.

10. The publishing history of this work in English is somewhat complicated. Published in Japan originally in *Weekly Young Magazine* (週刊ヤングマガジン) from Dec. 20, 1982 to June 25, 1990, *AKIRA* was later collected in six volumes of approximately 300–400 pages each, published by Kodansha from 1984 to 1993. The Japanese term for any such collection dedicated to a single comic series is called a *tankōbon* (単行本). These *tankōbon* were later translated into English and published by Dark Horse Comics from 2000 to 2002. A second edition of these volumes was published in English by Kodansha Comics from 2009 to 2011.

The large size distinction has been preserved for both of these English language versions. An earlier English version of *AKIRA* with colored images was published in 38 editions of approximately 50–60 pages each by Epic Comics from 1988 from 1995, with anthologies of those colorized editions appearing in ten volumes from 1990 from 1993; the last five editions were never anthologized into these volumes, and so the collection of this early English version remains incomplete; the individual colorized editions and their anthologies remain out of print. The editions referred to in this essay are the Dark Horse Comics versions.

11. *Kami* (神) is a particularly difficult word to translate, as it encapsulates a much wider array of meanings than the English "god" or "spirit." A *kami* can be any divine entity or force worthy of reverence, and can be an abstract concept, the spirit of a tree or waterfall, a particular deity or host of deities belonging or not belonging to the Japanese pantheon, a Supreme Being, or the spirits of the dead. The most infamous shrine in Japan is Yasukuni Shrine, where the souls of all those who died in the service of the Empire of Japan are deified; over 2.4 million souls are enshrined who died in wars spanning from the Boshin War (1868–69) to World War II (1939–45) ("History"). The webpage for Yasukuni Shrine conveniently fails to include the information that even convicted war criminals from World War II are among the deified. Approximately 1,000 war criminals from World War II are among the millions of kami enshrined at Yasukuni, deified in a secret ceremony in 1978 (Christopher Woolf n.p.).

12. One might be tempted to make an analogy between this bubble and the Bubble Economy here, but I feel this is an incorrect vehicle for such an analogy. The bubble mirrors the initial psychic blast which destroyed Tokyo in the first pages of the manga, which first appeared in 1984, before the Bubble Economy had begun to rise.

13. Visions of both Tetsuo and another slain friend and member of the motorcycle gang, Yamagata, appear on their motorcycles as Kaneda, Kei, and his other living members ride off away from the defeated UN peacekeeping forces; as they continue to ride with these ghostly companions, the rubble of the city falls away and a pristine vision of Neo-Tokyo takes its place in the final few pages (6.429–433). The final moments imply a restoration of Neo-Tokyo not based off of obligation to others *in general*, but rather *in specific*, which is a narrower understanding of *giri* than would normally be accepted. These teenagers do not recognize "a social obligation or moral duty or debt" to any group outside of their newly established and revolutionary way of life (Davies and Ikeno 97). The do-it-yourself attitude of punk is reaffirmed in this ending in ways missing from the movie's conclusion.

Works Cited

Ape and HAL Laboratory. *Mother 2: Gīgu Strikes Back* (マザー2 ギーグの逆襲). Nintendo, 1994. Rpt. As *EarthBound*. 1995.

"Biker Gang Ranks Fall Below 10,000." *Japan Times*, 11 Feb. 2011, http://www.japantimes.co.jp/news/2011/02/11/national/biker-gang-ranks-fall-below-10000/. Accessed 30 June 2013.

Brinton, Mary C. *Lost in Transition: Youth, Work, and Instability in Postindustrial Japan*. Cambridge UP, 2010.

Cavallaro, Dani. "The Nightmare of History: *Belladonna of Sadness*, *Grave of the Fireflies*, and *Like the Clouds, Like the Wind*." *Anime and the Art of Adaptation: Eight Famous Works from Page to Screen*. McFarland, 2010, pp. 19–37.

Davies, Roger J., and Osamu Ikeno, editors. "Giri: Japanese Social Obligations." *The Japanese Mind: Understanding Contemporary Japanese Culture*. Tuttle Pub, 2002, pp. 95–101.

"Fall in Traffic Offense Arrests Linked to Police Being 'Busy.'" *Japan Times*, 2 Feb. 2001.

Fujisawa, Tōru. *Great Teacher Onizuka* (グレート・ティーチャー・オニヅカ). 25 vols. Kodansha, 1997–2002. Rpt. As *GTO: Great Teacher Onizuka*. TokyoPop, 2002–2005.

_____. *Shōnan Jun'ai Gumi* (湘南純愛組). 31 vols. Kodansha, 1991–1996. Rpt. As *GTO: The Early Years: Shonan Junai Gumi*. TokyoPop, 2006–2009. Vols. 1–10. And *GTO: The Early Years*. Vertical, 2012. Vols. 11–15.

Hein, Laura. "The Cultural Career of the Japanese Economy: Developmental and Cultural Nationalisms in Historical Perspective." *Third World Quarterly*, vol. 29, no. 3, 2008, pp. 447–465. *Business Source Complete*. Accessed 6 November 2014.

"History." *Yasukuni Shrine*, 2008, http://www.yasukuni.or.jp/english/about/index.html. Accessed 4 November 2014.
Johnston, Eric. "Lessons from When the Bubble Burst." *The Japan Times*, 6 Jan. 2009, http://www.japantimes.co.jp/news/2009/01/06/reference/lessons-from-when-the-bubble-burst/. Accessed 27 June 2013.
Kase, Atsushi. *Kamereon* (カメレオン). 47 vols. Kodansha, 1990–1999.
Lamarre, Thomas. "Born of Trauma: *Akira* and Capitalist Modes of Deconstruction." *Positions*, vol. 16, no. 1, 2008, pp. 131–156. *Project MUSE*. Accessed 23 August 2014.
Lee, Andrew. "*Botchan*." *The Japan Times*, 4 Jan. 2014, http://www.japantimes.co.jp/culture/2014/01/04/books/book-reviews/botchan/#.WsbybOvyupo. Accessed 30 May 2014.
Miller, Gerald. "'To Shift to a Higher Structure': Desire Disembodiment, and Evolution in the Anime of Ōtomo, Ishii, and Anno." *Intertexts*, vol. 9, no. 1–2, 2008, pp. 145–166. *Literature Online*. Accessed 23 August 2014.
Miyashita, Akira. *Sakigake!! Otokojuku* (魁!!男塾). 34 vols. Shueisha, 1985–1991.
My Neighbor Totoro (となりのトトロ). Directed by Hayao Miyazaki, Walt Disney Home Entertainment, 2010.
Morimoto, Marie T. "The 'Peace Dividend' in Japanese Cinema: Metaphors of a Demilitarized Nation." *Colonialism and Nationalism in Asian Cinema*, edited by Wimal Dissanayake, Indiana UP, 1994, pp. 11–29.
Napir, Susan J. "*Akira* and *Ranma ½*: The Monstrous Adolescent." *Anime from* Akira *to* Howl's Moving Castle: *Experiencing Contemporary Japanese Animation*. 2nd ed., Palgrave MacMillan, 2005, pp. 39–62.
Natsume, Sōseki. 坊っちゃん. 1906. Natsumesosekiwww, http://www.natsumesoseki.com/home/botchan. Accessed 30 May 2014.
_____. *Botchan*. Translated by Alan Turney, Kodansha International, 1985.
Ōtomo, Katsuhiro. *Akira*. 1984–1993. Translated by Yoko Umezawa, Linda M. York, Jo Duffy, and Studio Proteus, 6 vols., Dark Horse Comics, 2000–2002.
_____, director. *Akira*. Pioneer, 2001.
Spike Chunsoft. *Danganronpa* (ダンガンロンパ). Spike Chunsoft, 2010. Rpt. As *Danganronpa: Trigger-happy Havoc*. NIS America, 2014.
Takahata, Isao. *Eiga o Tsukurinagara, Kangaeta Koto*. ANIMAGE June 1987. Rpt. By Tokuma Shoten, 1991. Rpt. As "Takahata and Nosaka: Two Grave Voices." Translated by *Animerica* staff. *Animerica*, vol. 2, no. 11, 1994, pp. 6–11.
_____, director. *Grave of the Fireflies* (火垂るの墓). Central Park Media, 2002.
Woolf, Christopher. "Why is the Yasukuni Shrine so Controversial?" *Public Radio International*, 26 December 2013, https://www.pri.org/stories/2013-12-26/why-yasukuni-shrine-so-controversial. Accessed 4 November 2014.
Yahoo!Finance. *Nikkei 225*. Yahoo! Inc., 5 July 2013, https://finance.yahoo.com/chart/%5EN 225. Accessed 5 July 2013.

Schoolgirls and *Sukeban*
Representations of Punk Women in Contemporary Japanese Manga

ALICE VERNON

The contemporary Japanese imagination mixes traditions, themes, and discourses of both Eastern and Western origin. The uniquely Western punk movement in Japan—its style, attitude, and music—influenced a subgenre of manga displaying scenes of cultural and social rebellion and apocalyptic anxieties. Thirty years after the emergence of punk, its aesthetic continues to feature in Japanese visual narratives, but its focus is constantly evolving in accordance with new issues and ideas. Punk's rebellious attitude universally supports or even permits participation of women in their fight to transgress social oppression. As Naomi Griffin suggests, punk provides a space for "a negotiation of expectations of women and femininity" (75). If this is the case with the Western punk movement, can the same be said of its Japanese interpretation? This essay aims to explore how the role of women in punk manga both mirrors and deconstructs their position in the traditional patriarchal structure of Japanese society.

Looking first at Ōtomo Katsuhiro's *Akira* (1982–1990), published during the prime of the punk movement, I will examine whether manga of the 80s permitted space for women's involvement. I will then observe the changes and continuations of attitudes to punk women in Ōkubo Atsushi's *Soul Eater* (2004–2013) and Narita Ryōgo's *Durarara!!* (2009–ongoing). Finally, I will compare these series to a woman's perspective of punk in Hayashida Q's *Dorohedoro* (1999–ongoing). In this essay, I intend to demonstrate the opportunities created by the punk aesthetic for experimentations of gender and, in particular, expectations of feminine behavior, as well as identify punk's ironic tendency to maintain the sexist ideologies of the society it supposedly despises.

Neo-Tokyo's Invisible Women: *Akira* and Female Exclusion in Punk

In 1982, Ōtomo Katsuhiro's *Akira* began serialization. It is a futuristic, post-apocalyptic vision in which teenage gangs fight barrel-chested military men in an epic struggle between scientific advancement and ethical boundaries. Ōtomo's fictional space is the year 2019 in Neo-Tokyo—a city built near the ruins of its original after what seemed to be a nuclear explosion. He creates a setting with careful mingling of scientific development and urban decay; a visually realistic image of the future that is neither wholly advanced nor utterly chaotic. Ōtomo does not, however, fantasize beyond the 1980s in terms of including a developed space for women, punk or otherwise. He imagines military robots, superior technology, and even a discovery of heightened psychological power, but while writing nearly forty years into the future, *Akira* does not present a significant shift in women's social position. There is a rarity of background women as soldiers, scientists, politicians, young rebels, and in scenes of conflict. For example, any crowd scene seems to be made up of boys and men, such as the congregation gathering around Akira in volume 4 (Ōtomo 4: 20–21). A further example includes the scene just before Tetsuo frees Akira from the secure facility: on a page featuring twelve characters (a mixture of scientists, soldiers, The Colonel, and others), Kei is the only female (Ōtomo 2: 232). While Ōtomo has included several important women in *Akira*, it is difficult to spot others in the background. It could be said that each woman is a key figure representing a larger idea of femininity—Kei as the young punk woman, Chiyoko as the physically powerful, independent adult—yet they still do not occupy a significant public space in the series. Some of the clearest evidence for the gender bias is presented in the heavily vandalized sign above Kaneda's club. Among other punk slogans, the sign reads: "No women's bathroom" (Ōtomo 1: 44). It demonstrates an almost childish exclusion of female presence and participation while playing to an ingrained idea that women are stereotypically repulsed by dirt. Here, the club is a rebel space; it is a loud, alcohol- and drug-fueled, broken world that provides respite from the oppressive society outside. However, in rejecting women, it acts as an ironic parallel to a patriarchal sphere. If, as David A. Ensminger believes, punk graffiti serves as a "call to arms," as a way to gather a rebellious force, then in *Akira* it is an invitation that does not extend past the masculine gender (18).

The most major female character appearing throughout *Akira* is Kei— an androgynous young woman working for an anti-government organization. Her appearance is intriguing in its gender neutrality, and while it could be argued that Ōtomo uses Kei's character to embody women's involvement in

1980s punk groups, in light of the sexist club sign, Kei's androgynous design becomes problematic. On the one hand, she is navigating a male-dominated space with a stylistic attempt to blend into the punk aesthetic. It was not uncommon for early punk women to adopt a masculine disguise or "hide first names"—such as Hayashida Q—so as to avoid being caught in sexist discourses both within and outside the underground subcultures (Ensminger 189). In order to contest against the oppression of wider society, Kei must first break from the gendered ideals that restrain her from acts of rebellion. But even so, amidst a sea of teenage boys causing chaos, she is the only clearly visible young woman doing the same. Kei is, of course, joined by her aunt Chiyoko in volume three but again, Chiyoko is a middle-aged, brutishly tall and strong woman. Kei has no female anti-establishment contemporaries her own age and does not belong to any sort of gang as Kaneda did. Ōtomo may have designed her to fit in with the masculine punk image, but rarely is Kei allowed to forget her gendered Otherness in Neo-Tokyo society.

Kei's "progressive" androgynous appearance and participation in the Neo-Tokyo conflict means very little during moments celebrating Kaneda's pubescent boy humor. When the two first meet in volume one, Kei orders Kaneda to come with her at gunpoint. Kaneda snaps his fingers and replies, "My pleasure!" (Ōtomo 1: 78). This sexualization occurs throughout the series as a kind of comic relief, but one which appeals only to sexually-charged adolescent immaturity. It is a joke recurring often throughout the manga, such as the moment when Kaneda barks like a dog and throws himself on top of Kei in volume one (Ōtomo 1: 195) and again when he wraps his handcuffed arms around her in the second volume, trapping her in his embrace (Ōtomo 2: 57). In reality, Ōtomo uses punk bravado as a way to negate the idea of the threatening woman. As Laura Miller and Jan Bardsley describe, a Japanese media tactic of dealing with socially transgressive women is to "trivialize or neutralize the behaviour" by verbally transforming them into "laughable objects of ridicule" or, in Kaneda's case, a sexualized object (5). It shows 80s punk sexism declaring the uselessness of women's participation in the sense that, to Kaneda, a gun is as dangerous as a banana when handled by Kei, and he feels confident enough in this opinion to make a crude remark straight into the barrel. Ōtomo avoids giving Kei true heroic responsibility, and only allows her to take independent action during Kaneda's absence in volume four.

What is perhaps most disconcerting when discussing the rarity of female representation in *Akira* is the fact that women's rights groups were emerging in Japan *before* the original serialization of the manga. For example, the International Women's Year Action Group appeared in Japan following the 1975 International Women's Year conferences. Just as Anglo-American culture had an effect on the Japanese youth population, so too did it influence Japanese feminism (Gwynne 326). Feminist organizations were making themselves known during the time of *Akira*'s publication, but Ōtomo does not appear to acknowledge this collective voice in 80s cultural conflict or that this voice will grow in strength in the near future. As Vera Mackie writes of contemporary Japanese feminism, "Women demonstrated alongside their male comrades, but often came to feel dissatisfied" or, in the case of *Akira*, almost entirely removed from the scene (600).

Manga's Monstrous Punk Women

While continuing to be overshadowed by apocalyptic paranoia to a certain extent, recent manga built on punk foundations is influenced not by wider political concerns but a more internal, domestic anxiety. In *Akira*, Kei's feminine expression, or lack thereof, was not pivotal to the plot. Tetsuo's angst-ridden dictatorship and Kei's androgynous appearance were not mutually exclusive. Now, however, Japan's literary imagination often reflects these recurring stories in the media. The newspaper campaigns of twenty-first-century Japan pertain to national crises such as the 1990 birth *shokku*—when it was revealed that Japan's birthrate took a troubling dive to 1.57 (White 26). Women, of course, were seen as the cause for this decline, and the media has since blamed the independent, working woman as the root of the population trouble. This section will examine portrayals of punk women in light of twenty-first-century media influence. I will continue to show examples of punk women in manga, identifying representations which regurgitate the national anxiety. Here, I will look at *Soul Eater*'s Medusa Gorgon and Celty Sturluson of the *Durarara!!* franchise and observe the contrasting behaviors of two undoubtedly monstrous punk women.

Ōkubo Atsushi's immensely popular *Soul Eater* series began publication in 2004. Heavily influenced by Western punk and pop culture, it is a standard but rather stylized story of good-against-evil. Young teenagers transform into weapons and fight the threat of personified madness with partners. The recurring villain in the series is the evil witch, Medusa Gorgon. She is a ruthlessly ambitious, intelligent, cunning woman who is as resilient as she is emotionally cold. Yet, throughout the story, Ōkubo continuously highlights a particular abhorred characteristic in Medusa: that she is both a villain *and* a mother. In other words, she is a stock antagonist in terms of her sly scheming, but the root of the reader's hatred for her character lies in her disrupted gender roles.

Soul Eater uses the punk image not as an aesthetic symbolizing social rebellion, but instead utilizes its traditional symbol of troubled adolescence. The main characters work together in pairs—one as the weapon and the other as the wielding meister—and attend the Death Weapon Meister Academy where they work to keep the rest of the world safe while staying away from normal society's prejudice against them and their unusual abilities. In other words, the punk image—their heavy boots, spiked hairstyles, and accessorized outfits—represents the idea that the heroes here are the outsiders, the monsters, the unwanted in mortal human opinion. The teenagers protect a society that rejects them, and adopt the punk image and attitude to declare their awareness of being set apart. However, they ultimately hold patriarchal conventions in place, and in turn reject the woman who dismantles tradition.

The *ryōsai kenbo* feminine ideal was a celebrated template particularly in the early twentieth century that taught women to be good wives and wise mothers. When girls in Japan were allowed a high school education, it was this mode of behavior that made up their curriculum. As Takahashi Mizuki explains, girls did not learn "how to function independently as adults" but were instead taught "the *shōjo*[1] ideal—the dream of becoming future happy brides, isolated from real-life public world outside the family" (116). While this ideal is arguably disregarded in Japanese schools today, the *ryōsai kenbo* image still seems to loom over modern women. In *Soul Eater*, however, Medusa obliterates the *ryōsai kenbo* dynamic. As the opposite of the "good wife," she is wholly independent and subservient to nothing and no one. During a fight in volume six, the heroic scientist Stein tells Medusa that it is impossible for her to "understand" love (Ōkubo 6: 181). She displays neither the propensity for emotional engagement on a marital level nor the skills transferable into domestic settings.

Medusa's emphasized deviation from the "wise mother" ideal is intended to shock the reader. Japan is currently in a grave population crisis. Its baby-boom generation is ageing without an adequate number of children to replace them in the workforce. Furthermore, with the ever-developing technology industry, the careers chosen by young people, both men and women, are moving away from sectors such as medical care. The act of having children, and the bond between mother and child, has always had particular prevalence in Japanese society. Indeed, this dynamic is regarded as the very "core" of the family unit (White 88). In Medusa's case, that core is undoubtedly rotten. She is mother to Crona, a genderless and melancholic child biologically infused with a rather boisterous weapon. Crona has nothing of their mother's intelligence or ferocious ambition. Ōkubo makes it explicit that Crona's purpose for existence is one wholly dictated by Medusa and for Medusa's own scientific pursuits. She refers to the child as "it"—dehumanizing her child and shifting her role from mother to researcher and Crona from child to lab rat (see Figure 1). The crucial observation here is that for a story with roots in social Otherness and confrontational attitude to accepted normality, Medusa's decon-

Schoolgirls and Sukeban (Vernon)   193

Figure 1: In this image from Atsushi Ōkubo's *Soul Eater* (2004–2013) Medusa refers to her child as "it" (Ōkubo 6: 26) (courtesy Square Enix).

struction of the role of mother is expressly demonstrated by Ōkubo as an act of rebellion *not* to be celebrated (6: 26).

It could be said, then, that Crona is merely one of a small army of fictional children characterized by neglect; the victims of the so-called selfish mothers demonized by the Japanese "male press" mentality Sharon Kinsella describes as "charting and disciplining signs of feminine evolution" (145). In soap operas, the commercials between them, newspaper articles and their neighboring advertisements, on billboards and big screens on city skyscrapers, Crona and their many hundreds of brothers and sisters look down on women for asserting their independence from the claustrophobic housewife lifestyle. For example, a series of uncanny commercials for Tarako Pasta Sauce depict a group of giant cod ovaries with kewpie doll faces singing to children (luduslove, "Tarako Compilation"). The children appear in a cheerful, domestic setting and are shown enthusiastically digging into a plate of spaghetti. Not only do these commercials present a small army of baby faces, but also show an idealized image of family life that is stereotypically happy. Ōkubo has the opportunity, the forum, and the audience of young Japanese adults to graffiti over this guilt-inducing, pro-motherhood propaganda. Instead, he chooses to endorse it. Medusa could be the scientist *and* caretaker. She could be independent *and* successfully raise a child. For Ōkubo, the worst, most diabolical essence of villainy he can imagine is linked to Medusa's failure as a traditional mother. During the fight of volume six it is the male heroes, Stein and Spirit, who storm forwards to confront Medusa but *only* when she describes Crona as a disposable object. Her evil plans to spread madness throughout the world are merely met with expected pre-battle rhetoric, and similar to *Akira*, Ōkubo attempts to mock Medusa through his inclusion of sexually "trivializ[ing]" dialogue (Miller & Bardsley 5). Before their fight begins, Spirit announces: "I thought I was the only one who was going to take that [lab] coat off for you, but now you've gone and taken it off yourself" (Ōkubo 5: 112). Medusa's position as scientist is reduced to the symbol of her attire, which in turn is treated as a prop in the strip-tease imagined by Ōkubo's hero. It is Medusa's cool dismissal of Crona as a worthless tool, however, that provokes Spirit and Stein into finally using force against her. This is the sort of Japanese "male-press" mentality that suggests one mother's neglect is infinitely worse than worldwide disaster.[2]

As though Ōkubo's transgressive portrayal of motherhood was not reason enough for the reader to loathe and fear Medusa, her infiltration of the Death Weapon Meister Academy also represents a wider anxiety plaguing Japan's patriarchal mindset. Medusa is introduced in the first volume as the snake-woman, the witch, the first true villain of the series. It is only a brief glimpse, but when we see her again it is in her disguise as a school nurse. She chooses a dress instead of her hooded jumpsuit and transforms into a kind, bashful caretaker and healer trusted too easily by the students. Is Ōkubo presenting Medusa as a parody of expectations of women in the workplace? In keeping with the punk attitude of the series, is he demonstrating Medusa's refusal to be shoehorned into a stereotypically feminine career? I want to argue that, unfortunately, this is not the case. As already discussed, Ōkubo is keen to depict Medusa as the definitively evil woman. Rather than a shift from nurse to scientist, then, Ōkubo creates a transformation from matron to monster. For example, the end of the second volume sees main character Maka worrying over her partner Soul's injuries. She blames herself, but seems to be comforted by Medusa in her nurse's disguise. Medusa places her hands on young Maka's shoulders and exclaims: "Cheer up!! You'll get stronger, Maka-chan!!" (Ōkubo 2: 182). While Maka's back is turned, however, Medusa's face morphs into a smirking, grotesque expression. Her nose disappears, her eyes become dark with serpentine pupils, and from her thin and sneering mouth coils a wisp-like snake with fangs bared to strike. This facial transformation is a recurring motif in *Soul Eater*. Ōkubo feels he must constantly remind the reader that her adherence to the accepted female ideal is purely superficial, and not even Medusa herself can fully control her monstrosity from coiling out of her mouth. Not only that, but it seems to be a reminder to the reader that Medusa is *not* a sensual person. Arachne—the eldest Gorgon sister—is arguably more dangerous, but since she displays maternal instincts she is also presented with an alluring, femme-fatale aesthetic. Medusa is never allowed to be considered attractive. Arachne is the mother, the gatherer of armies, the matriarch. Arachne is revered but remains within a certain limit that, while in this case for evil purposes, still stands within the traditional roles of women. Medusa is simply a scientist and is detested for it. It echoes the anxieties of Japanese mythology, the skeletal *hone onna* (bone woman) and the *yamanba* (mountain witch), featured in cautionary tales and ghost stories and generating the idea Rebecca Copeland describes as "the terrifying image of a woman alone ... left to roam the fringes of society" (22). Medusa, independent in her social transgression, is terrifying.

This manga may adopt the punk aesthetic in its narrative, but in no way does it permit Medusa room to demonstrate a woman's rebellion against society. She transgresses from notions of female gentleness, maternity, and matronly care. She pursues science to a point of obsession, no different from the character of Stein. For example, an internal observation from Spirit describes Stein as a "sadistic hedonist" and, in response to a provocation from Medusa, Stein declares: "I want to dissect you" (Ōkubo 6: 100). But the assignation of the label of "villain" goes to Medusa because her personal and intellectual pursuits are not within the scope of Japanese feminine tradition and resonates with the independent working women seen to be at the root of the problematically low birth rate. Medusa, then, is presented as a thoroughly unpleasant monster because she seeks to tear society apart. If there is a direct fictional opposite to Medusa in punk manga, I would argue that she takes form in Celty Sturluson of Narita Ryōgo's *Durarara!!* series.

Durarara!! is a twisted rope of a story exploring the lives, loves, and gang culture of Tokyo's Ikebukuro ward. Amidst alleyway brawls roars the urban legend of the Black Rider—a motorcyclist believed to be a monster without a head under their helmet. This is Celty, a fictional re-imagining of the headless horseman, the dullahan of Irish mythology. Celty's head was stolen from her while she slept, and her search for it has taken her to Japan. She spreads unease wherever she rides, but in reality she is a nervous, clumsy chatroom-user and television-addict. From her neck billows uncanny black smoke—the empty space where her head should be stands as a reminder that she is a monstrous figure not unlike Medusa. This section will examine Narita's exploration of feminine identities and Satorigi Akiyo's artistic representations of women's bodies. In comparison with *Akira* and *Soul Eater*, I will identify Celty's successful participation in Ikebukuro gang culture and her navigation of feminine conventions and deviances.

As witnessed in Ōkubo's deployment of Medusa in *Soul Eater*, Celty belongs to a Japanese tradition of casting women with demonic aspects of the "unknown, the uncontrollable, that which invites desire and inspires dread" (Copeland 16). Desire for Medusa was shown again and again to be an error of judgment on the reader's part. If ever she was presented as attractive, she would transform into something grotesque on the next page. Celty, however, *does* exude an air of feminine desirability despite her monstrous

196   Part IV: Punk Manga

Figure 2: This image from volume one of Ryōgo Narita's *Durarara!!* (2009–ongoing) shows Celty as an androgynous figure, in her zipped-up bike leathers (courtesy Square Enix).

form. Narita creates a modernized vision of an historic myth; Celty rides a motorbike instead of a skeletal horse, and the distinctive cat ears on her yellow helmet bring a much more personable, punk-customized edge to her image. Her first appearance in the manga is both interesting and somewhat problematic. In her zipped-up bike leathers, Celty is shown as an androgynous figure. Satorigi's presentation of Celty's jumpsuit blurs the feminine shape and it is only when Celty returns to the apartment she shares with young

Figure 3: This image from Ryōgo Narita's *Durarara!!* (2009–ongoing) depicts Celty stepping into the shower. A full page is reserved for this image of Celty censored only by steam, while Shinra's speech bubble to the right reads: "It doesn't suit a girl like you" (Narita 1:166) (courtesy Square Enix).

underground doctor Shinra that she is revealed to be a woman. Revealed in a very literal sense—after a hard day's ride around the city, Celty steps into the shower. A full page is reserved for this image of Celty censored only by steam, while Shinra's speech bubble to the right reads: "It doesn't suit a *girl* like you" (Narita 1: 166).

On one hand, Narita and Satorigi establish Celty's uncanny power and street presence *first* and then present her as a woman either to unsettle the reader's expectations or to ensure she is not trivialized by being identified as a woman before an unsettling urban myth. However, the voyeuristic attention to Celty's displayed gender does not inspire the same kind of punk progressiveness. Despite her missing head, this page is intended to titillate the reader. In her essay analyzing the transforming body in manga, June M. Madley argues that a morphed physical body can simultaneously "offer both traditional and transgressive gender models to readers" (800). I feel this strongly applies to Narita and Satorigi's depiction of Celty. She successfully navigates her identity as the uncanny Other—the silent angel of death walking among Japanese skyscrapers and spreading unease wherever her motorbike takes her—but she is in equal parts domesticated and idealized for her feminine physical shape. Whereas Medusa was spurned from both the punk subculture and mainstream society, Celty lives a kind of compromising dual-life in which her shadow dominates the Ikebukuro underground and yet she conforms to the very ordinary, comfortable and accepted modes of domestic feminine behavior. From this, then, there is a sense that Narita is demonstrating a kind of ability to blend between the street and the sofa. Celty's public identity resonates with the *sukeban*—the leader of female street gangs and *bōsōzoku* motorcycle gangs of Japan—and it is this image, emphasized by her memorable helmet, that is displayed prominently throughout the series. Furthermore, the first opening sequence to the 2010 anime adaptation focuses on Celty riding through the streets; an energetic punk drumbeat introduces her tires rumbling over the road, and later she is shown crashing through a window while her name in patchy graffiti is displayed across the screen. It is important to note, therefore, that while her punk aesthetic is celebrated, her personality is too sweet and naïve to be shamed for her transgressive behavior by Narita unlike Ōkubo who shames Medusa. *Durarara!!* is, however, a series about gang wars and the anti-heroes truly are criminals to some degree, whereas *Soul Eater* merely uses the punk image to demonstrate teenage Otherness, as Ōkubo's young characters are genuinely heroic. Perhaps, then, Celty's participation as the spectral one-woman *bōsōzoku* is celebrated as the very foundations of *Durarara!!* because she is surrounded by shifty characters and teenage gang members who are similarly idolized for their violence and underground involvement. Here, gang culture moves from the mythological and historical to the modern *yakuza* form and finally to the Internet forum.

Celty weaves between three teenage leaders as a kind of culmination of each of their gangs. The Yellow Scarves display a more traditional group of thugs led by teenage troublemaker Kida Masaomi. Then there is the almost zombie-like mob controlled by Saika, a maternal demonic spirit living symbiotically within Sonohara Anri. Anri's group is uncanny yet still has the idea of a mother as its figurehead, permitting women not just to participate but also to lead. The Dollars, organized by Ryūgamine Mikado, are a vast online group admitting anyone regardless of gender, age and occupation, which interestingly translates the Internet's capacity for anonymity back onto the street. It is only Kida's gang that maintains the *yakuza* form and the hypocritical punk attitude thriving in a brutal, misogynistic dynamic. I would argue that these three gangs represent Narita's ideas of shifting street crime. As David Kaplan and Alec Dubro write: "The place of women in the *yakuza* has long centered around their roles as prostitutes[…]" (115). While Celty and Anri do display aspects of traditional feminine ideals, Narita creates a punk gang setting in which they ultimately rule the streets. Narita and Satorigi do not aim to celebrate or condemn women based on their acceptance or transgression of the Japanese feminine ideal. This is a social debate in which the series does not involve itself. Its main concern is demonstrating women's successful navigation of underground culture. *Durarara!!* presents its women characters participating in, leading, and dictating the Ikebukuro gang wars. If Yagiri Namie, head of Yagiri Pharmaceuticals, represents the emergence of women in managerial positions in the *Durarara!!* world, then Celty and Anri do the same on the street. While Narita does not use the punk space to question modes of femininity, he does use the narrative to emphasize and celebrate social development that no longer forbids a woman's career or involvement in a traditionally masculine sphere.

Narita does show a range of ideas of femininity but ultimately they converge, whether intentionally or not, on a form of the *ryōsai kenbo* ("good wife/wise mother") model. The three main women of the series, therefore, stand on a kind of threshold between punk rebellion and domestication. Narita's fictional space embodies Naomi Griffin's description of the punk aesthetic as a space for "a negotiation of expectations of women and femininity" (75). But does this mean that women in punk must appease male onlookers? Was Medusa so viciously condemned in *Soul Eater* because she refused this negotiation of behavior? In *Durarara!!*, it could easily be argued that Celty, Anri, and Namie maintain feminine qualities to raise the manga's appeal to male readers preferring character designs over plot. Celty's shower introduction, for example, provides evidence to argue that this is the case. Were she a male character, I highly doubt the reveal would have involved full (albeit artfully censored) nudity. On the other hand, Narita's presentation of them as figureheads of Japanese gang culture suggests that he aims to show progression in the manga female stereotype. Celty is a monster and transporter working the underground circuit, but she actively seeks to be accepted as human and, more importantly, as a woman. The more time she spends in the crowded chaos of Ikebukuro, the more she experiences human emotions and realizes her love for Shinra. In volume two, her internal monologue reads: "Recently.... I have on more than one occasion found myself acutely aware of Shinra's masculinity. At first, I did not understand what this meant, but ... gradually, I came to understand its import" (Narita 2: 25). This scene involves an interesting reversal in which Celty, watching Shinra sleep, is aware of her own sexuality as a woman. Despite the problematic shower image, here Narita shows Celty gazing at Shinra as she thinks about her attraction towards him. She is not rising to meet Shinra's sexual energy—she is working out her own feelings, sexuality, and femininity for herself. To argue that true punk women should fully abandon their own identities as women and adapt to a fully androgynous and socially disruptive lifestyle is both an unrealistic and unfair standard. In this respect, I want to return to Griffin's use of "negotiation." If this negotiation exists, it is a privilege available only to women participating in punk. Wearing a dress does not make their protests any less valid if the dress was chosen by them and not in an answer to social requests. But while *Durarara!!* is important in its inclusion of this progressive negotiation, to some extent Narita's women characters are still used to appeal sexually to male readers.

Punk Women Writing Punk Women: Dorohedoro *and Female Participation*

The manga examples analyzed earlier in this essay have not provided sufficient evidence to show that, at least in Japan, the punk movement universally allows female participation. Male writers and artists dominate Japanese media, creating images of society and of women they find acceptable and comfortable. Carolyn M. Byerly's investigation for IWMF showed that in a sample of 8 Japanese news companies, 85.2 percent of full-time, regular employees were male (241). Simply because women are a rarity in Ōtomo's Neo-Tokyo, are seen as the villain in Ōkubo's mind, or are only beginning to be accepted as long as a degree of femininity is maintained as seen in Narita's fictional world, it does not mean rebellious women do not exist in wider Japanese society. It does not mean that because women cannot navigate the male-dictated social and media space, they do not make spaces dictated by themselves. Consider Hayashida Q's provocative *Dorohedoro* series to identify how and where women can fit into true punk groups free from ingrained patriarchal values and hypocritical rules for participation.

Hayashida Q's *Dorohedoro* began publication in December 2000. It is an obscure, gristly story about a war between sorcerers and the mortal subjects on whom they experiment with their magic. The victims of sorcery live in a place called The Hole, a slum underworld full of disfigured and broken people. The land of sorcerers, however, is no less filthy and chaotic—with an established but frequently contested power hierarchy. This manga embodies the punk aesthetic more than any other series discussed in this essay; Hayashida employs themes of urban degradation and corruption with gang wars, conflict, and social Otherness. But what makes *Dorohedoro* such an important text, and the reason why I have chosen to end my discussion on punk manga with this series, is that as a woman, Hayashida creates a forum to demonstrate female participation in socially rebellious movements.

There are no heroes in this series, but there are no clear villains, either. Both the sorcerers and the magic victims are in a constant struggle not only with each other, but with simply surviving in their respective lawless, polluted, and dirty societies. The cast of characters is immense, but for this analysis I want to focus mainly on Noi, a high-ranking sorcerer working for the sorcerer-lord En.

En's gang is constructed like a typical *yakuza* syndicate. As described by David E. Kaplan and Alex Dubro, the traditional *yakuza* dynamic has a "godfather at the top and new members adopted into the clan as older brothers, younger brothers, and children" (8). In *Dorohedoro*, En is the most powerful, a godfather figure, and his underlings are either related or of similar incredible strength with an internal hierarchy from adults to teenagers to children. They live in luxury and their names spread fear through magic-victims and sorcerers alike. Noi is En's cousin and one of his top underlings along with her partner, Shin. Together, Shin and Noi are responsible for disposing of troublemaking magic victims. Noi takes gleeful enjoyment in dealing with her targets in an array of stomach-churning, darkly comic and gratuitously violent methods. She is not afraid to leave a scene covered in blood. Her masked appearance is also quite disturbing. Noi wears her mask not simply because, like sunglasses in the *yakuza*, it is a mark of her identity as sorcerer, but it serves as a way to be rid of false, ironically sexist acts of chivalry during her fistfights with other men. When Noi wears her mask and jumpsuit, she is indistinguishable as a woman, and can therefore brawl in the street without being refused in response to her gender. In other words, Noi's behavior as a character trivializes cultural reactions to femininity. I want to suggest here that Hayashida Q appropriates the punk aesthetic to parody, reclaiming and restyling overly masculine *shōnen*-genre protagonists in Noi.[3] For example, during her encounter with female Hole resident Nikaido in volume two, Noi towers over her opponent and declares, "You know, it isn't my style to rough up a woman" (Hayashida 2: 42). In Noi, Hayashida translates *shōnen* manga's exaggerated male strength seamlessly into her depictions of femininity to show how the idea of gender binary systems exists only in the patriarchal imagination. Furthermore, she similarly presents this idea in the gender-anonymous Q of her pen name and the gruesome and violent scenes she depicts. If Noi is the gender-progressive character of the manga, then Hayashida Q is the gender-progressive figure of the manga industry.

As with Narita's introduction of Celty, Hayashida employs the technique of demonstrating Noi's power *before* presenting her as a woman. Hayashida's reveal, however, is much less voyeuristic than in *Durarara!!* After witnessing the tall, muscular, foul-mouthed figure in the grotesquely punk disguise commit acts of extreme violence, Hayashida shows Noi first revealing her feminine shape and then releasing an abundance of white curls from the back of her mask. Finally, her face is revealed and Noi is, of course, incredibly beautiful. The reader's reaction is mirrored in Fujita, a young new member to En's gang. During Noi's dressing-down, he is pictured in the background—his feelings reflected by the growing number of exclamation marks above his head. His only coherent thought is: "A woman?!" (Hayashida 1: 112). Noi, on the other hand, stands with confidence and says to the room, "See? Told you I dressed up" (Hayashida 1: 113). Unlike Celty's titillating shower scene, this sudden jolt from muscular monstrosity to alluring woman is a deliberate attack intended to confuse the reader's expectation. Whereas Celty in the domestic space is shown as a timid, somewhat geeky and excitable woman, Noi emanates a raw confidence and power no different to how she behaves in the street. Yet, to some extent, it could be argued that Fujita also represents the reader eagerly looking at naked Celty. How is Noi's undressing any more acceptable, if Hayashida is still reserving space for this surprising reveal of femininity? I would stress that it is Noi's attitude and her apparent enjoyment in making Fujita squirm that makes this depiction more progressive than in *Durarara!!*. Celty is more of a reserved woman, whereas Noi demonstrates full control over her personality and her body. In other words, Hayashida's idea of punk resides in behavior rather than dress code alone, and Noi embodies punk through her unapologetic confidence. Furthermore, unlike the parallel moment in *Durarara!!*, Noi's reveal is entirely on her own terms and she presents *herself* with assurance in her own sensuality and appearance as a woman. Noi's comment on dressing up, too, suggests that her femininity is dictated by no one but herself. Much like the punk attitude to clothes, Noi's dress sense answers only to her own decisions and not to a certain guideline set by social values. Hayashida shows Noi effectively navigating a spectrum of behavior from the hyper-masculine to hyper-feminine, and Noi stands exactly where, how, and when she wants. In discussing Japanese women creating art outside the boundaries of polite society, Miller and Bardsley argue that these "mind blowing acts transform bodies from objects into sassy subjects that disconcert the onlooker" (10). Noi, then, is the product of punk women writing punk women. Hayashida reclaims female agency from the Japanese male media, and encapsulates within Noi the possibility for women's absolute autonomy over their own bodies, choices, and social participation and rebellion. *Dorohedoro* is not simply a matter of Hayashida exploring and blurring the line of acceptable feminine behavior. Rather, she presents a world *without* this line to begin with, successfully showing the pointlessness of gender binary ideals and traditional roles dictated to women.

Conclusion

Certainly, the Japanese punk aesthetic, with some similarity to its Western cousins, adheres to accepted feminine ideals defined by cultural values. Despite the advances in laws securing equal opportunities for women, there is significant evidence to suggest that Japanese patriarchal mentality remains several decades behind. The punk influence in the male Japanese imagination has mingled with traditional phallocentric ideas of power and marginal social roles for women rooted in the domestic sphere. However, women creating their own punk fantasies demonstrate the success of female participation and the diminished validity of gender binary systems. While there is some hope that male manga creators are breaking away from enforcing feminine ideals in their work, it is still hindered by historic social prejudices. It unfortunately remains necessary for Japanese punk women to continue to rebel against their own issues of gender oppression before they can participate in the same battles as punk men.

Notes

1. The term *shōjo* can refer either to girls' romance manga or to a kind of gender image idealizing the polite, demure, innocent girl on the cusp of becoming a woman and therefore housewife.
2. Ironically, Spirit claims his anger is rooted in his own experiences and responsibilities "as a parent" (Ōkubo 6: 26), despite the running gag of the series involving his daughter Maka catching him in the act of boyish infidelity with various women.
3. *Shōnen* as a manga genre refers to stories aimed at young boys. These series often feature heroic male protagonists and sexually attractive women characters, although the genre is not limited to these archetypes.

Works Cited

Byerly, Carolyn M. *Global Report on the Status of Women in the News Media*. International Women's Media Foundation, 2011.
Copeland, Rebecca. "Mythical Bad Girls: The Corpse, the Crone, and the Snake." *Bad Girls of Japan*, edited by Laura Miller and Jan Bardsley, Palgrave MacMillan, 2005, pp. 15–32.
Ensminger, David A. *Visual Vitriol: The Street Art and Subcultures of the Punk and Hardcore Generation*. UP of Mississippi, 2011.

Griffin, Naomi. "Gendered Performance and Performing Gender in the DIY Punk and Hardcore Music Scene." *Journal of International Women's Studies*, volume 13, issue 2, 2012, pp. 66–81.
Gwynne, Joel. "Japan, Postfeminism and the Consumption of Sexual(ised) Schoolgirls in Male-authored Manga." *Feminist Theory*, volume 14, issue 3, 2013, pp. 325–343.
Hayashida, Q. *Dorohedoro: Volume 1*. VIZ Media, 2010.
_____. *Dorohedoro: Volume 2*. VIZ Media, 2010.
Kaplan, David E., and Alec Dubro. *Yakuza: Japan's Criminal Underworld*, 25th Anniversary ed. University of California Press, 2012.
Kinsella, Sharon. "Black Faces, Witches, and Racism Against Girls." *Bad Girls of Japan*, edited by Laura Miller and Jan Bardsley, Palgrave MacMillan, 2005, pp. 143–158.
Madley, June M. "Transnational Transformations: A Gender Analysis of Japanese Manga Featuring Unexpected Bodily Transformations." *The Journal of Popular Culture*, volume 45, issue 4, 2012, pp. 789–806.
Miller, Laura, and Jan Bardsley. "Introduction." *Bad Girls of Japan*, edited by Laura Miller and Jan Bardsley, Palgrave MacMillan, 2005, pp. 1–14.
Narita, Ryōgo (w), and Satorigi Akiyo (a). *Durarara!!: Volume 1*. Yen Press, 2012.
Ōkubo, Atsushi. *Soul Eater: Volume 2*. Yen Press, 2010.
_____. *Soul Eater: Volume 5*. Yen Press, 2011.
_____. *Soul Eater: Volume 6*. Yen Press, 2011.
Omori, Takahiro, director. *Durarara!!*. Brain's Base, 2010.
Ōtomo, Katsuhiro. *Akira: Volume 1*. Kodansha USA Publishing, 1984.
_____. *Akira: Volume 2*. Kodansha USA Publishing, 1985.
_____. *Akira: Volume 4*. Kodansha USA Publishing, 1987.
Takahashi, Mizuki. "Opening the Closed World of *Shōjo* Manga." *Japanese Visual Culture: Explorations in the World of Manga and Anime*, edited by Mark W. MacWilliams, Routledge, 2008, pp. 114–136.
"Tarako Compilation." *YouTube*, uploaded by luduslove, 23 Feb. 2011, https://www.youtube.com/watch?v=4G_JaddTUT0. Accessed 14 May 2015.
White, Merry Isaacs. *Perfectly Japanese: Making Families in an Era of Upheaval*, University of California Press, 2002.

Punk Bodies and the "Do It Yourself" Philosophy

FRANCESCO-ALESSIO URSINI

Introduction: Punk, the Do It Yourself Philosophy and Comics

The goal of this essay is to outline a theory of punk culture and its constituting principles that allow us to individuate punk comics. We focus on one specific aspect: the "Do It Yourself" (henceforth DIY) philosophy, usually defined as the desire to modify and design objects, possessions and parts of the environment (Wolf and McQuitty 1–2). Although certainly not specific to the punk movement, this philosophy played a key role in the evolution of punk culture. With respect to its use in comics, we address a central question about the role of this philosophy/principle: whether and how the DIY philosophy, acting as a core principle of punk culture, can crucially individuate "punk comics." The essay is organized as follows: section two introduces core theoretical notions; section three presents a discussion of comics that acted as "precursors" to the genre; section four presents a discussion of punk comics, while section five discusses "contemporary" works in this genre; section six concludes.

Core Theoretical Notions

The punk movement has often been characterized as a patchwork of styles, ideas and concepts borrowed from other sub-cultures (Savage 3–7), raising doubts about its status as a culture *tout court* (Thompson 5–10). However, standard definitions of "culture" focus on the social nature of the practices that community members (re-)elaborate in creative ways (Deacon 3–14).

According to this definition, punk culture qualifies as such, given its re-elaboration of various themes, from music to narratives to comics, but also grass-roots forms of social organization. The chaotic nature of punk, especially in its emergent phase, has slowly led to a highly flexible and yet distinct culture (O'Hara 10–15). Consequently, a key challenge has been to define core cultural principles that identify punk culture. A recent proposal is found in Prinz (583–584), which suggests the three following principles as the core pillars of punk culture. The first principle is *irreverence*: punks do not accord any respect to any authority, normative practice and cultural precept. The second principle is *nihilism*: punks focus on the individual, cultural and societal collapse against the tides of time (the "no future" motto: Hanscombe 2–3; Moore 3–10). The third principle is *amateurism*: punks do not buy commodified goods, but produce their own products and songs, for distribution and benefit of other punks (Atkinson 1–3; Triggs 70–72).

It is easy to notice that Prinz focuses on the negative aspects of punk culture: irreverence, nihilism and amateurism underpin the lack of adherence to preconceived norms of society. However, Prinz and other authors also indirectly suggest that positive counterparts to these principles can be defined, although they do not explicitly formulate such principles. For this reason, I suggest that by simply inverting these three principles we can obtain positive, mirror principles. I use the labels *independence, authenticity* and *creativity* for these three mirror principles, and define them as follows. Independence consists of punks being their own leaders and guiding figures, as indirectly argued in previous analyses (Moore 11–15; Cross 3–4). Authenticity consists of punks seeking their own future, rejecting pre-made plans or the oblivion (compare also to Moore's "Postmodernism" 308–310; Thompson 30–35). Creativity consists of punks seeking *new* elaborations of old ideas, methods and practices (Triggs 73; Prinz 586).

Overall, punks and punk culture do not seem to simply reject the *status quo*, but also aim to create freer, more inclusive types of societies, starting from emancipated individuals in charge of their own individualities and lives. A natural consequence of this argument, then, is that we can interpret punk principles as being inherently "dual." Irreverent punks chastise authorities and dogmas because they pursue independence of thought and action. Nihilist punks reject hollow plans and goals, only to create new, authentic goals. Amateur punks do not buy commodified goods and methods, because they want to learn and create their own methods and artifacts. In other words, I suggest that for each negative principle that defines how punks reject the old, a positive principle defines how punks create the new.

From this suggestion, I would like to extend my proposal by contending that we can individuate principles other than "simple" negative and positive punk principles. I also suggest that they can also explain the more complex aspects underpinning punk culture. I label these forms as "compound" principles, since they consist of the combination of two of the simple principles that we have discussed, negative and positive alike. For each compound principle, I would also like to propose a specific label, and explain how it is connected to its constituting principles. I first define the negative compound principles, then the positive ones.

First, I propose that irreverence and nihilism combine into an "existentialism" principle: punks may critically question the purpose of society and life. A similar relational analysis has been made in Hanscombe (3–4), although he does not explicitly use this label. Second, irreverence and amateurism combine into a "collage" principle: punks renovate and radically interpret established practices. Authors such as Thompson (70–80) and Triggs (73–75) discuss at length the importance of collage practices in the creation of punk fanzines and other cultural artifacts. In my proposal, though, the collage principle is explicitly connected to the amateurism and irreverence principles. Third, I propose that nihilism and amateurism combine into an "irony" principle. Punks refuse to take anything too seriously, as discussed in Moore (5–15) and other works, but they do so when they reject societal rules and propose their own rules. Thus, we have a set of three negative, compound principles underpinning punk culture.

Positive compound principles can be defined as well. First, I propose that independence and authenticity combine into an "autonomy/anarchy" principle. Punks do not need leaders, as they are their own genuine leaders, as indirectly discussed in previous works (O'Hara 21–24; Moore "Postmodernism" 311–313). Second, independence and creativity combine into the "renovation" principle: punks re-elaborate not only ideas but also methods (Atkinson 1–4). Third, I propose that authenticity and creativity combine into the "DIY principle": punks create their own artifacts, ideas and methods, compelled to define their original contributions to society (again, Thompson 70–80; Triggs 74–77). In our discussion, however, we go beyond fanzines, records and other musical artifacts, and discuss whether or not the DIY principle plays a key role in punk comics since it has not been investigated so far.

We come now to the main thesis I would like to argue for in this essay. If this interpretation of punk principles is on the right track, then we can motivate the importance of the DIY principle in differentiating punk comics from other closely related genres. Consequently, we can offer an answer to our two questions: whether and how the DIY principle, acting as a core principle of punk culture, can crucially individuate "punk comics." The main reason for answering these two intertwined questions, I suggest, is that punk characters in comics can instantiate the DIY principle in a very direct way. They can modify and create anew both their bodies and personalities: in a sense, they "do" their new identities themselves. This is a factor that seems to differentiate punk comics from other genres of comics, as I am going to discuss in the remainder of the essay.

Before I move on to the analysis of the selected texts, I would like to draw one further theoretical connection between this interpretation of the DIY principle and physical/intellectual identity. Punk comics seem to incarnate a principle that has been amply discussed in the literature on philosophy of the mind. Modern theories of consciousness suggest that our identities as individuals are flexible and dynamic, and can be seen as the result of the daily intellectual, physical, emotive experiences that we undergo (Chalmers 5–45; Metzinger 7–66). Individuals can change political, social, ethnic, or gender allegiances and even their biological sex, insofar as the societal norms and regulations allow them to do so. Individuals can change their physical and psychological "selves" in various manners, often as a result of the experiences they face over time. However, individuals cannot re-create their bodies and personae from scratch, as the technological know-how for such radical changes is still beyond the reach of modern societies (Clark 35–58).

In the fictional space of comics a much greater flexibility can be expressed since current technological limits can be ignored. Body modification can be an opportunity for characters to reshape their own identities, possibly escaping from the identities imposed by external forces. Hence, voluntary, "do it yourself" body modification can be seen as a quintessential application of the DIY principle as a way to assert one's identity and autonomy. In other words, punk characters can "do" their identities themselves, given their fictional status, and in doing so they can create new, authentic bodies, identities and futures for themselves and their fellow punks. I discuss whether and how they do so in the remainder of the essay.

Punk Precursors

The goal of this section is to discuss some cases of punk comics- precursors, which feature some but not all of the punk principles we discussed in the previous section. Our choices fall on one manga, *Cyborg 009* (Ishinomori) and one American comic, *Doom Patrol* (Drake, Haney & Premiani). I choose these two works for two reasons. First, each of them features some but not all of our punk principles, in a sense anticipating punk culture. Second, these works can give us an indication as to how these themes developed across distinct, but closely related, traditions.

I start with *Cyborg 009*, published in Akita Shoten's *Young Shōnen King* from 1964. This manga features nine individuals who are kidnapped by "Black Ghost," an underground conglomerate that produces weapons and fuels conflicts, with the support of "powerful nations" that support a *status quo* of perennial war. The nine victims are turned into powerful war cyborgs (the "00X" series). However, they rebel against their masters, thanks to the aid of renegade Dr. Gilmore, and attempt to find a freer, non-violent life. Thus, *Cyborg 009* is a typical *shōnen* manga of the post-war period, featuring lots of action scenes interspersed with more reflective passages (Gravett 60–70).[1]

Although it may not be obvious at a first reading, certain punk principles seem to emerge as key themes in the narration. Throughout the series, the cyborgs show no respect for their creators and the institutions they represent, actively fighting for their independence and that of other Black Ghost victims (e.g., Vietnamese people in the Vietnam conflict) (5: 1–72). The protagonists are originally misfits and outcasts, living goalless lives before their transformation into cyborgs. For instance, 002 was a "street punk" from New York, prior to his kidnapping. When he is introduced, he is seeking a fight with a rival gang. In a few panels, the situation escalates and he is quick to extract his knife, in a sequence of panels that parody *West Side Story* (1: 18–30). Another cyborg, 008, is a young African man reduced to slavery by ruthless mercenaries, who kidnapped innocents and sold them to diamond mining companies (1: 48–56). Since 008 does not want to become a slave, he attempts to escape from his kidnappers, and is saved from certain punishment when the rest of the cyborgs come to his rescue.

By becoming cyborgs and rebelling against their fate as war machines, the cyborgs move from a state of nihilism to one of authentic autonomy. However, they do not really follow a DIY principle to their identity: they passively accept their new selves and use them to their own advantage, as per classical manga tropes (Gravett 100–110). Thus, *Cyborg 009* represents a work that acts as a precursor to science fiction manga featuring cyborgs (e.g., *Ghost in the Shell*: Orbaugh 151–153). However, it also acts as a precursor to punk comics, since it features rebellious characters that seek a new, authentic life via their cyborg bodies, even though their body modifications are imposed by other forces. While the cyborgs do not "do" their bodies themselves, they certainly seek autonomy and renovation in their lives, especially since this autonomy amounts to escaping from the control of Black Ghost.

A similar picture emerges from the comic *Doom Patrol*. This comic first appeared in issue #80 of the anthology *My Greatest Adventure* (April 1962), and ended its first run with issue #121 (September-October 1968). The first incarnation of this comic features a group of misfits who received superpowers after horrific accidents permanently crippled them (Beatty 278). The adventures of the Doom Patrol involve battles against even more bizarre enemies such as the Brain and Monsieur Mallah, a disembodied brain and a genius communist chimp, respectively. In most battles, the Doom Patrol acts as a "last bastion" against forces that would trump the *status quo* that also shuns the Patrol members as misfits, not unlike the cyborgs in *Cyborg 009*.

The most pervasive punk principles that permeate the adventures of the original Doom Patrol are nihilism and authenticity, as well as some forms of creativity. Cliff Steele ("Robotman"), Rita Farr ("Elasti-girl") and Larry Trainor ("Negative Man") see their powers as curses and try to use them to help others, even if the powers inevitably cause alienation. Although these characters certainly do not embody a punk aesthetic, they often need to use their powers and bodies in creative ways. It is not rare that in his attempts to work for a greater good, Cliff's body is mangled, partially destroyed and reconstructed again by the Chief (e.g., issues #111–113). In this regard, *Doom Patrol* is certainly best seen as a superhero comic (compare also Reynolds 8–14), since its main characters fight to preserve the *status quo*, and do not actively seek any independence. However, it also anticipated certain punk themes, creating a conceptual base on which Grant Morrison built his more punk-oriented run of this series. Unlike their more modern incarnation, the original Doom Patrol did not "do" or re-elaborate their own bodies.

Overall, our selected punk precursors seem to feature several punk principles, both negative and positive. The tight connection with science fiction, in particular in the use of cyborg and post-apocalyptic themes, often acts as a prelude to the emergence of a fruitful interaction between the two genres, under various forms. However, we have also observed that our precursors do not seem to feature a DIY principle, since most "embryonal" punk characters accept their status and do not attempt to reshape their identity or environment. Hence, in order to answer our central question we need to discuss examples of "genuine" punk specimens, and evaluate the presence and role of this principle.

Punk Pinnacles

The goal of this section is to discuss comics that were produced during the period from the late '70s to the period of the late '80s/early '90s, hence covering the heyday of the punk movement to its affirmation as an alternative, but well-established form of popular culture (Thompson 90–110). Given the powerful influence that punk culture had on comics of this period, clear cases of punk comics include *V for Vendetta* (Moore and Lloyd) or several stories and characters from the magazine *2000 AD* (e.g., *Dredd* and *Rogue Trooper*). However, we focus on works whose punk themes have not been explored in due detail: the fumetto *RanXerox*; the manga *Akira* and *Nausicaä of the Valley of the Wind*; and the comic *Doom Patrol*, focusing on Grant Morrison's run.

RanXerox (Tamburini and Liberatore *Volume 2*) features an eponymous cyborg built during student riots with the spare parts of a Ranx Xerox copy machine. RanXerox's cyborg body is left loose after a fight between its crea-

Punk Bodies and the "Do It Yourself" Philosophy (Ursini) 211

tors and the anti-riot police, with his aggression levels set up at maximum. He is lured by Lubna, a 12-year-old female drug addict, who lives in the lower echelons of a future Rome that looks much like the stratified metropolises of *Blade Runner* or *Brazil*. RanX (his nickname) is involved in bizarre plots featuring video-clips for punk-riot bands (Tamburini and Liberatore *Volume 2*: 24–48), fights between an artist father and his harshest critic (his son) (1–24), and his becoming a celebrated Broadway star in a Fred Astaire revival (37–48). In between, RanX abuses drugs, sex and anyone who stands in his way, including innocent children selling roses (4).

As a *fumetto* published in an anarchist magazine, during the punk heyday (*Frigidaire*, 1978: Raffaelli 200–201), *RanXerox* wears its punk identity on its sleeve. RanX always appears wearing soldering goggles and a perennial grimacing face (see Figure 1).

Figure 1: This image is from the cover for Volume 1 of the French complete collection of *RanXerox* © Glenat (courtesy Glenat).

To an extent, RanX's looks, and the looks of other characters in the series, mirror punk and other fashion styles of the early '80s (Castaldi 90–95). All the characters are deeply irreverent and nihilist, abusing drugs and surviving by scraping together money, technology and other necessities as they can. The series is permeated with a deep sense of irony, as RanX never takes seriously the bizarre events he partakes in. RanX seems to live his cyborg life in an authentic, creative and independent way, while also being in love with Lubna. Case in point, RanX can refill his own batteries and control his behavioral programs: he is a fully independent cyborg, although a peculiar one. Thus, RanX incarnates a different facet of the DIY philosophy, as he decides to live a low-key life that is nevertheless his own, much like his feelings for Lubna and a penchant for ultra-violence and drugs.

A different punk picture seems to emerge in *Akira* (Ōtomo), however. In some of its key themes, *Akira* is a quintessential punk manga, since it features biker gangs, young misfits, anarchistic groups fighting against the government and a pre- and post-apocalyptic neo-Tokyo. As the plot unfolds, Kaneda's *bōsōzoku* ('bike gang'), the Capsules, and his rival bikers, the *bozu* ('Clown') gang, uncover the complex governmental web of lies behind Akira, a child with immensely powerful extra-sensory abilities. Furthermore, Colonel Shikishima, military leader of the governmental squad that keeps Akira a well-guarded secret, becomes disillusioned with the government's actions, and joins Kaneda and the anarchists' fight against the U.S.-led United Nations military intervention, which aims to take control of what is left of Tokyo (*Volume 5*: 1–20). Tetsuo inadvertently awakens his enormous powers by coming into contact with Akira, and he uses these powers to slowly become a threat to everyone, while also developing a drug addiction (*Volume 4*: 73–144). As his drug addiction progresses, though, his control on his body deteriorates, and he succumbs to uncontrollable mutations, while cataclysmic events engulf and devastate Tokyo (*Volumes 5–6*).

Although *Akira* features several sub-plots, its central themes are inherently punk. Several works have analyzed these themes, stressing in particular how irreverence and nihilism feature prominently, and how the main characters Tetsuo and Kaneda incarnate the youth angst and rebellion of the time (Kwok Wah Lau; Napier; Orbaugh). Most characters, including Shikishima, display or develop a strong irreverence towards the *status quo*, whether it be the government or the United Nations, with the perfect example being the anarchist group aiming to uncover the Akira secret. Characters such as Kaneda, Tetsuo and their friends and other gang members live aimless lives at the beginning of the story, producing and using cheap, amateur drugs and driving modified bikes. Tetsuo and Akira perfectly embody the self-destructive, rebellious tendencies of early punks, and the children with extra-sensory powers only wait for premature death to come. Once the Akira secret is uncovered, however, the events this sets in motion center on Kaneda, Shikishima and other characters' desperate attempts to stop Tetsuo's descent into madness and the consequent, inevitable second destruction of neo-Tokyo at the hands of a re-awakened Akira.

As a direct or indirect consequence, each character discovers a way to find freedom and create their own identity and future. For instance, the re-awakened Akira spends most of his time in an apparently catatonic-like state, since his artificial powers are so vast they apparently cancel his identity. Akira recovers his own identity as a child once he is shot during a fight and can be freed of his immense powers. Akira experiences pain again and becomes conscious of his body and mortality, from which his immense powers have shielded him. In a sense, this event acts as a trigger, allowing him to "do" his own identity, after years of oblivion. Similarly, although Tetsuo apparently dies, the story suggests that he is reborn in some other dimension, perhaps as its creator. Kaneda, Shikishima and other characters survive to live in neo-Tokyo's apocalyptic ruins (the "Great Tokyo Empire"), and stubbornly refuse any help from external sources, declaring full independence from the "external" world. Thus, the quest for a new identity and future leads the characters to re-appropriate the ruins of that world in which they were at the mercy of the *status quo*. Kaneda and the other characters are willing to do their identities and future, even if it means facing a harsh, brave new life.

Differently from *Akira* and *RanXerox*, Miyazaki's *Nausicaä of the Valley of the Wind* (*Kaze no Tani no Naushika*) does not appear to be a work with explicit punk themes. It was Miyazaki's only (intermittent) foray into manga (McCarthy106–165). The world in which Nausicaä lives has been ravaged by a millennium of heavy pollution and the expansion of a mysterious "sea of sickness" (*fukushoi*), a semi-organic miasma that kills all living beings except various species of giant mutated insects and fungi. As a consequence of a mysterious accident that occurs in her small kingdom Eftal (the "valley of the wind"), Nausicaä plays a key part in a series of cataclysmic events that permanently reshape her world, revealing its peculiar and mysterious nature.

Given its central theme as a post-apocalyptic blend of fantasy and sci-fi manga, *Nausicaä* features several punk principles both in its aesthetic and thematic realizations. Nihilism and amateurism are strong initial themes. The surviving humans try to survive by scavenging the remnants of the past civilizations, recycling technologies (e.g., flying and fixing planes, *Volume 1*: 1–40). Most human tribes dress often in garish, patchwork outfits (e.g., the outcast "worm-handlers" who become fiercely loyal to Nausicaä, *Volume 6*: 20–24). Similarly, many of the events that occur in the series are based on Nausicaä's crucial form of irreverence, and desire to independently determine her fate. In a world in which giant insects ("Ohmu") can easily crunch humans, Nausicaä suggests that humans and insects can co-exist, and should do so, if they wish to survive (*Volume 2*:1–20). As the series progresses, Nausicaä becomes pivotal to the downfall of the old order that created the *fukushoi*, and she ends up destroying the very creators of her world, using the biological weapons they created, "the god warriors" (*Volume 7*:110–130).

This ultimate gesture of autonomy and renovation comes at an exorbitant price, like in *Akira*'s case. Nausicaä and the other human beings of the tragic millennium have been genetically altered to cope with their polluted environment, and would not survive the cleansed world that would emerge next (Napier 219–220). Nevertheless, Nausicaä commits an act of "deicide" by guiding a fearsome god warrior to destroy the crypt in which the scientists who created her world resided as disembodied memories (*Volume 7*: 200–220). The god warrior, here reduced to a maimed body, takes the pulsating, semi-alive crypt and crushes it, destroying the scientists' ambitions to resurrect in a purified world created by them. By ordering this "deicide," Nausicaä entrusts to the future the possibility that humans may find a way to adapt their bodies to this new environment, perhaps "doing" new bodies that can withstand a purified world (Haas 128–129). Thus, Nausicaä follows the DIY principle in a fairly radical way. Even though she has no idea how to cope with the new world, she nevertheless rebels against her destiny of nothingness and slavery, and decides that humans' destiny is in their own hands alone.[2] Much like Kaneda and Shikishima, she is willing to face an apocalyptic scenario, gambling on the possibility to "do" her own future and body, and that of everyone else around her (see Figure 2).

A different picture emerges in Grant Morrison and Richard Case's run of *Doom Patrol*, given Morrison's strong bonds with punk culture (Callahan 220–230). In the first 18 issues of the new run, written by Paul Kupperberg, the Doom Patrol was presented as a prototypical and somewhat bland team of superheroes. Since the series' sales were plummeting, the up and coming Grant Morrison was asked to jumpstart the series, and to also bring it within Vertigo's publication themes (Callahan 200–210). Morrison revitalized the series in a 43-issue run (January 1989 to July 1992). In this run, Morrison retains Cliff Steele, but also introduces Crazy Jane, a schizophrenic woman with 64 personalities, and a new version of negative man, known as "Rebis," born as the union of three "alchemic" entities: the negative spirit, Larry Trainor (a "white" man) and Dr. Eleanor Poole (a "black" woman). Aside from these new characters, Morrison introduces a long series of adversaries and stories (e.g., the brotherhood of Dada), that are very surreal even by *Doom Patrol* standards.

Several principles permeate this version of *Doom Patrol*, as the series was written in a period in which Morrison was still deeply influenced by punk culture, including the DIY principle (Callahan 230–240). Not only do

NAUSICAÄ
Of The Valley Of The Wind
7

HAYAO MIYAZAKI

Figure 2: In cover art for *Volume 7* of *Kaze no Tani no Nausicaä* (*Nausicaä of the Valley of The Wind*), Nausicaä and the worm-handlers are a clear example of DIY dress (courtesy Viz Media).

"enemies" such as the brotherhood of Dada show no respect for authorities, but also the Doom Patrol, together with their allies Flex Mentallo and Danny the Street, fight against enemies such as the Pentagon and the men from N.O.W.H.E.R.E. (issues #36–39 and #49–52, respectively), dangerous representatives of the *status quo*. Furthermore, all of the characters fight against the existential nothingness that their lives as super-powered but nevertheless handicapped individuals involve, battling their way out of the existential wreckage of their own lives. Rather than punks' nihilism and/or irony, the Doom Patrol seem to simply battle against their own self-destructive tendencies, with Cliff's emblematic action of banging his head against the wall as a key example (issue #19). To a considerable extent, Morrison's run recovers the original spirit of the first series and its darker themes, before developing a more distinctive and punk approach as the series unfolds.

Although the series is rife with instances of punk principles, the final narrative arc represents a particularly fitting example. This arc features the chief's surreal plan to create an apocalyptic future in which all matter is reduced to a chaotic, primordial state. Cliff, Jane, Rebis and the other members can thwart this plan, but only once they can accept their nature as "handicapped" individuals, hence creating their own new identities (Callahan: 231–233). For instance, Cliff survives the chief's attempt to kill him by destroying his physical brain, because his *mind* has been turned into software and downloaded into his body. Once Cliff accepts this new identity as authentic, and not "just" a mechanic simulation, he is able to create his own future, along with the other members. Similarly, Rebis is able to fight against the chief and the Candlemaker and win the fight once his old body is dead, and his new, more powerful alchemic body emerges. Unlike the cyborgs in *Cyborg 009*, or the Doom Patrol from the first original series, these Doom Patrol members take firm control of their new bodies, and "do" their own new futures via this basic, creative step of physical and intellectual reappropriation. Thus, they can also be seen as genuine punk characters, much like the other characters discussed in this section.

We can now take some stock. As our discussion shows, punk comics crucially differ from their precursors in featuring characters that create their own identities, principles, futures and environments. From RanX to Cliff Steele, punk characters decide their life independently, rejecting any form of authority that attempts to block their plans of independence. Women also lead the way: Nausicaä can be seen as a leading, emancipated and empowered punk "heroine." The characters we discussed do not simply rebel against the *status quo* of their fictional worlds, but attempt to create their own futures, which they wish to share with everyone. In each work, a discriminating factor is the commitment that characters display in creating their own identities, destinies and goals. Thus, *RanXerox*, *Akira*, *Nausica*ä and *Doom Patrol* are punk comics, since they feature characters that are very determined to follow the DIY principles to their logical and radical consequences.

Punk Heirs: A Case Study

The goal of this section is to discuss comics that further elaborate punk themes, despite being produced beyond the "core" punk wave. For reasons of space, I concentrate on one anime, *Kemonozume*, which does not appear to be a punk work, at least at a first, superficial glance.

Kemonozume is a 13-episode series directed by Maasaki Yuasa, a celebrated anime author who started his career as a director with this "midnight anime" show.[3] The plot of the story centers on the complex and extremely troubled romantic relationship between Toshihiko and Yuka, a skydiving instructor and a member of the *shokujinki* ("man-eating ogres"), a group of humans cursed with a need to eat other humans' flesh. The *shokujinki* can transform into ferocious ogre-like creatures when their cannibalistic urges emerge, but can otherwise live hidden amidst other members of society. Most *shokujinki* only discover their true nature once some emotionally intense event (e.g., the first kiss, as shown in the preamble to episode #8) triggers their transformation into ogres. Against the *shokujinki* stand the *Kifūken* ("ogre-sealing sword"), a group of samurai-like fighters who hone their fighting skills in their attempt to exterminate the *shokujinki* once and for all. This, however, changes when Toshiko and Yuka meet by chance, fall in love and elope, setting a catastrophic turn of events in motion.

Toshihiko, while eloping with Yuka, discovers that the claws that the *shokujinki* have in their ogre-like form have a parasite-like, distinct existence, and can consume their "host" if their negative emotions become overwhelming. As parasite-like entities, the claws can be removed from a *shokujinki* and attached to a human without arms, acting as new host. The *kifūken* have used this technique, known as the *kemonozume* ("beast claw"), as a dangerous weapon against the *shokujinki*. In a bizarre twist of events, it is also revealed that one of the three executives of the *kifūken*, Ōba, is killing *shokujinki* and harvesting claws to create drugs, medicines and other substances including the claws' powder. His goal is to cause a mass "epidemic" of *shokujinki* mutations, and take control of Japan. Only when Toshihiko, Yuki and Ōba's son, the albino giant Jōji Bon, defeat a completely mutated and insane Ōba, can they escape from this terrible fate, save Japan, and build a family.

The key aspects that make *Kemonozume* a punk series, or at least a series with strong punk undertones, are the relationships that the characters have with their bodies. Both Toshihiko and Yuka have very different, but quite specific, physical problems. Toshihiko is a fine swordsman, but he loses control of his bowels in actual fights. Yuki is a *shokujinki* who spends most of series desperately fighting her urge to eat other human beings, while at the same time engaging in physically intense activities, such as working as a skydiving instructor. Their love is, for most of the series, very physical and passionate, although sex is a concern for Yuka, since pleasure can awaken her *shokujinki* side.

To a certain extent, Toshihiko and Yuka act as a post-modern Romeo and Juliet couple and, as a consequence, embody a specific type of anarchist (punk) lover. Before they elope, both live hollow, nihilistic lives as a sheltered, idealistic samurai (Toshihiko), and a risk-seeking *shokujinki* in denial (Yuki). Their lives are initially bound to the "authority" of their clan and the claws as parasites, respectively. From this they desperately attempt to escape, which is an act of irreverence and independence. Furthermore, in pursuing this new life, Toshihiko and Yuka experience a radical change. Both follow daily, shallow routines until the fateful day of their meeting. After eloping, they desperately fight to forge a new authentic life as lovers, created by patching together whatever sources of happiness they can find. Via their love, they seek to create a new, authentic future by themselves. The iconic flyer of the series captures this fact in an elegant way. Toshihiko the *kifūken* heir and Yuki the *shokujinki* kiss, while their weapons (a katana and a claw), symbols of their societal constraints they try to become independent from, loom large in the background. Importantly, Toshihiko and Yuka follow the DIY principle to also reshape their personal physical and social identities. Yuka fiercely resists her urge to eat human flesh, and only does so during the "mutation" epidemic. Toshihiko never truly masters his inability to constrain his bowels, but he uses this flaw as a weapon in his fight against Ōba. More importantly, Toshihiko never falls prey to the temptation of transplanting the *Kemonozume* onto his body, even when Yuka offers him her arms. He wins a desperate battle against Ōba after losing one arm, and uses the maimed limb to extend the reach of his other arm, thus cutting off the head of an irremediably mutated and insane antagonist.

As our discussion suggests, then, *Kemonozume* is a series that features characters who embody a DIY principle in a fairly radical manner, although in a different manner than the *Akira* or *Doom Patrol* characters. By not appropriating these bodies but seeking new ones, they affirm a distinct identity, which they "do" themselves. Again, Toshihiko refuses to change his body to fight Ōba, who modified his body to grotesque levels in order to obtain power. Yuka refuses to eat other humans, hence refusing to give in to the curse imposed on her by an old tragedy. The other characters in the other works we have discussed also follow different paths when they create their futures. Cliff Steele can overcome his pain once he renounces his old body, and appropriates a new, synthetic one. Akira regains his consciousness by accident, and only once he is shot. RanX simply pursues his own life, according to his own decisions. Thus, regardless of the path taken, all of these characters affirm their identity by "doing" their new identity themselves.

In most of these cases, however, these choices have far reaching consequences, since the Doom Patrol, Nausicaä, Toshihiko and Yuka also save the world (or at least Japan, in some cases) from the destructive forces of their enemies, the incarnation of the *status quo*. These punk characters "do" their bodies, identities and destinies themselves. Contemporary punks do not simply mock and rebel against the corrupt *status quo*; they strive for independence and an authentic, *better* future than the empty ones determined by the authorities they fight. If early punks such as Kaneda would take their lives in their hands and only fight for their own future, then modern punks fight this fight for everyone around them, leading everyone by example. Thus, these punk characters challenge pre-conceived views and re-create their own identity as a means of freedom, thereby creating everyone's freedom as a logical consequence.

In doing so, punk characters strictly follow a DIY principle, which seems to indeed act as the crucial trope that distinguishes punk comics from their precursors (e.g., *Cyborg 009*). Hence, we can offer a positive answer to our central question, as the DIY principle seems to critically identify punk comics, and distinguish them from their "DIY–less" precursors. Punk principles have been used not only as aesthetic choices for the visual representation of punk characters in comics, but also as tropes/themes that represent punk identities, specifically identities based on the DIY philosophy. Punks in comics can be easily recognized as they create their own identities, futures and goals and, in doing so, permit others to seemingly reach emancipation, as unlikely but more genuine heroes.

Conclusions

In this essay we have attempted to answer the question of whether and how punk principles can be found in comics. In order to answer these questions, we have proposed a set of negative and positive punk principles, in which irreverence, nihilism and amateurism find a counterpart in the positive principles of independence, authenticity and creativity. We have discussed how these principles interact and combine together, focusing particularly on the interaction of creativity and authenticity, which we dubbed the DIY philosophy/principle. We have then seen that this principle seems to identify genuine punk comics, and also place this genre close to the related genres of cyborgs, and post-apocalyptic science fiction. Punks do not just fight to decide their own identities, but also for their own future and independence, helping other fellow human beings along the way.

The works we have discussed in this essay, then, show that punk protocomics already appeared before the punk movement officially emerged, anticipating most but not all of its principles, as the DIY philosophy did not feature strongly (e.g., *Cyborg 009*). Comics that were contemporary with the movement added this principle, thus becoming full-fledged punk comics (e.g., *Nausicaä*). Modern punk comics, then, interpret these ideals in even more radical terms, showing that punk characters can represent full-fledged heroes rather than misfits and rebels (e.g., *Doom Patrol*). It should be obvious that our discussion does not cover all the works that can indeed qualify as "punk": once more, we opted not to discuss works that seem more "straightforward" examples of punk comics in section 4. However, if this analysis is on the right track, future works may shed light on many other punk comics, as well.

Notes

1. *Shōnen* in this context can be translated as "boy": *shōnen manga* are generally aimed at male teens. The distinction between *shōnen* and *seinen* ("male adult") *manga* was popularized in the early '80s (Gravett 60–70; Bryce and Davis 38–40).

2. Interestingly, both Ōtomo and Miyazaki cited in several occasions Moebius as a very important source of inspiration for these works; however, Moebius (Jean Giraud, although this "pen name" was conceived as a distinct artistic persona) never produced truly punk works (Schodt 200; 220). The fact that Moebius, as one of the authors behind the *Métal Hurlant* movement, had a deep influence on these authors, among many others across the world, is not surprising. We do not discuss this point here, though, since it would lead us too far afield.

3. The label "midnight anime" is an informal term used for shows that are usually presented at a time slot that usually starts at 23:45 onwards (Bryce and Davis 58). It is fairly common that these anime feature mature themes, such as complex philosophical questions, but also explicit sex scenes.

Works Cited

Atkinson, Paul. "Do It Yourself: Democracy and Design." *Journal of Design History*, vol. 19, no. 1, 2006, pp. 1–10.

Beatty, Scott. "Doom Patrol." *The DC Comics Encyclopedia*, edited by Alastair Dougall, Dorling Kindersley, 2008, pp. 278–279.

Bryce, Mio and Davis, Jason. "An Overview of Manga Genres." *Manga: An Anthology of Global and Cultural Perspectives*, edited by Toni Johnson-Woods, Continuum, 2010, pp. 34–61.

Callahan, Timothy. *Grant Morrison: The Early Years*. Sequart, 2007.

Castaldi, Simone. *Drawn and Dangerous: Italian Comics of the 1970s and 1980s*. University of Mississippi Press, 2012.

Chalmers, David. *The Conscious Mind: In Search of a Fundamental Theory*. Oxford UP, 1996.

Clark, Andy. *Natural-Born Cyborgs: Minds, Technologies and the Future of Human Intelligence*. Oxford UP, 2003.

Cross, Rich. "'There Is No Authority but Yourself': The Individual and the Collective in British Anarcho-Punk." *Music & Politics*, vol. 4, no. 2, 2000, pp. 1–20.

Deacon, Terrence. *The Symbolic Species: The Co-evolution of Language and the Brain*. W.W. Norton, 1997.

Drake, Arnold, Bob Haney, and Bruno Premiani. *The Doom Patrol Archives: Volume 1*. DC Comics, 2002.

Gravett, Paul. *Manga: Sixty Years of Japanese Comics*. Harper Design, 2004.

Groensteen, Thierry. *The System of Comics*. Translated by Bart Beaty and Nick Nyuyen, University of Mississippi Press, 2007.
Haas, Daniel. "Why Nice Princesses Don't Always Finish Last." *Anime and Philosophy: Wide Eyed Wonder*, edited by Josef Steiff and Tristan D. Tamplin, Open Court Publishing Company, 2010, pp. 212–130.
Hanscombe, Stuart. "Do It Yourself: Existentialism as Punk Philosophy." *Café Philosophy*, June 2014, http://cafephilosophy.co.nz/articles/do-it-yourself-existentialism-as-punk-philosophy/. Accessed 18 May 2017.
Ishinomori, Shōtarō. *Cyborg 009: Volume 1*. Tokyopop, 2003.
_____. *Cyborg 009: Volume 2*. Tokyopop, 2003.
_____. *Cyborg 009: Volume 3*. Tokyopop, 2004.
_____. *Cyborg 009: Volume 4*. Tokyopop, 2004.
_____. *Cyborg 009: Volume 5*. Tokyopop, 2004.
_____. *Cyborg 009: Volume 6*. Tokyopop, 2004.
_____. *Cyborg 009: Volume 7*. Tokyopop, 2004.
_____. *Cyborg 009: Volume 8*. Tokyopop, 2004.
_____. *Cyborg 009: Volume 9*. Tokyopop, 2005.
_____. *Cyborg 009: Volume 10*. Tokyopop, 2005.
Kemonozume. Directed by Masaaki Yuasa, Madhouse. 2006.
Kwok Wah Lau, Jenny. *Multiple Modernities*. Temple UP, 2003.
Mahmutovic, Adnan, David Coughlan, and Blake Erwin. "Ecce Animot Or, The Animal Man That Therefore I Am." *ImageTexT*, vol. 8, no. 2, 2015, http://www.english.ufl.edu/imagetext/archives/v8_2/mahmutovic_et_al/. Accessed 18 May 2017.
McCarthy, Helen. *Hayao Miyazaki Master of Japanese Animation*. Stone Bridge Press, 1999.
Metzinger, Thomas. *Being No One: The Self-Model Theory of Subjectivity*. MIT Press, 2004.
Miyazaki, Hayao. *Nausicaä in the Valley of the Wind*. Viz Media, 2012. 2004.
Moore, Ryan. "Anarchy in the USA: Capitalism, Postmodernity, and Punk Subculture Since the 1970s." Dissertation, University of California, San Diego, 2000.
Moore, Ryan. "Postmodernism and Punk Subculture: Cultures of Authenticity and Deconstruction." *The Communication Review*, vol. 7, no. 3, 2004, pp. 305–327.
Morrison, Grant (w) and Richard Case (p). *The Doom Patrol Omnibus*. DC Comics, 2014.
Napier, Susan. *The Fantastic in Modern Japanese Literature*. Routledge, 1996.
_____. "Vampires, Psychic Girls, Flying Women and Sailor Scouts." *The Worlds of Japanese Popular Culture: Gender, Shifting Boundaries and Global Culture*, edited by Dolores P. Martinez, Cambridge UP, 1998. pp. 91–109.
O'Hara, Craig. *The Philosophy of Punk: More than Noise*. AK Press, 1999.
Orbaugh, Sharalyn. "Cyborg Affect and the Limits of the Human." *Mechademia*, vol. 3, 2008, pp. 150–172.
Ōtomo, Katsuhiro. *Akira: Volume 1*. Kodansha US, 2009.
_____. *Akira: Volume 2*. Kodansha US, 2010.
_____. *Akira: Volume 3*. Kodansha US, 2010.
_____. *Akira: Volume 4*. Kodansha US, 2010.
_____. *Akira: Volume 5*. Kodansha US, 2011.
_____. *Akira: Volume 6*. Kodansha US, 2011.
Petersen, Robert. *Comics, Manga and Graphic Novels: A History of Graphic Narratives*. ABC-CLIO, 2010.
Prinz, Jesse. "The Aesthetics of Punk Rock." *Philosophy Compass*, vol. 9, no. 9, 2014, pp. 583–593.
Raffaelli, Luca. *Il fumetto*. Il saggiatore, 1997.
Reynolds, Richard. *Superheroes: a Modern Mythology*. Mississippi UP, 1992.
Savage, Jon. *Teenage: The Creation of Youth Culture*. Viking, 2007.
Schodt, Frederick L. *Dreamland Japan: Writings on Modern Manga*. Stone Bridge Press, 1996.
Shirow, Masamune. *Ghost in the Shell*. Dark Horse Comics, 1997.
Singer, Marc. *Grant Morrison: Combining the Worlds of Contemporary Comics*. University of Mississippi Press, 2012.
Tamburini Stefano, and Massimo Liberatore. *RanXerox: Volume 1*. Edizioni del Grifo, 1992.

_____. *RanXerox: Volume 2*. Edizioni del Grifo, 1992.
Thompson, Jason. *Manga: The Complete Guide*. Del Rey, 2007.
Thompson, Stacy. *Punk Productions: Unfinished Business*. SUNY Press, 2004.
Triggs, Teal. "Scissors and Glue. Punk Fanzines and the Creation of a DIY Aesthetic." *Journal of Design History*, vol. 19, no. 1, 2006, pp. 69–83.
Wolf, Marco & Sergio McQuitty. "Understanding the Do-It-Yourself Consumer: DIY Motivations and Outcomes." *Academy of Marketing Science Review*, vol. 10, no. 1, 2011, pp. 1–20.

About the Contributors

Spencer **Chalifour** is in the English P.hD. program at the University of Florida with a concentration in comics and visual rhetoric. He is a member of the UF Graduate Comics Organization and was the lead organizer for the 14th Annual UF Comics and Graphic Novels Conference.

Jodie **Childers** has published essays on folk music, self-taught art, and other topics related to the intersection of culture and politics. Her creative work has been featured in *Poetry East*, *Feral Feminisms*, and *The Portland Review*. She is pursuing a Ph.D. in English at the University of Massachusetts, Amherst.

Jill **Dahlman**, a graduate of the University of Hawaii system: Hilo, is an assistant professor at the University of North Alabama. She sits on the editorial board for *Rocky Mountain Review*, the peer-reviewed journal of the Rocky Mountain MLA. Her research interests include student self-efficacy and the first-year composition classroom.

Christopher C. **Douglas** is an instructor at the University of Alabama. His scholarly interests include the creation of community in fiction, non-human narration, and the history of the novel. He has published in *ESQ*. He's working on contextualizing Natsume Soseki's first novel *I Am a Cat* (1905–1906) into modern it-narrative discourse.

Christopher B. **Field** is an assistant professor in the Languages, Literature, and Philosophy Department at Tennessee State University. His research and teaching interests include contemporary American literature, twentieth-century American literature, early American literature, popular culture, and rhetoric and composition.

Keegan **Lannon** is an adjunct English instructor at Dominican University and North Central College. He has published and presented on comics and narrative theory, but he still harbors fantasies of playing bass for the Ramones.

Michael David **MacBride** received his Ph.D. in English from Southern Illinois University, Carbondale, in 2014. Since 2005, he has taught a variety of English, literature, and humanities courses at universities in and around the Midwest.

About the Contributors

Francesco-Alessio **Ursini** is a research fellow at Sun Yat-Sen University. His work in linguistics focuses on spatial expressions across languages, and his scholarship on comics focuses on the representation of places, and coherence and narrative relations underpinning stories. Together with Frank Bramlett and Adnan Mahmutović, he is the editor of a special issue of *ImageTexT* dedicated to Grant Morrison.

Louie Dean **Valencia-García** is an assistant professor of Digital History at Texas State University. He earned his Ph.D. from Fordham University in 2016 and has been on the teaching faculty in arts and sciences at Harvard University. His book *Antiauthoritarian Youth Culture in Francoist Spain* was published in 2018.

Alice **Vernon** is a Ph.D. student in creative writing at Aberystwyth University. Her research interests include comics, graphic novels, and manga—particularly the comics of Carol Swain and women mangaka such as Q Hayashida and Satsuki Yoshino.

Russell **Weber** is a Ph.D. candidate at the University of California, Berkeley. His dissertation explores the relationship between emotions, rhetoric, print media, and identity politics in colonial North America and the early American republic. His research interests also include the political and cultural history of American comic books.

Can **Yalçınkaya** is a Turkish-Australian academic, writer and cartoonist based in Macquarie University, Sydney. He is the editor of *ResistComics*, an anthology inspired by the Occupy Gezi movement in Turkey. He researches the cultural history of comics, film and popular music in Turkey and co-convenes the Graphic Social Science Research Network.

Index

Numbers in **bold italics** indicate pages with illustrations.

Aaron, Jason 12, 49, 50, 52–57, 59, 60, 107n4
The ABCs of Autobio Comix 129
Ablak, Emrah 159, 165
Abraham Erskine 30
An ABZ of Love **121**, **122**
Acid Eaters 6
Adam, Eddie 3
Adelman, Bob **118**, 119, 131n6, 131n9
Adorno, Theodor 161
The Ages of Superman: Essays on the Man of Steel in Changing Times 151n3, 151n6
Akdeniz, Tünay 154
Akira (anime) 14, 171–173, 176–178, 181, 185n9
Akira (character) 178, 180–184, 189, 212, 213, 218
Akira (manga) 10, 14, 15, 131n5, 171, 173, 174, 176, 181, 185n4, 185n10, 186n10, 188–191, 194, 195, 210, 212–214, 216, 218
Akira, Miyashita 176
"Akira and Ranma ½: The Monstrous Adolescent" 172
Akiyo, Satorigi 195
Akiyuki, Nosaka 176, 185n8
Alamo 12, 88, 89, 105, 106, 107n2
Alaska y los Pegamoides 148
Albuquerque, Rafael 107n4
All-Star Superman 79
Allen, Woody 135
Altamont Free Concert 2
Althusser, Louis 62
American Vampire 107n4
anarchy 1, 4, 9, 12, 62, 66, 88, 106, 108n8, 115, 156, 165, 207
Anarchy for the Masses 77, 82
Anarchy in the UK 59, 82, 83
Anatolian Pop 154
Anderson, Benedict 140–142
Animal Boy 6 Animal Man 76, 79
anti-authority 1, 9, 13, 20, 24, 25, 27, 44, 63,

73n1, 91, 93, 96, 97, 101, 102, 119, 123, 128, 129, 134–137, 140–143, 147, 150, 156, 157, 182, 206, 216
Appleseed 173
Aptullica 156; see also Elçioğlu, Abdülkadir
Aral, Oğuz 156
Aratan, Kemal 157
Arkham Asylum 79
Asahi Shimbun 9
"Aşık Memo" 161, 163, 167
Astaire, Fred 211
Astro Boy 9
Atkinson, Paul 206, 207
Atsushi, Kase 176
Atsushi, Ōkubo 14, 188, 191, **193**
The Avengers 33, 35, 36, 37, 40
Aydın, Suavi 153

Babas, Kike 151n7
Bad Religion (band) 62, 115
Bagge, Peter 80
Bakhtin, Mikhail 66, 136, 143, 163
La Banda de Moebius 147
Bangs, Lester 4
Barcelona 144, 145
Bardsley, Jan 190, 194, 202
Baroja, Julio Caro 135
Barslan, Can 157
Baruter, Bahadır 158, 159, 160, 165–167, 168n6
"Basket Case" 54
Batman 65
Batman: The Dark Knight Returns 83
Battle Angel Alita 173
Baudelaire, Charles 65
Beatles (band) 75
Beatty, Scott 209
"Ben Bir Eşşeğim" 165
Ben Grimm 43
"Beni ilgilendirmez" 155

225

226 Index

Benton, Mike 37
Berlanga, Carlos 148
Bermejo, Lee 53
Berry, D. Bruce 26
Bill Foster 43
Binky Brown 113, 119, *121*, 123–126, 128, 130
"The Binky Brown Matter" 126
Binky Brown Meets the Holy Virgin Mary 13, 113, 114, 119, 120–*125*, *127*–129, 131n12
Bisley, Simon 56–59
Black Flag (band) 115, 116
Black Jack 9, 15n6
Black Jack (character) 15n6
Black Panther 35
Blade Runner 185n4, 211
"Blank Generation" 54, 67
Boot, Adrian 3
"Born of Trauma: *Akira* and Capitalist Modes of Destruction" 173
bōsōzoku 14, 171, 172, 174–177, 181, 182, 184, 185n2, 198, 212
Botchan 175, 176
bourgeois 136, 137, 159, 166
bourgeoisie 136, 137
Bowie, James 88, 107n2
Boynik, Sezgin 154, 155, 160, 161, 166
Brain Drain 6
Brazil 211
bricolage 86, 135
Brinton, Mary 174
Brother Eye 20–23
Bruce, Lenny 2
Bryce, Mio 220n1, 220n3
Bubblegum Crisis 173, 185n4
Bucky Barnes 35, 36, 38, 39, 46n4
Buddy Blank 20–22, 24, 25, 27, 131n5
Bukatman, Scott 64, 65
Burbey, Mark 120
Büstün 159; see also Üstün, Bülent
Byerly, Carolyn M. 200
Byrne, David 146

Callahan, Timothy 75, 214, 216
Campoamor, Manolo 148
Cantek, Levent 156, 163, 166
Canut, Nacho 148
capitalism 8, 20, 24–27, 59, 61–63, 69, 72, 73n1, 109n11, 142, 145, 173
Captain America 11, 12, 25, 29–46; see also Steve Rogers
Captain America **31**
Captain America and the Falcon 38–40, 46n4
Captain America: Red, White & Blue 30, 32
Captain America: Sentinel of Liberty 30
Carajillo 148, **149**
Carlin, George 2
carnivalesque 13, 66, 134–137, 139–143, 146, **149**, 150, 163
Cascorro Factory 146

Case, Richard 214
Castaldi, Simone 212
Cavallaro, Dani 177
CBGB 66
Ceesepe 146–148; see also Pérez, Carlos Sánchez
Celty Sturluson 191, 195–200, 202
censor 1, 8, 70, 71, 83, 84, 86n6, **121**, 122, 141, 142, 144, 145, 151n5, 197–199
Chalmers, David 208
The Chief 210, 216
Chikamatsu 177
Çığrışım 154
Civil Rights Movement 3, 38, 41, 114
Civil War 29, 41, 43–45, 46n5
Civil War: Casualties of War 40, 42
Clark, Andy 208
Clark, Dylan 68
The Clash (band) 62, 67, 79, 101
Cliff Steele 210, 214, 216, 218; see also Robotman
Clowes, Daniel 86n3
Cobalt Man 41
Coldheart 41
"Come On Now" 6–8
Comic Book Character: Unleashing the Hero in Us All 32
The Comic Book in America: An Illustrated History 37
The Comic Book Legal Defense Fund 86n6
Comic Book Nation 46n2
The Comics Code 8, 36, 128
The Comics Journal 78
El Comix Marginal Español 145, 147
commodification 12, 49, 50, 61, 62, 67–72, 135, 154, 206
A Confederacy of Dunces 63
conformity 14, 24, 35, 36, 40, 66, 68, 89, 92, 101, 126, 161, 198
Constantine 11, 12, 49–60
Copeland, Rebecca 195
Coşkun, Mehmet 158, 165, 168n5; see also Memcoş
Costa, Salvador 147
counterpublic 137, 139–143, 148, **149**
Cowe-Spigai, Kereth 77, 81
Crass (band) 62, 108n8, 115
Crazy Jane 214
Creem 3
Critique of Everyday Life 150n2
Crockett, David 88, 89, 107n2
Cross, Rich 206
Crumb, Robert **117**, **118**, 119, 120, 129, 131n8, 131n11, 135, 144, 145
A Cultural Dictionary of Punk: 1974–1982 82
"Cümbür Cemaat" 159
cyberpunk 9, 10, 12, 61, 62, 72n1, 73n1, 73n2, 173, 185n4
Cyborg 009 15, 208, 209, 216, 219, 220

Dabak, Gökhan 157
Dadaism 161
Damned (band) 54
Dane McGowan 76, 83, 85
Danganronpa: Trigger Happy Havoc 176
Danny the Street 216
Danzig, Glenn 9
Daredevil 35
Dark Horse Comics 81, 185n10, 186n10
Darkseid 28n1
Davis, Jason 220n1, 220n3
Day-Glo 82
"The Day the World Turned Day-Glo" 78
DC Comics 11, 12, 19, 20, 22, 26, 27, 28n1, 49, 57, 78–81, 83, 86n6
De Espaldas al Kiosco: Guía Histórica de Fanzines y Otros Papelujos de Alcantarillas 151n7
De Qué Va el Rock Macarra 137, **138**
Deacon, Terrence 205
Dead Kennedys (band) 115
Debord, Guy 65
De Certeau, Michel 142
DeConnick, Kelly Sue 107n4
de Fonseca, Javier Rodríguez 147, 148
Delano, Jamie 50, 51
The Demon 28n1
détournement 62, 65, 67, 69, 156
Devilman 9, 173
DEVO (band) 115
DiDio, Dan 19
Dillon, Steve 12, 88–90, 92–106, 107n4, 108n9, 109n12
Dini, Paul 30, 42
do-it-yourself (DIY) 5, 8, 14, 15, 15n6, 20, 25–27, 68, 71, 73n1, 80–91, 97, 99, 108n8, 141, 158, 160, 165, 171, 186n13, 205, 207–210, 212, 214, **215**, 217–220
Doom Patrol 15, 79, 208–210, 214, 216, 218, 220
Doom Patrol (characters) 209, 210, 214, 216, 219
Doors (band) 2, 5
Dorohedoro 14, 188, 200, 201, 203
Dragotta, Nick 107n4
Drake, Arnold 208
The Drifting Classroom 173
Dubro, Alec 199, 201
Duin, Steve 33, 37
"Dünyanın En İğrenç İnsanı Memo Tembel Çizer" 163, **164**
Durarara!! 14, 188, 191, 195–200, 202
"Duvar" 168n5

East of West 107n4
Eastwood, Clint 7, 91
Eightball 86n3
Elasti-girl 210; *see also* Rita Farr
Elçioğlu, Abdülkadir 156; *see also* Aptullica
Eleanor Poole 214

Ellis, Warren 12, 51, 52, 61, 63–66, 69–72
Emre, Kumru Berfin 167
En 201, 202
End of the Century 6
Englehart, Steve 38, 39, 46n4
Ennis, Garth 12, 50, 52, 88–90, 92–106, 107n2, 107n4, 108n9, 109n12
Ensminger, David A. 189, 190
Erdem, Alpay 165
Erdoğan, Recep Tayyip 168
Ergönültaş, Engin 157, 158, 165, 168n4
Ertem, Kaan 161, 163 Esparbe 145, 146
espers 172, 178, 181–183, 185n3
Estren, Mark James 131n9
Evanier, Mark 19, 20, 22, 23, 25–27
Everyday Life in the Modern World 70
Evren, Kenan 153
Exploited (band) 155

The Fabulous Furry Freak Brothers 156
The Factory 82, 146
Falcon 38, 39
Fantastic Four 26, 42, 43
Farriol, Josep 144
Farriol, Miquel 144
Fashion Beast 131n5
Fear and Loathing in Las Vegas 63
Federal Bureau of Investigation (FBI) 5, 107n4
Fermuar 167
The Filth and the Fury 85, 86n7
Fingeroth, Danny 32
Flex Mentallo 216
Fourth World 19
Franco, Francisco 13, 134–137, 139–143, 145, 151n3, 151n6
Francoist 134, 136, 137, 141–144
"Frankie Teardrop" 68
Frazier, Nancy 143
Frigidaire 211
Fugs (band) 2

Gage, Christos N. 42
Gaiman, Neil 78, 155
García-Alix, Alberto 146, 147
Genesis Survivor Gaiarth 173
Ghost in the Shell 173, 209
Ghost Rider 68
Gibbons, Dave 83
Gimarc, George 3
Giraud, Jean 220n2; *see also* Moebius
Gırgır 156, 157
giri 14, 15n5, 171–174, 177–184, 186n13
Gō, Nagai 9, 173
God (character) 9, 13, 89, 93, 95–97, 101, 104–106, 109n12
"God Save the Queen" 59, 69, 82
Goliath 42, 43; *see also* Bill Foster
Goodman, Martin 26
Gotham City 65

Göxel 165
Gramsci, Antonio 150n1
Grant Morrison: Combining the Worlds of Contemporary Comics 76
Grave of the Fireflies 171, 172, 176, 177
Gravett, Paul 209, 220n1
Great Teacher Onizuka 176
Green, Justin 13, 113, 114, 118–129
Green Day (band) 54, 55, 79
Griffin, Naomi 188, 199, 200
grotesque 136, 155, 162, 163
Groth, Gary 26, 27
Grosz, George 161
Gruenwald, Mark 37
Grundy, Bill 68, 83–85, 86n7
Grup Perişan 156
Guéra, R.M. 107n4
Güldallı, Tolga 154, 155, 161, 166
Gülmen, Yetkin 165
Guns N' Roses (band) 30
Gwynne, Joel 191

Haas, Daniel 214
"Haftanın (Göt) Laleleri" 157
Halfway to Sanity 6
Hand of Fire: The Comics Art of Jack Kirby 19
Haney, Bob 208
Hannon, Sharon M. 22, 24, 25, 91, 92, 101, 108n8, 109n10, 109n11
Hanscombe, Stuart 206, 207
Harry, Debbie 146
Hasted, Nick 78
Hate 80
Hatfield, Charles 19
Hawkeye 40
Hayvan 166
H.B.R. Maymun 155, 157, 159, 160
Headbangers (band) 155
Hebdige, Dick 29, 30, 32, 41, 46, 56, 64, 86, 135, 161
hegemony 1, 46, 62, 67
Hein, Laura 184
Hell, Richard 54, 62, 67, 146
Hellblazer 12, 49, 50, 51, 52, 53, 58
Hells Angels 2
Hendrix, Jimi 2, 4
Henry, Tricia 62, 158
Herbert, Mark 23, 26
Hercules (character) 45
Here Are the Sonics 114
Hernandez, Los Bros 11
"Hey Joe" 68
Hıbır 156
Hickman, Jonathan 107n4
Higgins, John 51, 52
hippies 3, 23, 82, 85, 134
Historia de la Censura 145
historietas groseras 144
A History of Underground Comics 131n9
Hitler, Adolf 12, 21, 32

homology 30
Hong Kong Virus (band) 168n3
How to Read Superhero Comics and Why 31
Hughes, Rian 81, 82
Hulk 19

I Am a Cat 175
"'I Like Hate and I Hate Everything Else': The Influence of Punk on Comics" 78
Ibars, Eduardo Haro 150
Iggy Pop and the Stooges (band) 114
Image Comics 81
Imagined Communities: Reflections on the Origin and Spread of Nationalism 141
International Women's Year Action Group 190
The Invisibles 11, 12, 75–83, 85, 86, 86n3, 86n4
Iron Man 40, 41, 43–45; *see also* Tony Stark
Isao, Takahata 176, 177
Ishinomori, Shōtarō 15, 208
Iyuka, Sato 174

Jackson, Jack *117*, 131n8
Jansen, Klaus 83
Jarman, Derek 67, 68
Jesse Custer 13, 89, 90, 93–106, 108n9, 109n11, 109n12
jidaigeki 174
John Constantine 11, 12, 49–60
Johnny Storm 42, 43
Johnston, Eric 173, 174, 181
Jones, Steve 84, 85
Joplin, Janis 2
Jova, Olvido "Alaska" Gara 148
Joy Division (band) 135
Jubilee (film) 67
Jubilee 40
Judas Priest (band) 7
Judge Dredd 131n5
Justice League 28n1

"Kabız Kuğu" 159, 160
Kahn-Egan, Seth 2, 5
"Kahraman Barut" 165
Kaka De Luxe 148
Kamereon 176, 185n7
Kamikaze Biker 174
Kaneda 178, 179, 181–184, 186n13, 189, 190, 212–214, 219
Kaplan, David 199, 201
Karabulut, Ersin 159, 167
Karahasanoglu, Songül 168n2
Karataş, Hakan 165
Katsuhiro, Ōtomo 9, 10, 14, 15, 15n5, 171–173, 176–181, 184, 188–191, 200, 212, 220n2
Kaze no Tani no Naushika 213, **215**
Kazuo, Umezu 173
Kei 178, 182, 186n13, 189–191
Kemonozume 217, 218
Kennedy, John F. 2, 37

Index   229

Kennedy, Robert 2
Kevin Kho 19
Keyder, Çağlar 154
Kick Out the Jams 114, 130n1
Kifûken 217, 218
King, Dave 115
King, Martin Luther, Jr. 2
King, Stephen 7
King Cat 80
King Mob 75, 76, 83
Kingsmen (band) 5, 114
The Kinks (band) 114
Kinsella, Sharon **193**
Kirby, Jack 11, 19, 20, 22–28, 28n1, 35, 36
Kirby: King of Comics 26
Kitchen, Denis 119
Klock, Geoff **31**, 46
"Know Your Rights" 67
Kochira Katsushika-ku Kameari Kōen Mae Hashutsujo 15n7
Korean War 33
"Kötü Kedi Şerafettin" 159, 161–163, 165, 168n7
"Kunteper Canavarı" 161, 163, 167
Kupperberg, Paul 214
Kurtzman, Harvey 119
Kwok Wah Lau, Jenny 212

L-Manyak 13, 153, 155–163, 165–168, 168n7
Lágrimas 148
Lamarre, Thomas 173
Larry Trainor 210, 214; see also Negative Man
Latour, Bruno 151n4
Lawley, Guy 78, 86n2, 155, 156
Led Zeppelin (band) 154
Lee, Andrew 176
Lee, Stan 26, 27, **31**, 33–36
Lefebvre, Henri 70, 149, 150, 150n2
"The Legend of Nick Detroit" 146
Leman 156–159, 161, 165–167; see also *Limon*
Leman Kültür 157
"Lemanti-Medya" 157
Lennon, John 147
Leslie, Ester 82, 83
Lewis, Jerry Lee 4
Liberatore, Tanino 15, 210, 211
Limon 156, 157, 159; see also *Leman*
Lipstick Traces 73n3
Liviandad del Imperdible 148
Lloyd, David 210
Lobo 131n5
Lombak 153, 155, 156, 158–161, 163, 165–168
"Lombak Kerizleri" 165
Lorrio, Félix 150
Los Saicos 114
"Louie Louie" 5, 114
Louvin, Ira 4
Love and Rockets 131n5

low culture 7, 136, 137
La Luna de Madrid 141
Luque, Nazario 144, 147, 150
Lydon, John 57

Machiko, Hasegawa 9
Mackie, Vera 191
Mad Magazine 7, 118, 119, 120, 156
Madley, June M. 198
Madrid 13, 134–136, 140, 141, 144, 146–150
Madriz 141
Manrique, Diego 137, **138**
Marcus, Greil 4, 73n3, 161
Mariscal, Javier 144
Márquez, Fernando 148
Marsh, Dave 5, 15n2
Marvel Comics 11, 19, 20, 22, 25–27, **31**, 33–35, 37, 40, 41, **44**, 45, 81
Marvel: The Characters and Their Universe 46n1
Marzinger Z 9
Masamune, Shirō 173
Maus 120
MC5 (band) 3, 68, 114, 130n1
McCaffery, Larry 72
McCarthy, Helen 213
McLaren, Malcolm 67, 73n2
McNeil, Legs 158
McQuitty, Sergio 205
Meaney, Patrick 75–77, 82
Medusa Gorgon 191–195, 198, 199
Melnick, Monte 7
Melody Maker 3
Memcoş 158; see also Coşkun, Mehmet
Mesela Mesele 154
Métal Hurlant 220n2
Metropolis 65
Metzinger, Thomas 208
Microbe 41
Mikrop 168n4
Millar, Mark 40, 42–45
Miller, Frank 78, 83
Miller, Gerald 172
Miller, Laura 190, 194, 202
Milligan, Peter 12, 49, 50, 52, 56–60, 78
Minima Moralia 161
Miró, Joan 135
The Misfits (band) 9, 115
Miyazaki, Hayao 213, 220n2
Mizuki, Takahashi 192
Moebius 220n2; see also Giraud, Jean
Mohawk 11, 19, 20, 22–24, 27, 28, 58
Mohr, Melissa 84, 85
"Mokar Hastası Nihan" 163
Mondo Bizarro 6
"Mongollar" 165
Moon, Keith 4
Moore, Alan 50, 78, 83, 210
Moore, Ryan 49, 206, 207
Morimoto, Marie 174

230 Index

Morrison, Grant 12, 15, 75–81, 83–86, 86n2, 155, 210, 214, 216
Morrison, Jim 2, 4
Movida Madrileña 13, 134–137, 139, 141, 143, 144, 148, 150
Murphy, Sean 52, 57 *My Greatest Adventure* 209
My Neighbor Totoro 171, 172

Namor 41, 45
Namorita 41, 45
Napier, Susan 10, 172, 214
Narita, Ryōgo 14, 188, 195–200, 202
Nausicaä 213–216, 219
Nausicaä of the Valley of the Wind 210, 213, *215*, 216, 220
"Neat Neat Neat" 54
Negative Man 210, 214; see also Larry Trainor
Neighly, Patrick 77, 81
Neo-Tokyo 173, 178, 180–182, 186n13, 189, 190, 200, 212, 213
Never Mind the Bollocks Here's the Sex Pistols 53
New Musical Express 3
New Statesman 3
The New Warriors 41
New York Dolls (band) 1, 3, 79, 114
New York Magazine 6
The New Yorker 3
Nick Fury 43
Night Thrasher 41 96
Nitro 41
Noi 201–203
Noisey 79
Noisy Mob (band) 168n3
Nomad 29, 38–40; see also Captain America
"Not Waving but Drowning" 63
N.O.W.H.E.R.E. 216
Nyberg, Amy Kiste 86n6

Obsessive Compulsive Disorder 120, 121, 124, 126, 128, 129
Oky 159, 165, 167
OMAC (character) 11, 19–25, 27, 28n1; see also Buddy Blank; Kevin Kho Öncü, Ayşe 161, *162*
One Man Army Corps (OMAC) 11, 19, 20, 22–28, 131
Optic Nerve 80
Orbaugh, Sharalyn 209, 212
Orhon, Göze 167
Ortega, Juan Rodriguez *149*, 151n8
Osamu, Akimoto 15n7
Osamu, Tezuka 9, 10 *Our Sentence Is Up* 75–77, 82
Oxford English Dictionary 2–4, 82
Özal, Turgut 154, 160, 161
Özgür, Yiğit 167
Ozzi, Dan 79

P-Orridge, Genesis 4
Panter, Gary 11, 155
Paraíso 148
Pattison, Robert 52
Paul Revere and the Raiders (band) 4, 5
Penguen 166, 167, 168n6
penis 13, 114–*117*, 119, 123–126, 128–130, 130n2, 163
Pérez, Carlos Sánchez 146; see also Ceesepe
Perry, Mark 3
Peter Pank 131n5
Pettibon, Raymond 13, 115–*117*, 120, 124, 129
Phoenix 9
Picasso, Pablo 130n4, 135
Pink Floyd (band) 147
La Piraña Divina 142
Pişmiş Kelle 155, 157–159, 165, 168n4
Plastic Man 118
Pleasant Dreams 6, 7
Police (band) 50
The Politics and Poetics of Transgression 136
polysemy 29, 30
Porcellino, John 80
Preacher 11, 12, 88–90, 92, 94, 99–106, 107n4, 107n6, 109n12
Premiani, Bruno 208
"Prensiplerim Vardır" 165
Pretty Deadly 107
Prinz, Jesse 206
Prison Notebooks 150n1
Proinsias Cassidy 13, 89, 90, 95–98, 100, 101, 103–105, 108n9, 109n12
Publics and Counterpublics 137
Punk Diary 3
Punk Magazine 147
"The Punk Paper: A Dialogue" 82
Punk: The Illustrated History of a Music Revolution 3
Punks: A Guide to an American Subculture 22, 108n8

Q, Hayashida 14, 188, 190, 200–203
Queen (band) 83
Quesada, Joe 44
Quinto, Manuel 145

Raffaelli, Luca 211
Rag 3
Ramone, Dee Dee 6, 7, 15n3
Ramone, Joey 6
Ramone, Johnny 6, 7
Ramone, Tommy 7
Ramones (band) 3, 6–8, 27, 80, 102
RanXerox (character) 210–212, 216, 218
RanXerox (fumetto) 15, 210, *211*, 213, 216
Rashit (band) 166
Reagan, Ronald 51, 116, 154
Reassembling the Social: An Introduction to Actor-network-theory 151n4
rebellion 9, 10, 15, 24, 29, 38, 40, **44**, 46,

Index

46n2, 49, 51, 53, 58–60, 62, 68–70, 83, 88, 91–93, 100–104, 109n11, 123, 174, 176, 179, 188–191, *193*, 195, 199–201, 203, 209, 212, 214, 216, 219, 220
Rebis 214, 216; see also Negative Man
Recio, Juan Luís 147, 148
Reed, Lou 147
Reed Richards 42, 43, 45
Reynolds, Richard 210
Reynolds, Simon 4
Richardson, Mike 33, 37
Ridgway, John 50
Rimbaud, Arthur 135, *149*, 150
Rios, Emma 107n4
Riot Grrrl 92, 108n8
Rip It Up and Start Again 4
Rita Farr 210; see also Elasti-girl
Rivett, Miriam 25
Robertson, Darick 12, 61, 63–66, 69–72
Robotman 210; see also Cliff Steele
Rock Comix 147, 150
rock *macarra* 137
Rocket to Russia 6
Rogue Trooper 210
Rolling Stone 3, 6
Rolling Stones (band) 84, 147
Rollins, Henry 116
Rombes, Nicholas 82
Rorty, Richard *31*
Rosenkranz, Patrick 129
Ross, Alex 30, 42
Rotten, Johnny 4; see also Lydon, John
Royer, Mike 26
el *Rrollo* 144, 148
El Rrollo Enmascarado 144, 145
Runaways (band) 92
Ryōgo, Narita 14, 188, 195–200, 202
ryōsai kenbo 14, 192, 199

The Saga of the Swamp Thing 50
Sakigake!! Otokojuku 176, 185n7
Salak 154
Salewicz, Chris 3
San Reprimonio y las Pirañas 150
Sanders, Ed 2, 3, 15n1
Sanders' Truckstop 2, 3
Sandman 80, 86n4
Sarıkaya, Umut 167
Satan (character) 9
Saturday Night Live 134
Savage, Jon 205
Sazae-san 9, 10
Scalped 107n4
Schodt, Frederick L. 220n2
The Searchers 100
Seduction of the Innocent 1
sell out 51, 52, 54, 57, 61, 79, 80, 166
Sells Like Teen Spirit 49
Şen, Necdet 156
Sentinels of Liberty 33

SEX 67
Sex Pistols (band) 2–4, 33, 49, 50, 52, 53, 59, 65, 68, 69, 73n3, 79, 80, 82–85, 86n5, 86n7, 92, 101, 108n10, 115, 129, 155
Shaviro, Steven 65
Shelton, Gilbert 156
Shin Devilman 9
shōjo 10, 192, 203n1
shokujinki 217, 218
Shōnan Jun'ai Gumi 176
shōnen 10, 201, 203n3, 209, 220n1
Shōtarō, Ishinomori 15, 208
Sierra, Enrique 148
Simon, Joe 37
Singer, Marc 76
Sioux, Siouxsie 83, 84
Sirc, Geoffrey 4
Situationist 65, 70, 73n3, 156
Skinn, Dez 131n9
Skoog, Gabriel 168n2
Slits (band) 92
Smith, Patti 68, 135
Smith, Stevie 63
Smith, Winston 115
Sniffin' Glue 3
Snyder, Scott 107n4
Society of the Spectacle 65
Sola, Emilio 148
Solmaz, Fatih 158, 159
The Sonics (band) 114
Sōseki, Natsume 175, 176, 185n5
Soul Eater 14, 188, 191–195, 198, 199
Spanish Civil War 135, 137, 140, 148
Speedball 41, 46n5
Speedfreak 41
Spider Jerusalem 12, 61–72, 73n1, 73n2
Spider-Man 41, 43, 45, 65
Spiegelman, Art *117–121*, 124, 131n6, 131n9
Spinners (band) 168n3
Stallybrass, Peter 136
Stamford Incident 41, 42
Steranko, Jim 37
Steve Rogers 30–32, 37, 39–43, 45
Sting 50
Stokes, Martin 154
Stonewall Riots 3
The Stooges (band) 3, 114
Styrene, Poly 78
Subculture: The Meaning of Style 29, 41, 56, 135
Subterranean Jungle 6
Sue Storm 43, 45
Suicide (band) 2, 3, 68, 114
sukeban 15n5, 198
Supergods 76, 78, 79, 80
Superhero Registration Act 12, 29, 40–43, 45
Superman 65
Superman 144
Superman on the Couch 32
"Suratına işemek istiyorum" 155

232 Index

Swamp Thing 50
"Synthesising Identity: Gestures of Filiation and Affiliation in Turkish Popular Music" 168n2

Take No Prisoners 147
The Talking Heads (band) 67
Tamburini, Stefano 15, 210, 211
Taşkın, Yüksel 153
Tekelioğlu, Orhan 154
Tembelçizer, Memo 158, 159, 161, 163–165, 167, 168n8
Temple, Julien 85, 86n7
Testis (band) 159
Tetsuo 178–183, 186n13, 189, 191, 212, 213
Thatcher, Margaret 51, 52, 58, 154
"Theory of the Dérive" 65
Thompson, Hunter S. 63
Thompson, Stacy 62, 65, 66, 205–207, 210
Thor 43, 45
Throbbing Gristle (band) 4, 115
Tijuana Bibles **117**–119, 121, 123, 131n7, 131n9
Tijuana Bibles: Art and Wit in America's Forbidden Funnies, 1930s–1950s **118**, 119, 121, 131n6
Time 3 "'To Shift to a Higher Structure': Desire, Disembodiment, and Evolution in the Anime of Ōtomo, Ishii and Anno" 172
Tomine, Adrian 80
Tony Stark 40, 41, 42, 43, 45
Toole, John Kennedy 63
Top of the Pops 78
Tōru, Fujisawa 176
Toshihiko 217–219
Totleben, John 50
Townshend, Pete 4
Transmetropolitan 12, 61, 62, 64–69, 72, 72n1
trigger trio 90, 103, 104, 105, 106, 107n3, 109n12
Triggs, Teal 206, 207
The Triumph of Vulgarity 52
Triunfo 150
"Truth, Justice and the American Way in Franco's Spain" 151n3, 151n6
Tulip O'Hare 89, 90, 93–96, 98, 99, 101, 103–106, 108n9, 109n12
Turkey: A Modern History 168n1
Turrón, Kike 151n7
2000 AD 78, 210

Uncanny X-Men 131n5
Üstün, Bülent 159–**162**, 165, 167, 168n7; see also Büstün
Üstün, Cengiz 155, 157–159, 161, 163, 165
Uykusuz 167

V for Vendetta 131n5, 210
La Vaquería 147–**149**
Vaucher, Gee 115
Veitch, Rick 50
The Velvet Underground (band) 82, 114
Vera, Nazario Luque 144, 147, 150
Vertigo Comics 12, 49, 80, 81, 86n4, 89, 214
El Vibora 141
Vibrators (band) 54, 115
Vicios Modernos 146–148
Vicious, Sid 50, 52, 53, 56–59, 108n10
Vietnam War 3, 33, 35, 36, 37, 38, 85, 93, 102, 209

Warhol, Andy 7, 81, 82, 135, 146
Warner, Michael 137, 139
Watchmen 83
Wayne, John 13, 90, 94, 95, 100–102
"We Vibrate" 54
Weekly Shōnen Jump 15n7
Weekly Young Magazine 10, 185n10
Wertham, Fredric 1
West Side Story 209
Westwood, Vivienne 67
White, Allon 136
White, Merry Isaacs 191, 192
White, Ray 103, 104, 107n3, 109n12
Who (band) 5
Wolf, Marco 205
Wolverine 33
Woodstock 2
Wright, Bradford 38, 46n2

X-Men 33, 41, 42
X-Ray Spex (band) 78
Xerox 141, 142, 210

yakuza 198, 199, 201
Yarar, Kenan 159
Yeowell, Steve 81
Yılmaz, Ahmet 159
The Young Ones 156
Young Shōnen King 208
Yuasa, Maasaki 217
Yuka 217–219
Yukito, Kishiro 173

Zappa, Frank 147
"Zıçan Adam" 161, 163
Zimmerman, David 32
zine 64, 68, 80, 108n8, 140–144, **149**
"Zort" 161, 163, **164**
Zürcher, Erik Jan 168n1

www.ingramcontent.com/pod-product-compliance
Lightning Source LLC
Chambersburg PA
CBHW051220300426
44116CB00006B/654